Maise M.D. ✓ **W9-AWX-541**

SEARCHING

FOR A

DIFFERENT

FUTURE

Searching for

a Different Future

THE RISE OF A GLOBAL

MIDDLE CLASS IN

MOROCCO

SHANA COHEN

Duke University Press   Durham / London / 2004

© 2004 Duke University Press

Printed in the United States of America on acid-free paper ∞

Typeset in Carter and Cone Galliard by Keystone Typesetting, Inc.

Library of Congress Cataloging-in-Publication Data

appear on the last printed page of this book.

All rights reserved

Contents

Preface

As I told you from the beginning, an evening of poetry
is a party of fireworks that preys upon me and upon you at the same time . . .
Oh, my male and female friends, do not fear the fire
of poetry, a great human being is the human being that can burn . . .
— Nezar Qabbani, from *Birds Do Not Require a Visa for Entry*, 2000

About the middle of May 2003, I was preparing for a trip to Morocco and revising this manuscript for publication. During that week, four bombs hit downtown Casablanca, killing more than forty people and wounding dozens. These were places I knew, that I became familiar with during my many visits to the country and the three years I lived in Casablanca.

At the same time this horrific violence became part of a global confrontation, a confrontation consisting of multiple levels and actors, it also suggested how inseparable our interests and fears had become. Globalization implied not only interconnectedness through media, consumption, and terrorism, but also a more profound sense of being in a world where economic and political insecurity had become normal and no place remained singular or distinct.

When I first arrived in Morocco, I came with a plan to analyze how the global agenda of market reform had changed the specific comportment of the Moroccan middle class. Had the Moroccan middle class become more consumer-oriented, more attached to a liberal market economy, more global in its perspective? After a few months of preliminary interviews, I changed my focus to address the alienation prevalent among young high school and university graduates. I changed focus due not only to the information I attained in my conversations but also to my own sympathy, in fact my own participation, in this alienation. I understood uncertain identity and economic insecurity and I knew that being an American of the same age had only relative value. The two experiences of facing transformation in national institutions, class identity, and economic opportunity had much in common.

Intellectually, I asked how this alienation related both to national identity and material circumstances induced by market liberalization. To find answers, I read political economy of development, economic sociology, cultural studies, and social theory. The concept of a middle class itself became a theoretical challenge for me. I searched for a way to integrate a sense of life possibility with social structure, returning, I thought, to the early Marx of *The Economic and Philosophic Manuscripts*, where consciousness directly relates to position in the labor market.

Eventually, I came to adopt the theoretical methodology of Critical Theory, intersecting a Marxist analysis of social relations and class within the evolution of market capitalism with psychoanalytic approaches to the constitution of subjectivity and social consciousness. Not completely satisfied with the ability of psychoanalytic theory to interpret the fragile subjective position inherent in global market capitalism, I turned to contemporary Arabic literature and philosophy and social thought. I borrowed from Mahmud Darwish's poetic image of the nomadic, unwanted traveler in *Yowmiyyat il-huzn il-ʿdi* (Days of ordinary sadness) and the ideas of Emmanuel Levinas and Franz Rosenzweig. Levinas contemplated subjectivity without preceding, foundational totality (the nation-state) that brings together universal and singular in the same conceptual framework. Both Rosenzweig's and Levinas's discussion of the relation between the infinite and the subject allowed me to theorize the rise of an omnipresent, non-located global market and its consequences for individual subjectivity, social relations, and the stability of the global market as a social institution.

More specifically, the alienation of young Moroccan graduates became a symptom of underlying loss of attachment to the social structure, material possibilities, and the ideologically driven system of meaning offered by the nation-state. The push to join the global market economy as white-collar labor and the inability to conceptualize or experience identification with a historically and geographically located collectivity became the structure and consciousness of the new middle class. Meaning came not from membership in a nation or, more indirectly, position within a hierarchy of social and political power, but rather from its converse, from nonlocation, from rootless participation in transnational paths of opportunity and social validation.

All of this theoretical labor was possible only as the consequence of years of research in Morocco and knowledge of research and theory in other disciplines. I went to graduate school to become a sociologist, yet the theoretical framework I developed for my dissertation reflects a long, aggressive pursuit for ideas across disciplinary borders. At the end of the process, I became convinced that the time in Morocco and the years of culling concepts and ideas from very diverse literatures allowed for a stronger, more insightful analysis of the social impact of global market capitalism. In other words, I became an advocate for interdisciplinary research methodology and social analysis. I also came to believe in distinguishing policy and material differences among local, national, and transnational levels while acknowledging conceptually and practically experiential inseparability.

For my research, I interviewed seventy unemployed men and women, bureaucrats, professionals, entrepreneurs, and managers over the course of almost three years (1995–1997). I separated the interviewees by gender, employment, education, and age. To single out the effects of market reform and allow time enough after university to stabilize professionally and personally, I distinguished men and women between the ages of 25 and 40 and above 40, the former maturing with market reform policies initiated in 1983. I also conducted ethnographic research and analyzed secondary sources on demography, social history, and economic and social development. I followed networks of friends and family members, people I knew well and people I met in passing during the years I spent in Morocco. I listened to conversations everywhere, from the homes of neighbors with unemployed children to the train, as a way of understanding the experience of this population.

Their alienation and economic difficulties did not in any way substitute for or overshadow the alienation or often worse material circumstances of farmers, factory workers, and merchants on the street. Their experience was distinctive because of attachment to the goal of social mobility through education, to the ideal of human fulfillment for the pride of family and individual. They represented transference of the modern ideal of progress from nation to globalization, and their discourse likewise offered insight into the existential implications and the social possibility of this transference. If moving through the institutions of social mobility set them apart from agricultural and industrial workers, it also set them apart from the children of elite families. These children could gain access to capital and to contacts to find a job or set up a company or, importantly, leave Morocco for better opportunity elsewhere.

In chapter 1, I outline the theoretical framework of the book and situate my analysis of a global middle class within sociological theory as well as political economy of development and cultural studies, the two dominant literatures on liberalization and globalization today. In chapter 2, I provide a more analytic-historic interpretation of the rise of a modern middle class out of colonial and postcolonial policies of modernization and development. With chapters 3 and 4, I return to the global middle class, analyzing its sociostructural foundations in the former and existential experience in the latter. I end with speculation on how an emerging global middle class might affect the evolution of global market capitalism. For this kind of study, of class formation, and this type of theoretical approach, drawn from Critical Theory, must consider the political consequences of social change for a system that engenders both unequal distribution of resources and pervasive and socially destructive alienation.

Acknowledgments

I once told a friend that I felt isolated defending my work. She responded, "At some point, you have to believe in your ideas," meaning that I had to continue if I wanted those ideas to have life. I have remembered those words for years. I am grateful for her advice and confidence, as well as that of other friends and colleagues, during the period from dissertation research to book publication.

The research for the dissertation was funded by the Social Science Research Council, American Institute of Maghrib Studies, and the Fulbright IIE Fellowship. I received financial support during the writing period from the Department of Sociology at the University of California, Berkeley, as well as the Institute of International Studies. While in Morocco, I developed ideas for the thesis through many, many conversations with Aziz, Fatimah, Sofia, Mouna, Saïd, Omari, Chaoui, Katya, Aïcha, and my English-language students. I also relied on the counsel and intellectual guidance of Khalid Jamaï, Larbi Jaïdi, Nourredine El Oufi, Abdelhafid Boutaleb, Ahmed ben Chemsi, Amina Yazimi, Susan Ossman, Stefania Pandolfo, and Driss Benzekri. Susan helped as a friend and as a colleague, especially through her persuasion to reconsider a few conceptual ideas.

Anyone who has conducted research in a foreign country, particularly in a foreign language(s), knows how important it is to be able to turn to other researchers, even, or especially, regarding the simplest experiences. I am glad that I was in Morocco at the same time as David Zaffran, Sarah Levin,

Raffaele Cattedra, Katherine Hoffman, Bryan Daves, Luz Martin del Campo, Diana Davis, Jim Housefield, and Jamila Bergach.

To Marti, Rafi, and most of all Amina B. and Driss, I owe much more than gratitude.

In the United States, during the arduous and rewarding period of writing and revising, Nancy, Jane S., Jane T., Iona, Steve, Susan L., Jackie, Lynne, Will, Michelle, Eddy, Matt, Sarah, Emily, Gil A., and Barb provided generous encouragement. Todd Gitlin expressed appropriate doubt about some of my conceptual innovations but enthusiasm and conviction about the subject and its importance. Intellectually, I never would have taken the risks I did, struggled to articulate blurred ideas or refine immature theoretical instincts, had Peter Evans not been my advisor. His opinions and his advice contributed fundamentally to the theoretical framework presented here. Natasha Kraus, Jonathan Cutler, and Charles Lemert offered camaraderie and professional support during the process of revising for publication. Natasha, Jonathan, and Charles in particular played a critical role in maintaining the life of those ideas. Tracie and Annie pushed me to continue while handling phone calls and seeking job placements at Jubilee Jobs. Diana Bauer and Will Tiao just pushed me to continue, believing wholeheartedly in the necessity of the effort.

During the last stage of revision, Ivy Kennelly, Fran Buntman, Tom Medvetz, Matt Wray, and two anonymous reviewers for *Comparative Studies in Society and History* wrote insightful and very useful critiques of either specific chapters, related talks, or an article I published that was derived from the dissertation. Muhammed Kassab helped in translating both the quote from Nezar Qabbani at the beginning of the preface and the quote from Mahmud Darwish at the beginning of chapter 1. Our discussions concerning contemporary Arabic literature and Arab thought proved invaluable in refining and improving the theoretical framework of the book. My editor at Duke University Press, Raphael Allen, whose smile and teasing nature always proved reassuring, demonstrated a genuine integrity in his job. As I came to the end, relieved, happy, and surprised at hitherto unknown qualities of endurance and resistance, I met Rupert. He and my family have helped me to appreciate what this process can bring.

Translations and Transcriptions

The interviews cited in this book were conducted in French, the Moroccan dialect of Arabic, Modern Standard Arabic, Spanish, and English. I have translated the interviews, occasionally retaining expressions in French that seem inadequate in English. I have also translated texts from French and Arabic, with the exception of those of Abdellah Laroui, that do not have an English translation. For transcriptions in Arabic, I have used ' to represent the 'ayn except when citing other texts that use 'a or â. Admittedly, my focus in the research was not on language per se and I thus must assume any and all responsibility for inadequacies in translation and less than perfection in transcription.

I

Global Market Capitalism

and Social Change

Economic insecurity is a broader and subtler question
than it seems at first sight. — "Learning to Cope," *The Economist*, April 6, 1996

Bend, *ya habibi,* until the storm passes.
In the force of the bow my back became a bow. When do you release your arrow? . . .
When the storm dispersed both of them, the present was screaming to the past: you are
   the reason.
The past was changing its crime into law. Yet the future alone was a neutral witness.
When the storm quieted, the arc was completed. It changed into a circle where you could
   not tell the beginning from the end.
—Mahmud Darwish, "The Bow and the Circle," in *Yowmiyyat al-huzn al-ʿdi*, 1988

A hotel clerk in Morocco once explained how his friends would fantasize
about the lives of relatives or friends working in Europe in order to temper
anxiety about the present and find hope in the future:

> When I was a kid of 14 or 15, Moroccans would come from Belgium
> with soap and chocolates. They were heroes. We never imagined that
> they would suffer during the winter because they came in the summer.
> We never imagined that they worked hard, that it was cold in Belgium
> during the winter. They were heroes. My friends that have gone to
> Saudi Arabia, they go just to get on a plane, to breathe, to have space.
> They say we want space. But most of them that have gone to Saudi

Arabia come back after four months. The pay was weak, they were near to the border with Yemen and they said that there were no cafés, no women, no movies. We couldn't breathe, they said. Driss stayed a year and a half. Sometimes when he is weak, he thinks about going back.

The problem in Morocco is a crisis of identity. People are afraid. Once they get a job, they want to take revenge. They go out and buy expensive clothes, shoes, a car. They are not cool. I say take it easy, calm down. They are afraid of being the last person on a full bus and being cheated. That is why they go to a public space like a park and they destroy it. They see it as being private, that when they return, it won't be there. They do this in buses. That they will come back and they won't have it.

A teacher gave her own impression of migration, real or desired, from Morocco:

I know people in a very good situation here, at least to me, who want to leave. They say that there is nothing to do in Morocco. But there are a thousand things to do. I have seven friends who are going to leave for Canada. One is a professor at the university. He wants to leave because he says that he cannot do research here. They have already left for Montreal to look for work. They are afraid that their children won't adapt, but the children don't want to come back. . . . There is a discrepancy in Morocco between what people see as their life and what is their life.

In the discussion that follows on the transformation of the middle class in Morocco during market reform, I attempt to analyze the restlessness and existential anxiety conveyed in these remarks. More broadly, I try to understand how younger generations in Morocco conceive of the present and future, how they interpret the material, social, and political conditions of their existence and their options to change them.

I situate individual interpretation of life circumstances within the study of class formation. Inherently, I am also suggesting that class analysis represents a viable and productive method of theorizing the social dimension of our contemporary era of globalization. In this class analysis, global market integration has led both to the decline of an older modern middle class fundamental to the legitimacy and historic evolution of the nation-state and to the rise of a younger global middle class critical in its alienation, awkwardness, and dislocation to the evolution of globalization.

In the theoretical approach outlined below, I distinguish conceptually between globalization as a period in process, and thus without precise definition, and global market integration. Global market integration implies the construction of a universal economic structure through the implementation of uniform reform policies, the dominance of neoliberal ideology, and the global production of consumer culture. Reform policies include liberalization of the financial sector, enforcement of efficiency and transparency in state management and corporate governance, establishment of an independent judicial system, deregulation of the labor market, and investment in general human capital through combating negative social trends like poverty and illiteracy. These policies contribute to the development of a liberal market economy by encouraging private sector growth while reversing historic political and social priorities in government spending and regulation. Ideally, market reform should attract greater foreign and domestic investment, provoke more domestic competition and consumption, and promote sufficient overall economic expansion to diminish social problems related to inequity.

If reform does not yield enough positive economic impact to compensate for declining state intervention and population growth, then it may lead to an increase in unemployment, poverty, and economic and social insecurity. Reform policies can also directly and indirectly affect critical social institutions like education and public health and disrupt social trends ranging from age at marriage to the transfer of funds between generations, whether formally through social security or simply through continued financial dependence.

This book is not a critique of market integration in itself, because market liberalization has produced positive results. Proponents of privatization and deregulation policies can offer plenty of examples of how good reform is for the general population, both regarding quality of life and educational and work opportunity.[1] Statistically, improvements in basic living conditions can correspond with economic growth induced by reform. For instance, Bangladesh's annual rate of GDP growth between 1990 and 2001 averaged 4.9 percent. From the mid-1980s to mid-1990s, access to an improved water source more than doubled in percentage, from 40 to 84. Although a crude comparison, between 1990 and 2001 Romania averaged a GDP growth rate of −0.3 and witnessed a decline in access to improved water source from 71 to 62 percent (*World Development Report* 2000–2001, 2003).

My concern is also not with the debate over the scope and speed of reform or the sum of negative versus positive effects. Comparing reform in China and Russia, Joseph Stiglitz (2002) praises how China's gradualist strategy of reform yielded average growth rates of 10 percent during the 1990s. For Stiglitz, the consequence of reform in China was "the largest reduction in poverty in history in such a short time span"[2] and in Russia, "the largest increase in poverty in history in such a short span of time (outside of war and famine)" (181–82). He criticizes IMF management of reform in Russia, where average annual growth in GDP declined at a rate of −3.7 during the 1990s and poverty exploded, leading the World Bank to estimate that every percentage point drop in GDP places 700,000 more people in poverty (*World Development Indicators* 1995, 6).

Instead of analyzing issues like poverty as part of a discussion internal to the process of market liberalization, I am interested in how together the positive and negative consequences of global market integration provoke social change. Trends in unemployment, economic insecurity, and the consumption of luxury goods become not just the effects of market reform policies, but also factors in the organization of social structure and the formation of self-identity.

For instance, Driss, an unemployed doctorate I met through researching the social movement of unemployed university graduates, declared, "If there is an opportunity to leave, I am going. I regret that I left [France]. I could care less about being Moroccan. I do not have work. I do not play a part. I am not a citizen." Driss assumed a positive connection between job and citizenship based on the principles of modernization and modernity that informed the nation-building period of the 1950s–1970s. Likewise, his conscious negative equation of unemployment and noncitizenship reflected the decoupling of national institutions of social mobility and economic security from modern ideological concepts.

Liberal market democracy, the political model disseminated in global market integration, theoretically institutionalizes rights to opportunity, representation, and happiness. However, the trajectory of liberalization lacks clear articulation of these ideals. We might in fact question in the political economy of development if the liberal conception of equality has become like Calvinism in the twentieth century, surviving just as the set of ideas that once informed the evolution of political and economic institutions.

In the Arab World, market reform has corresponded with the popularity of conservative Islamic thinkers like Yusuf Qardawi and Abdessalaam Yassine, both of whom favor religious-political control to create societies alternative and opposed to those in the West.[3] Liberal Islamic thinkers like Sadiq Nahum, who argues that conceptual and practical bases exist in Islam for popular government, and Mohammed Arkoun, Hassan Hanafi, and Nasr Hamd Abu Zeid, who encourage rigorous scholarship on Islam, have tried to fight conservative interpretations, but they have remained politically marginal. Liberal, secular thinkers like Farag Foda, who fought for a pluralistic, secular regime in Egypt before he was assassinated in 1992, have perhaps faced even worse opposition. In response to ideological battles over religion, socioeconomic problems like unemployment, and foreign pressure to reform politically and economically, states in the Arab World have pitted internal against external issues, using one at the expense of the other. Lost in ideological conflict and state action is a clear, overarching strategy for rejuvenating society.[4] Rather, elites, local and global, compete for the allegiance or the identification of a distant social objective of the "masses."

In my analysis of the transformation of the middle class in Morocco, I delineate a more detailed and complex portrait of social organization and social difference during market reform. I argue that classes emerge during the process of legitimizing institutions and ideologies of economic, political, and social change, whether modernization or market reform. These ideologies and institutions reflect distinctive philosophical and material connections between economy and polity and likewise produce social structures and a subjective perception in the world that support the force of one relative to the other.

For example, during the nation-building period, nationalism and modern institutions inherently promoted internal social cohesion and equalization, if only in name, among citizens. The developing power of the nation-state as an idea and as a political economic system engendered the rise of a modern middle class that saw itself in terms of its function within the nation, the domestic economy, and the scope of state authority. Today, the social power of public institutions, the state, and nationalism have shifted to the firm, globalization, and global market capitalism, which together impose an atomistic, nonlocated vision of social order. In the legitimization process of global market capitalism, the synthesis between structure and consciousness within the enclosed nation-state has given way to sociostructural organization dependent on local economic growth and real opportunity and self-consciousness within the expansive, amorphous context of the globe.

In arguing that the alienation of young, urban, educated Moroccans reflects the formation of a new kind of class, the global middle class, I do not focus specifically on demonstration of discontent, even though in places like Argentina and Indonesia the middle classes have protested rising inflation and unemployment. Bataille (1986, 373) contends, "In historical agitation, only the word Revolution dominates the customary confusion and carries with it the promise that answers the unlimited demands of the masses." Yet, revolution or open resistance can also hide order within the confusion. In Morocco, one unemployed young man told me that his situation was "worse than hard [*pire que s 'b*]." He was not raging in the streets to protest, but his understanding of his situation was still important to understanding larger themes of social change.

Continued political stability in Morocco through market reform is due in part to simultaneous liberalization of the market and the political sphere, the latter initiated by King Hassan II and followed by his son, Mohammed VI.[5] In principle, political liberalization should encourage nonelite groups to organize against continued concentration of capital and power, particularly if faced with the negative consequences of adjustment, such as unemployment. Yet, an absence of mass protest against market reform policies and the state and of clearly articulated, alternative political goals may not mean that the generation is "lost," similar to images of Generation X, empty and impotent. I once asked a professor for references to young Arab thinkers who are attempting to construct a voice for their generation; he responded, "If this generation had a voice, you would not have a dissertation." I suggest that the voice of this generation may not translate into conventional self-expression within the established public space. Instead, younger generations deny the relevance of this public space through their lack of participation in conventional politics, their sharp, reflective critiques of social and political life in Morocco, and, inversely, their idealization of alternative arenas and social relations that traverse the globe.

A *fonctionnaire*, a man set to retire after twenty-five years, criticized university graduates for demonstrative political passivity and for expecting a good job to come to them: "One needs to get up early in the morning and start to look for a job, not wait around. My nephew gets up early [*il bosse*] and earns money doing errands while he looks for a job." Likewise, a businessman explained to me, "We would have no unemployment if people would just accept the jobs that are available." A friend who is both a social activist and a teacher posed a rhetorical question: "Are there any young people in politics? When you look at the militants here, they are all old. Young people want the maximum of money with the minimum of effort.

There is a lot of creativity at the level of the individual, but a framework for this expression does not exist, one that would allow this creativity to change [something]."

In contrast, Khalid Jamaï, a prominent journalist, praised what he called *la nouvelle génération*. He saw hope in the *grain de folie* (element of madness) that possesses them, in their absolute frustration and their moments of refusal to obey rules of nepotism or bloated bureaucracy. He told me that a young woman doctor came to his office to protest obstructions in the court system and corruption that prevented her from settling family financial affairs. She wanted to launch a hunger strike to draw attention and possibly push her case through, a technique that eventually worked.

In this grain de folie that draws the whole world into individual madness, the younger generations of global market integration differentiate themselves from the generation of nationalist intellectuals born before World War II and the generation of leftist and Islamist activists of the 1960s and 1970s. Both of these older generations cited problems in economic, political, and social change as justification for their own ascendancy to power in Morocco.

Today, the university graduate resembles the isolated, stateless Palestinian Mahmud Darwish (1988) describes in *Yowmiyyat al-huzn al-'di*. Darwish depicts the lonely individual stuck at border crossings, wandering through airports, and creating a life in a foreign country. This figure engages in an internal, psychological battle over his or her relation to the nation and to the world, over definition of self both for others and for self. Darwish writes of a Palestinian joking about his residence status with a lawyer friend, "I am not a citizen here and I am not a resident. Therefore, where am I and who am I?" The problem the narrator finds, however, is that to have legal status, one must prove one exists: "You are shocked that the law is with them (the authority). That the law is set up so that you must prove your existence. You say to the Minister of Interior: I am present or absent? Give me an expert in philosophy to establish that I am present." The narrator then concludes, "You realize that you are present philosophically, but you are absent legally" (94).

The angst and anxiety of young men and women in Morocco parallel that of the narrator because they have become, within the processes of global market integration, simply individuals. They must negotiate the present and future outside of a system of collective representation, of a nation. For these men and women, the realization of the narrator that he is philosophically present but legally absent flips to become legal existence and philosophical absence. Their existential anxiety is due not to the loss of legal rights derived from loss of territory and citizenship but to the loss of philosophical purpose and meaning derived from the declining relevance of both territory and citizenship.

Alienation from the Sociological Perspective

Although this book explores how alienation, occupation, social identity, and growing inequality in control over material and social resources relate within global market integration, questions linking one to the other date to the evolution of classical sociological theory. Certainly Marx consecrated much of his work to this relation. And even if a theorist like Weber did not address alienation as a function of exploitation and labor relations, but rather of disenchantment and rationalization, he and other sociologists looked to subjective meaning and the use of human capacity within the social order as a critical theoretical and moral concern of the discipline. Sociologists sought to understand how modernization and industrialization had organized, and distorted, existential experience and human ability to situate capitalism and its consequences historically and to allow for the possibility of an alternative social order in the future. As Weber (1958, 182) postulates at the end of The Protestant Ethic, "No one knows who will live in this cage in the future, or whether at the end of this tremendous development entirely new prophets will arise, or there will be a great rebirth of old ideas and ideals, or, if neither, mechanized petrification, embellished with a sort of convulsive self-importance."

Contemporary social theorists such as Baudrillard and Foucault, as well as theorists of postcoloniality, such as Homi Bhabha, have critiqued in one way or another "mechanized petrification" and pointed the way out, namely, through the unintended consequences of modernity to social interaction and subjective meaning. Baudrillard (1988, 215) encourages the masses, dissected by polls and surveys, to turn away from a political leadership that seems to have little need for popular support to remain in power: "We might argue that there exists another philosophy of lack of will, a sort of radical antimetaphysics whose secret is that the masses are deeply aware that they do not have to make a decision about themselves and the world." In contrast, Bhabha (1994) focuses on subjectivity made unique through its specific hybridity. He looks to migrants, women, and minorities excluded from the discourse and temporal organization of modernity as actors in a new, promising social space. He offers a theorization of subaltern agency that originates in the temporal and discursive lag between symbols and concepts of domination and the process of reinscription and relocation (193).

The theorization of unintended consequences presented here returns to social formation in its most classic sense, the idea that transformation in economic and political organization can lead to a change in the nature of subjective meaning and in the organization of the social structure. The combination of new subjective meaning and social structure in turn allows for the emergence of a new social formation, specifically class. This class can, like the masses of Baudrillard or the migrant of Bhabha, both depend on the continued acceleration of economic integration, the advancement of media and communication systems, and cultural interaction, and challenge in its experience and action the evolvement of liberal market democracy that underpins the globalization of today.

Unlike sociological theory of the late nineteenth and early twentieth century, the theoretical framework developed through the following chapters does not locate the cause of social change in transformation of the economy, ideas, or social organization. As stated above, I relate social change to transformation in the relative power of economic and political institutions and to the force of the ideology(ies) that legitimates the transformation. In Morocco, subjective meaning and social action have altered with the declining power of the state and legitimating ideologies of nationalism and modernization and the concurrent rise of global market capitalism and neoliberalism.

Finally, Morocco, a lower-middle-income country in the Arab World and the Berber regions of North Africa, is far from the centers of Western modernity, the original location of analyses of class formation and class awareness. Slightly larger than California, Morocco's population consists of approximately 30 million people, more than 99 percent of whom are of Arab-Berber origin. The Alaouite dynasty, to which the current king belongs, came to power in 1660, one of a series of dynasties that has ruled Morocco since the end of the eighth century.[6]

I suggest that we can think about class formation in contemporary Morocco as a consequence of global forces, and that we can therefore think about a concept like class in relation to, but not subsumed within, geographic and civilizational specificity. In other words, we can think about the global middle class in Morocco as possibly not only Moroccan.

The Transformation of the Middle Class in Morocco

During the postcolonial period (1950s–1970s), development policy and nationalist ideology equated the evolution of the nation-state with fulfill-ment of the human potential of its citizens.[7] In more practical political terms, the state achieved legitimacy through exchanging opportunity and identity in a Westernized process of social mobility for labor and acceptance of authority.[8] This exchange propelled the formation of a middle class based on material security, a well-demarcated life trajectory of education to employment, and a subjective position constituted as agency within the contained space of postcolonial society. Overall, created through the ideol-ogy of nation building, the modern middle class perceived its identity as modern and therefore capable of understanding and grappling with social, economic, and political change.[9]

Men and women in colonial and postcolonial Morocco entered the edu-cational system and pursued jobs in professions like teaching or in state-owned enterprises to pass through stages of social maturation and eco-nomic security. Emancipation, the goal of modernity, could be measured through the steps of modern trajectories of social mobility and qualified through reflection on and realization of inner potential within these trajec-tories. Men and women pursuing modern social mobility saw each other as part of a status system, through a sideways glance at those in a parallel position. Their combined individual fulfillment was to lead to the fulfill-ment of the collectivity. Their political behavior and identity were bound up in realizing, whether through reform or support, the totality of the nation-state. In the end, the dominant frame of urban social space during the postcolonial era was triangular, connecting the regime, the bourgeoisie, and the modern middle class.

The adoption of a structural adjustment program in 1983 led to a climb in unemployment and temporary, noncontractual employment among uni-versity and high school graduates. Likewise, it pushed *diplômés* to seek employment in the evolving service industries in the private sector in ad-dition to the predominantly public sector occupations of the older middle class. Global market integration, in forcing reorganization of the labor market and more international control over material and social resources, also altered the structural organization of the middle class and changed its perception in relation to other social groups and to institutions enforcing political and economic power.

Such a profound social transformation has occurred because if political and economic elites required middle-class support for modernization and nationalization in the past, today corporate elites require participation in the organization of global market capitalism. Participation is founded in economic insecurity and consumption, with market actors strategizing to overcome insecurity through consumer choice, whether of a school, an appealing "look," an insurance plan, or a type of job. Instead of an exchange of middle-class political support for government intervention into economic security and social status, today social relations between political and economic elites and younger generations of high school and university graduates force material dependence without social concern for individual welfare. In other words, these relations between elites and nonelites form structural economic and political interests — namely, financial obligation, legal control, and economic utility — that leave well-being to personal responsibility or to the private life of the individual. Financial obligation can include debt, legal control, restrictions such as visas, economic utility, and wage and benefit suppression.

More broadly, whereas the postcolonial state influenced both hierarchy and homogeneity in social relations, its decline and replacement by multiple authorities of foreign governments, Islamist movements, financial institutions, and development organizations have led to the rise of a new diversity in social relations. These social relations traverse borders, language, and culture and present diverse obligations, social and material benefits, methods of exploitation, and forms of assistance. The complexity and heterogeneity characterizing social relations have made conflict between different types of authorities an inherent feature of social interaction and everyday experience. Likewise, the multiplying sources of authority and possibilities for opposing interests have made practices of power like law and surveillance simultaneously objects to thwart (illegal migration, fraud) and rules to follow.

The sociostructural impact of market integration has been to separate the young, urban, educated population into distinct career, and life, trajectories. First, the middle class has shifted from consisting of men and women in relative gradation of education and managerial or professional rank to an educated population fragmented among the unemployed and temporarily employed, salaried bureaucrats and professionals, and businesspeople and entrepreneurs. Second, neoliberal policies and ideology have contributed to a system of social evaluation based on quality of participation in the global economy, for instance, knowledge of financial instruments and techniques of marketing and manufacturing or contact with international actors. This system of social evaluation has become a self-reifying counterpart to structural position, creating social groups based on relation to global market capitalism as a whole.

Specifically, the generation of market reform has separated into two relatively more coherent groups of entrepreneurs and midlevel managers in the private sector and the unemployed and temporarily employed and one mixed, more incoherent group of bureaucrats, professionals, and informal business owners. Integrated as a social group through social networks and education, young entrepreneurs and company managers are those men and women who work in the service industries that have evolved with market liberalization, such as marketing, management consulting, and finance, or for large Moroccan and multinational manufacturing companies. In contrast, the unemployed come together due to their common marginalization as well as time spent in cafés, parks, and demonstrations demanding public sector jobs. Members of this group may also work as *stagaires*, or interns in often nonpaying private and state sector enterprises, and or in labor-intensive, low-skill service industries like tourism, where wages are often correspondingly low relative to other sectors.

The third group includes the men and women who work in the mostly public sector occupations of the older postcolonial middle class as well as teachers, doctors, and technicians in the private sector. These jobs differ in prestige and wage levels, but most require years of education and training. They also manifest negative trends in status and relative income, although public sector positions are typically more stable than those in the private sector.

Though separated by occupation, career possibility, and social status, these men and women together share the same loss of connection to the social space and existential purpose of the nation. They share this loss not only because of state retreat from economic and social intervention but also because their work does not contribute to self-representation within a social system (which fits most theories of the middle class that focus on relative position in society), but to becoming part of a noncontained market. The noncontained market, in its ambiguity and amorphousness, cannot support identification between a physically and historically defined totality and an individual within the totality. The inability to structure a relationship of identification leaves the younger generation without an external mirror that provides the contours and features of self-identity. More concretely, unlike a modern middle class that came together over a common sense of historical purpose, younger high school and university graduates share the inability to equate a geographic site or historical moment with themselves as individuals. Their existential challenge is to reconcile with this inability, to go beyond connecting a physical and temporal space to the realization of their own capacity as human beings.

They confront this challenge through pursuing wherever they can the psychically lingering ideals of emancipation and freedom. They chase these ideals across frontiers and with varying methods, from Internet to illegal labor. Their experience of time in the pursuit is not an unfolding of events and life stages within a stable system, but dissolving disappointment in the past and restlessness in the present into the possibility of the future. Politically, the disconnection of all three groups from the nation-state leaves both a project of national development and the more specific need in market reform for local institutional and organizational change without the middle class as a primary agent. Their professional position and existential distance also leave local economic and political elites without the middle class as an ally.

A Note on the Modern Middle Class

I borrow the term "modern middle class" from André Adam (1968), who distinguished this class as modern because it appeared after Moroccan independence and because it was "the fruit of westernization, both economic and cultural, of urban society in Morocco" (728). In Moroccan society, the new space of social mobility, the very possibility of mobility, transformed the structuration of classes (Giddens 1973) around the symbolic and material residue of the values of modernization, creating the Weberian social class of propertyless white-collar workers. For Adam, the formation of what he called the "bourgeoisie of the diploma" had two important consequences for Moroccan society. First, the path of social mobility engineered through education allowed the children of poor parents, of illiterate factory workers, to become intellectuals, even ministers in postcolonial Morocco. Recognition of this possibility created a mystique around university and secondary education, so that any threats to limit enrollment provoked an uproar. Second, the modern middle class represented "a more efficient and resolute factor of modernization than the bourgeoisie itself" (Adam 1968, 730). The latter still relied economically on commerce, a trade connected to traditional social networks and status, whereas the middle class "is built on that which made the essential of Western dynamism: science and technique" (732), or solely the creation of modern processes.

Therefore, in contrast to the traditional Berber and Jewish merchants and shopkeepers, labor, the subproletariat of unemployed and informal service sector workers, and the entrepreneurial and administrative elites, the modern middle class for Adam signified a rupture in family social, economic, and cultural capital. Lacking in economic resources as children, they took advantage of the expansion of the postcolonial state to ameliorate their social and economic position. They earned stable salaries with lifelong benefits and likewise established a certain lifestyle, buying homes and cars and taking vacations. When the state provided a quality education and a job or successfully ensured enough economic growth to permit job creation in the private sector, the middle class generally tolerated or even supported the regime. Certainly, students and intellectuals opposed the regime, as seen in the Marxist and leftist movements of the 1960s and 1970s, but they did so as part of state-led modernization, not outside of it. They formed their ideas in the public university and within the discourse of national progress and reform.

When the state began to lose its financial capacity during the 1980s to intervene in the social economy, the modern middle class faced deteriorating standards of living and the burden of unemployed children and other family members as well as the necessity of private education. Symbolic in their lives of individual and national potential and possibility, much of the modern middle class, namely those in the public sector, now fell into a path of social decline.

Theorizing Class and Globalization

The promises of the State were only a political maneuver to extinguish the anger of the dissatisfied and to appease their revolt. Nothing but bodies emptied of their energy, of their determination, and transformed into columns of skin and blood to support the walls of the cities. Youth leaving the belly of desperation and thrown into the arms of hazard, of interminable wait and desolation. A dead-end future, hermetically sealed to children without a voice, to people of the night and of cemeteries. . . . Children who take on alone a malevolent destiny. Youth: a disaster cornered by unemployment, disarray, a futile dream. God is merciful! Only He knows why He has given to some and deprived others. The promises of the State to employ unemployed *jeunes diplômés* succeed in resembling all that will never come about. Promises of circumstance that evaporate with time; immediately calm returns to the streets of our cities swarming with children, of legitimate malcontent and subterranean revolt. — Abdelhak Serhane, *Les Prolétaires de la Haine*, 1995

To what height shall I ascend? Of what severity shall I be afraid? For every thing that God has created, and that He has not created, is as of little account in my aspiration as a single hair in the crown of my head. — al-Mutanabbī, "Verses Recited Ex-tempore in His Youth," in *Poems of al-Mutanabbī*, 1967

I suggest that we can conceptualize class formation in two different time periods based on the connection between objective conditions and subjective perception because this connection reflects an underlying shift in the balance of power between economy and polity. The modern middle class evolved not as the result of a grasp for power or will toward political and cultural domination, but through the mutual dependence of the formation of a middle class, the development of an overall social structure centered on this class, and the validation of a society and an economy under a unified political authority. The state assumed authority over society and economy and invested in a self-reifying social structure because of the importance to the nation-state of acceptance in the world system and because of the corresponding philosophical belief that progress occurred through joining self with collectivity to control history. Within modernity, self-reflection and self-consciousness illuminated the world and thus allowed for the mastery of it, in this case through the nation's taking control after colonialism of its own territory and future.

The modern middle class reflected this belief because it translated change, development, in terms of itself. It acted as a social manifestation of the circular logic of modern ontology in which all experience affirms and is affirmed through the unity of the self. The modern middle class embodied what Emmanuel Levinas (1998, 12) calls the subject seeing itself "without exit. . . . Everything is absorbed, sucked down, and walled up in the Same." Within the nation-state, the modern middle class led the pursuit of authenticity, analyzing objective conditions through the prism of rational, reflexive abstraction, abstraction that would bring clarity to the desire to change these conditions.

The pursuit of clarity, where Levinas says "the very doing of being led to clarity, in the form of intelligibility, and then became an intentional thematization in an experience" (1989, 169), both structured the existential experience of the modern middle class and underscored their social prestige. First, the process of intellectual abstraction ("thematization") to understand Being established how the modern middle class interpreted and acted on the world, or through the lens of abstract progress. Second, the cultural and moral significance of modern knowledge, which represented "truth," contributed to the social prestige of a class that derived power from access to this knowledge. The relationship between the development of knowledge and the development of Being culminated politically in a challenge to the isolation of being through the creation of an ideal community. This challenge meant the pursuit of what Levinas calls "a term outside people to which each person can contribute. . . . An ideal, a collective representation" (1989, 164): the nation-state.

Global market capitalism as a project and a policy discourages conceptual identification between individual meaning and a collectivity under united political and economic authority and disassociates well-being from submission to the will of a localized, overarching body. In short, this process has weakened the fundamental principle of the social contract that Rousseau articulated in the eighteenth century and that became the philosophical and political basis of the legitimacy of the nation-state. Bridging the meaning of the life of the individual with the organization of the polity, the social contract mandates that "each of us puts in common his person and all of his power under the supreme direction of the general will; and we receive as a body each member as an indivisible part of the whole" (Rousseau 1992, 40). From the perspective of the state, it explains that "the State regarding its members controls all of their goods through the social contract, which in the State serves as the base of all of their rights" (44).

The decline of national political authority under the expansion of global market capitalism has forced the subjective position of the young, urban, educated to shift, in the formula of Levinas, from meaning originating in the self, in cogito, to the self before the Infinite. Subjectivity is now founded on the impossibility of identity between individual and totality (Levinas 1989), of identity constructed through the totality. Returning to Rousseau, individuals do not possess the possibility of placing themselves under the "supreme direction of the general will." The new subject of the global middle class exists with "the Infinite [that] can neither be posited as a correlate of the subject, nor enter into a structure with it, nor become its contemporary in a co-presence — but in which it transcends him" (176). Levinas (1989, 105) writes, "Here we are trying to express the unconditionality of a subject, which does not have the status of a principle. . . . The unity of the universe is not what my gaze embraces in its unity of apperception, but what is incumbent on me from all sides, regards me in the two senses of the term, accuses me, is my affair."

In terms of class formation, a class framed by the interdependence of individual, group, and totality, like that which existed in the nation-state, depends de facto on the possibility of identification among the three. Adorno (2000, 6) wrote, "Dialectics unfolds the difference between the particular and the universal, dictated by the universal." We could conceive of a dialectic of identity between universal and particular within the nation-state, where an exchange of material resources and collective and self-identity for popular legitimization of a national state and culture underpinned identification between the individual and totality.

The structural conditions for a similar exchange between the global market and the individual do not exist. Although necessary for the reorganization of companies pushed to compete in the global economy, the lack of a unifying political authority like the post-Independence state, the normalization of economic insecurity among the middle class, and the fluctuating or diminishing value of white-collar labor preclude the possibility of political exchange. As a result, in retreating from its Pygmalionesque role, the state has instigated the rise not so much of the inverse of the modern middle class, or a disenfranchised, rebellious class, but of its nihilistic other, still the young, educated, ambitious professional, but with ambivalent attachment to the modern state and society. The younger generation, lacking the preconceived mission of its predecessor, has collapsed upon itself, creating a new form of class, the global middle class.

The consciousness of the global middle class reflects the singular break between state authority and the modern path of social mobility and, implicitly, between state authority and individual and collective emancipation. In this break, educated, ambitious men and women have experienced a loss of the ideal of progress through the rational activity that constituted the social identity of the modern middle class.

The loss of the ideal of human potential offered in national development and the foreclosure of material possibility is the same loss and foreclosure of possibility that underpins the psychic condition of melancholy. It is the psychic imprint of the lost ideal of human potential and social symbolism within society, and thus what forms the self-reflection of an entire population and adds consciousness to a sociostructural understanding of class formation.[10] In Freud's (1957) theorization of melancholia, love of the object lost escapes extinction by "taking flight into the ego." At this moment, when the ideal becomes part of the consciousness of the subject rather than an external given, conscience takes on the function of critique and ego the function of the object of this critique. If we go further, and say, as Judith Butler (1997) has, that the reflexivity of the subject is formed at the moment of loss, then the subjective turn of the young, urban, educated renders human potential the object of consciousness and makes the reflexive process the critical examination of the fulfillment of this potential.[11] As the lost ideal and the lost social-symbolic role of modern leadership are inseparable from their function in society and political power, the nation-state is also incorporated into the object of consciousness.

The young, urban, educated identify themselves with the ideal without acknowledging the reality of its absence because political and economic power have not recognized or allowed for recognition of the loss. The discourse of the World Bank and development economics in general encourage the growth of a middle class. However, neither qualifies this class with anything but quantitative measurement — namely, according to income or functional prescription (Milanovic and Shlomo 2000) — or as a "democratizing" or "developmental" force. Power offering existential emptiness masked in the rhetoric of the middle class has only propelled the force of the psychic impact of loss. This population suffers the withdrawal of all that has justified and substantiated the middle class without having choice or power over that loss and without being able to admit that the progression of globalization has rendered historic the middle class itself, as part of the modern past.

Butler (1997, 185) writes of the undeclared loss, "A loss in the world that cannot be declared enrages, generates ambivalence, and becomes the loss 'in' the ego that is nameless and diffuse and that prompts public rituals of self-beratement." The young, urban, educated, expressing anger toward the modern arrangement of political and social organization that they simultaneously identify with and cannot have, act politically by leveling against themselves. By desiring to destroy the middle class of the nation-state the men and women of the global middle class contribute to the decline of both.

In melancholia, the subject avoids self-destruction by gradually abandoning the object. As Freud (1957) comments, "Each single struggle of ambivalence loosen[s] the fixation of the libido to the object by disparaging it, denigrating it and even as it were killing it." Freud adds that the resolution of melancholia comes "either after the fury has spent itself or after the object has been abandoned as valueless" (257). The will to survive of the young, urban, educated entails gradual distancing from the ideological and social role of the modern middle class. Distancing also pushes this population to separate itself from the nation-state, regard conventional political participation or confrontation as undesirable, and ultimately emerge as a social actor within the nebulous arena of the globe.

In fact, the new subjective position of the global middle class — of the individual facing the abstract, undetermined context of the globe replacing the individual contained within the modern quality of belonging to a society — could inform both a sociological approach to globalization and analysis of global politics and social movements built on middle-class support.

Sociologically, the lack of unity between forms of individual capital and political and social alienation means that we have to theorize alienation apart from a localized conceptualization of capital or socioeconomic status. I suggest that alienation in global market integration derives fundamentally from the loss of the ability to identify control over material and social resources with belonging to a collectivity or, more profoundly, with individual potential or possibility in the world.

Also, social relations, and the identity of the individual in social interaction, have changed in organization and substance with global market integration. A shrinking social and economic role means that the state no longer has the power it once did in providing a model for identity, or national authenticity and citizenship. The state thus intervenes less in the organization of social status and differentiation that frames interaction and maintains relations of power.

In fact, social relations that extend across the globe increasingly substitute for the state, in that the individual seeks a job through social networks, finds models to imitate through images in the media or stories of success, and looks for financial assistance from family and friends. While the retreat of direct state intervention gives local and global social relations more importance, the rise of global market capitalism as the source of opportunity makes these relations heterogeneous and contingent temporally, spatially, and culturally. On the other hand, the collective search for security, opportunity, and models for fulfillment of human talent provides a unifying framework for the substance of social interaction. Social relations contingent in form and similar in substance give rise to a social consciousness that mimics the nontotality of the globe while articulating shared expectations for a role in the evolution of a global economy or culture. We can interpret the meaning of these social relations for the subject according to the aspirations, opportunities, and possibilities they offer for exploring individual capacity, which remains the qualification of happiness. Inversely, we can argue that interpellation, or social assignation of meaning, occurs not so much through state action as through action offering or hindering entrance into the global economy as well as global politics.

Politically, the alienation of both entrepreneurs and the unemployed demonstrates that marginality and inclusion do not necessarily predict protest, conflict, or tension. Myriam, a former marketing agent and at the time an aspiring restaurateur, hinted in remarks about her own restlessness that we must think differently about the relationship between political action and dissatisfaction: "My dream is to leave again. But I am an idiot because I do nothing for that. Not France, as this is not much more comfortable than Morocco. Why go there? Morocco is truly a ghetto . . . we ask ourselves too many existential questions. Instead of living our lives. There is an incredible malaise. Morocco is null. I would really like it if there is a change in Morocco. I would be the first to go down to the streets and to combat if there is a revolution. But I am too cowardly to do it myself."

Her joint declarations of frustration with Morocco and her desire for change, for an alternative either elsewhere or after the desired "revolution" do not indicate the seeds of modern opposition based in regime reform. Rather, they indicate a naturalness in pursuing fulfillment in Morocco or elsewhere, giving social foundation to the politics of this pursuit.

Furthermore, young, urban, educated men and women do not seem to participate actively in Islamist parties beyond the university, although they sympathize with Islamist political activity because these movements address alienation from nationalist politics and ideologies and offer followers material support. Yet, I have found that who turns to Islam for personal strength and who becomes *mutidayyin* (religious) and *mutitarif* or *muta-shadid* (extremist) does not follow a neat line of statistical correlation with occupation, social origin, and education.[12]

For example, a man who had recently obtained his doctorate and was unemployed whispered to me in an aside that he had practiced fasting for Ramadan this year to prepare for the job he hoped to have in the university, where he would be forced to fast during work. He both joked about it and resented the lack of alternatives in public space. On the other hand, a successful entrepreneur sheepishly admitted he could barely read *fusha* (modern standard Arabic) and had rarely looked at the Quran, whereas his partner boasted of the scope of his memorization (*tahfidh*).

I would suggest that the social complexity behind sympathy with or participation in Islamist movements implies that if we want to arrive at a sociological explanation, we should attempt first to understand the consciousness that informs the choice to participate in movements opposed to official political institutions. Through enlarging the research scope beyond Islamist movements, we can avoid substituting marginal political activity and identity for the entire population and we can see that this consciousness can inform as well the desire to participate in liberal or other transnational social and political movements.

Social Differentiation, Structural Organization, and Class

Global market integration has affected the structural organization of the middle class through assigning new social and economic value to different forms of white-collar work. Opportunity to access these different forms of white-collar work depends on, as Bourdieu (1984) suggests in his work on France, combinations of cultural, social, economic, political, and educational capital. I rely on Bourdieu's theoretical work in analyzing characteristics of social inequality in market reform in Morocco. However, I emphasize that particular combinations of capital have led to career and life trajectories that form the basis of social groups, and not classes, and that capital takes on new meaning as job markets and ideologies change.[13] These external factors to social differentiation and structural organization themselves depend on the pressure market reform places on a local system characterized by narrow distribution of power and capital and on Morocco's position in the global market economy.

Since the advent of market reform in the early 1980s, combinations of social, material, educational, political, and cultural capital (Bourdieu 1984) have shifted in meaning to represent potential ability in the global market economy. New social groups have formed based on common potential ability, and eventually career trajectory, to negotiate the scarcity of resources in a lower-middle-income country like Morocco, a country still dependent on agricultural production, and thus climate, for significant economic growth. Through these groups, young men and women claim a positive position in the competition over resources. Incorporating the language of political discourse and international financial institutions like the International Monetary Fund, they also establish social identities that provoke elite interest, if not concern. These identities range from young entrepreneur to long-term unemployed.[14]

The competition for jobs, capital, and status created through declining state budgets and limited economic growth plays out both in the process of social reproduction and in the quality of the educational system, public administration, and company behavior. Young university, *lycée*, and professional school graduates fight for administrative posts threatened by budget cuts or management positions dependent on company stability and expansion. However, the competition is weighted by social origin, as most young Moroccans lack the funds to attend elite *écoles de commerce*, and thus the degree often necessary to secure even an interview with a company. In addition, faced with an educational system in which only the highest scores on the baccalaureate lead to marketable fields of study, most young men and women in Morocco today study liberal arts or hard, not applied, sciences at the public university. The mass quality of education in the liberal arts departments has diminished their reputation and thus, in a self-reifying logic, limited the possibilities for graduates.

Education, family status and economic resources, qualities of personal presentation cultivated through family and school, social networks, and local and international political and economic interest determine paths into business, administration, or joblessness based on their ability to translate into assets in the job market. For example, entrepreneurs and midlevel managers tend to be of Fassi or occasionally Soussi (Berber from the southwest region of Morocco) origin, whereas employed professionals and bureaucrats and the unemployed or temporarily employed are almost always of 'rubi (Arab, rural origin) or Berber origin.[15] Because Fassis dominated the post-Independence administration as well as professions and business, their children today benefit from family name and money and social networks in locating jobs.

If their parents can afford it, these Moroccans attend private primary schools to become bilingual in French and Arabic, travel to Europe or the United States for vacations, and study at expensive local business schools or overseas after the baccalaureate. At the end of their trajectory, they can use family ties and contacts made through school to set up a business or find a position in a company. In addition, the government under Abdellatif Filali (May 1994–February 1998) established a loan program for young entrepreneurs, which, despite its inherent flaws, indicated state support for entrepreneurism as an activity. Those men and women without the financial ability to attend private schools from the beginning become part of the first group by studying at the national business school, ISCAE, or at a technical school in France with the help of Moroccan government fellowships. Very rarely, if not educated at elite schools or overseas and not from a well-off, typically Fassi or Soussi family, they compensate by gaining experience early in developing sectors such as marketing. Economic capital and characteristics of personal presentation can thus, in a few cases, compensate for lack of social and educational capital.

Young entrepreneurs and company managers work in industries dependent on continued liberalization. They start businesses in such service niches as market research and advertising or they work for large Moroccan or multinational manufacturing companies. However, small-scale entrepreneurs face limited mobility due to narrow access to capital and insufficient internal resources. Midlevel managers themselves confront oligarchic economic practices that have not changed substantially with reform. The alliance between political and economic elites in Morocco has prevented legal restraint of practices such as corporate nepotism and industry monopolies. Inversely, this alliance has discouraged the organizational innovation necessary to combat mild economic growth and growing international competition. In other words, companies often either remain under the direction of family and intertwined social networks or they go out of business, leaving the labor market for midlevel managers unstable.

In addition to external constraints on mobility, entrepreneurs and midlevel managers face the limited resources of their own families. The parents of these young men and women often cannot assist beyond education and social contacts because of larger economic problems, their own dependence on state salaries and the income of a clientele (including corruption), and the charge of multiple children whose needs continue well into adulthood. Entrepreneurs and managers can thus acquire a job that offers a relatively high salary and the prestige of being connected to the global economy, but they must rise in the ranks on their own. They can buy cars, rent or buy apartments, eat out, and take vacations, but they can only do so on credit.

Professionals as well as the unemployed and insecurely employed do not have the bilingualism and skills of personal presentation that come from having studied at French schools and traveling overseas, critical skills necessary to find a job at management level in a multinational or domestic company. The parents of both groups often possess little or no education and work in manual labor jobs or as technicians, teachers, or lower-level bureaucrats and company managers.

Although these occupations appear too diverse to be analyzed as having a common origin, they fit into a particular historical trajectory of social mobility. Without excess resources, the parents cannot help their children to attend prestigious schools or travel overseas and thus accumulate the social and cultural capital necessary to find a post in a multinational corporation. They are like the parents of the modern middle class, in that they offer encouragement, even discipline, to continue with education as long as it holds the promise of a white-collar job. Generally, however, even with years of education, professionals are stuck, in their career and financially. With sometimes six to eight siblings, they have to contribute most of their earnings to the household or the education of their brothers and sisters. They cannot quit or risk launching their own enterprise because of this dependence, and they cannot accumulate enough resources to marry and start their own family.

Common social origins, education, language skills, personal presentation, and so on provide the sociocultural and structural origin and frame for the formation of social groups. The social groups materialize through collective discussion within social networks, through public and private behavior, and through personal and collective attitudes developed through the steps of particular career trajectories. For example, graduates of public universities and second-tier professional and business schools know they must compromise in their job search, that a doctorate in engineering cannot find a job in Morocco because companies do not fund research and development; a doctorate in French cannot find a teaching job because public universities advertise few openings. Entrepeneurs and midlevel managers, on the other hand, blessed with elite degrees, government support, media admiration, and family connections, typically perceive themselves as rational, forward-thinking businesspeople confronting a sometimes irrational business environment.

Therefore, the three groups distinguish themselves to each other and the rest of the population not only through their position within the division of labor, biographic characteristics, and attachment to the market economy but also through a conveyed sense of social position and social right. They take different positions on changing social mores and the influence of global culture and they engage with political actors according to the channels open to those with their social status and resources. For example, unemployed doctorates and university graduates hold sit-ins at the Rabat headquarters of Union Marocaine de Travailleurs (UMT), one of the politically independent unions in Morocco, to attract national and international media attention as well as local support. These activities are the most important form of political activity in this population, although the unemployed who participate state explicitly that they are apolitical, that they want only employment and not the acceptance of an ideological project.

Young entrepreneurs complain to each other, to aid officials, and (though less) to the media that they have difficulty establishing and maintaining an enterprise in light of corruption, nepotism, and anachronistic legal restrictions and business practices. Professionals and bureaucrats express a tempered political and social conservatism, typically defending their own good fortune of finding a job by criticizing the unemployed rather than the economic policies that caused joblessness in the first place. In fact, employees in the public sector or nongovernmental organizations usually spend some time after university unemployed but cannot, at least in my research, go on to access the position of the entrepreneurs and managers. As a population varied in composition, professionals and public sector employees typically organize only within their specific occupation, for instance, conducting a teacher's strike.

Socially, entrepreneurs and midlevel managers set themselves apart through the flash of their jobs and their lifestyles, and professionals, through the stable status of their administrative posts and professions. In contrast, the unemployed unfortunately mark their territory by ennui, by their public presence in cafés, parks, markets, and the streets of their neighborhoods. The unemployed search for work through family contacts and friends, and the temporarily employed wait for the firm or ministry where they are doing an internship (*stage*) to hire them full time.

Although these groups cannot be measured exactly, the unemployed and insecurely employed remain the largest group. By the year 2000, 46.3 percent of the cohort ages 25–34 with a baccalaureate or higher-level degree were unemployed (41.1 percent of the male and 54.4 percent of the female labor force). By comparison, the unemployment rate among men and women of the same cohort and without a diploma (not having finished the sixth year, or basic education) was 17.8 percent (*Activité, Emploi et Chomage* 2000). As to entrepreneurs and midlevel managers, the IMF has estimated that new investments in services related to industry have rarely generated over five hundred jobs a year (*Resilience and Growth through Sustained Adjustment* 1995, table A15), and elite business schools combined typically boast fewer than 10,000 students a year combined. In contrast, there are approximately 260,000 students a year enrolled in higher education at the public university, and employment in the public administration and public services represents about 9 percent of the total labor force (*Les Indicateurs Sociaux* 2000). Out of a population of about 3.5 million in greater Casablanca, perhaps .5 million make up the global middle class (*Les Indicateurs Sociaux* 2000).

These groups also divide internally between genders. Men become entre-preneurs or managers in both manufacturing and service sector companies. Women tend to work exclusively in service industries such as finance, mar-keting, advertising, and the media, and rarely, unless their family has money, become entrepreneurs. These women, unlike most of their professional or unemployed female peers, often distinguish themselves and each other socially by smoking, drinking, going out at night, wearing clothing brought from France or the United States, and traveling regularly overseas. They cultivate these markers of independence, using their income and the free-dom their work environment offers to separate themselves from familial and societal constraints toward marriage and "proper" feminine behavior. In contrast, women who are unemployed or who work in public administra-tion often wear more conservative clothing and do not smoke or drink, either because of social norms or religious practice. Marriage also takes on a greater significance in social status. Men who work as entrepreneurs typ-ically marry earlier than their peers because of their access to material re-sources; they devote their energy to buying and furnishing an apartment and saving money for their children's education. On the other hand, unem-ployed men or professionals often make a decision to marry later, in their thirties or even their forties, or perhaps not to marry at all.[16]

The Global Middle Class in the Sociology of Class

What I call middle-class society is any society that becomes rigidified in predetermined forms, forbidding all evolution, all gains, all progress, all discovery. I call middle-class a closed society in which life has no taste, in which the air is tainted, in which ideas and men are corrupt. And I think that a man who takes a stand against this death is in a sense a revolutionary. — Frantz Fanon, *Black Skin, White Mask*, 1967

The decline of the modern middle class should relativize historically Fanon's hostile conception. The middle class, the standard-bearer and champion of the nation that bears responsibility for both this stagnation and the exclu-sion of all who are different, has become hegemonic in its experience of alienation and detachment. The difference between the global middle class and the petite bourgeoisie of Marx or the self-satisfied, self-centered individ-ual of Alexis de Tocqueville, Frantz Fanon, or Anthony Giddens is that the middle class no longer takes center stage as a nation's achievement or, likewise, acts to defend its continuity and stability. No longer an agent of modern progress or a protector of tradition, the young, urban, educated force us to question theorizing a relation between the anxiety and self-absorption induced by a middle position and a politics of conservatism, if not stagnation or regression.

The conception that I put forward here of class formation in a new period of global market capitalism differs both analytically and politically from that of conventional conceptualizations of the middle class or the petite bourgeoisie. Most social theory that discusses the middle class focuses on its structure, distinguishing the "new" middle class from the older petite bourgeoisie by highlighting the growth of occupations based on knowledge, technique, and management that separate the working and capitalist classes (see, for example, Mills 2002; Dahrendorf 1959; Giddens 1973; Goldthorpe 1982; Abercrombie and Urry 1983; Esping-Andersen 1990). Erik Olin Wright (1997) goes further by subdividing the middle class in modern Western societies according to relation to money capital, physical capital, and labor. Managers control physical capital and labor, situating them closest to the capitalist class, whereas semiautonomous employees, in their exclusion from control over labor and money capital, are closest to the working class.

Politically, during the nineteenth and for much of the twentieth century, both conservative and leftist intellectuals perceived the middle class as a deterrent to social transformation. From Marx onward, critical thinkers argued that when faced with the erosion of economic and political power, the middle class or petite bourgeoisie reacted by turning inward, by rejecting social upheaval for the security of the past and political alliances for the safety of neutrality. Marx wrote, "The lower middle class, the small manufacturer, the shopkeeper, the artisan, the peasant, all these fight against the bourgeoisie, to save from extinction their existence as fractions of the middle class. They are therefore not revolutionary, but conservative. Nay more, they are reactionary, for they try to roll back the wheel of history" (quoted in Tucker 1978, 482).

Describing the "crisis of authority" that occurs when a state has failed at a promised task and can no longer represent the will of the masses, Gramsci (1971, 211) pointed his finger at party/state bureaucrats and labeled them "the most dangerously hidebound and conservative force." According to Gramsci, this "hidebound and conservative force" resisted organization among workers and peasants seeking to improve their own conditions, demonstrating remarkable homogeneity of intention in the protection of political position and social importance.

Making his case against the petite bourgeoisie in postcolonial Morocco

and the rest of the Arab World, Abdellah Laroui described the petite bourgeoisie as a historical artifact, a ragtag collection of actors drawn together
by common dedication to individual independence and private property
and shared political conviction in traditional social and cultural values
(1974, 202; see also Farsoun 1988).[17] For Laroui, the petite bourgeoisie
kept postcolonial Moroccan society and politics *en retard* because they, the
most likely candidates for progressive leadership, did not further the development of a society governed by reason. They fought for power over the
state apparatus through the military and the administration, and once satisfied with increased consumption and cultural authority, at least in urban
areas, did little to benefit the progress of the country.

Laroui specifically discusses three ideological positions that make up the
petite bourgeoisie: the technocrat, the cleric, and the politician. The politician was a lawyer, doctor, or public official who, with the cleric, sought an
explanation for "backwardness." The technocrat, on the other hand, dis-
missed what he saw as unending and ultimately unproductive self-reflection
on backwardness or other comparisons to the West and accepted uncondi-
tionally the value of Western models of industrialization and rationalization:

> For him, the Occident is not as opaque as it is for the cleric. He feels
> himself there, speaking its language, conforming himself to its logic
> and slowly obscuring in his spirit the past and its problems. He no
> longer asks himself: "What was our grandeur?" nor "Why our deca-
> dence?" [asked by the cleric and the politician]. Insipid questions, he
> decides, and he starts to shout: the truth is for tomorrow, the truth is
> the technique. He believes he has surpassed the cleric and the liberal
> politician; in fact, he has adapted himself to the Occident with a short
> jump and without effort, being relieved too easily of his past: the
> Occident has not become clearer for him, it is his history that for him
> has become more opaque. (1982, 26–27)

Laroui's vision of the technocrat was deterministic and cynical, as he
wanted to demonstrate how much postcolonial educated Moroccans evalu-
ated their lives through familiarity with the symbols and technology of the
West. The devotion of the technocrat for the West was not that of the
descendant of a known family who advertised status through Western symbols and products of luxury, but of a disciple of the ideas, rules, and values
of Western progress.

Today, the petite bourgeoisie of Laroui, *vite coupée* from the majority of the population, has aged, becoming senior, or retiring, bureaucrats and soldiers and teachers and small-scale businessmen. These men, and a few women, may still hold positions of power, but social reproduction depends now on success in new sectors like the media, finance, and advertising. The crumbling foundations of the older middle class, however, have given rise to a new middle class fundamentally unlike its predecessors. This is not to deny continuity between middle classes, as men and women in the global middle class certainly profess the same scope and substance of ambition as those in the modern middle class. They do so, though, only because of the loss of institutional support for these ambitions and not, as was the case in nation building, because these ambitions drive institution building.

In fact, although born more than a century later and in the northwest corner of Africa, university and lycée graduates in Morocco would probably find resonance in the desires and values of the Americans Tocqueville (1945) describes in *Democracy in America*. These Americans of the early nineteenth century believed in individual ability and power to move forward and sought a life of satisfied ambitions and quiet security.

I listened to a young man calling into a radio program complain that all young Moroccans want is the money to start a family and buy a car and take a vacation. A woman told me, when I asked how she perceived herself in terms of social position within Morocco, that she "lived a little better than the middle class." I asked how she defined this middle class, and she replied with the following: "I should have asked you the question before [knowing my research topic]. I will explain myself and you tell me what you yourself think. The middle class is not standard of living because that changes. It is rather the assurance of all that is necessary — housing, education, food, accompaniments like travel, luxuries, eating out, dressing well, not staying always at home, inviting others over, buying things for personal pleasure, doing sports." Tocqueville (1945, 256) wrote of the United States something remarkably similar: "The first thing that strikes a traveler in the United States is the innumerable multitude of those who seek to emerge from their original condition; and the second is the rarity of lofty ambition to be observed in the midst of the universally ambitious stir of society. No Americans are devoid of a yearning desire to rise, but hardly any appear to entertain hope of great magnitude or to pursue very lofty aims. All are constantly seeking to acquire property, power, and reputation; few contemplate these things upon a great scale." Tocqueville attributed this paucity of "lofty aims" to the end of aristocratic values in American society, to a society rejecting the structure of social hierarchy, the marking of time through family lineages and importance, and systems of economic and political patronage.[18]

Ultimately, for Tocqueville, Americans gave strength to the "democratic principle" because all they sought was a "middling standard" of knowledge and a professional career marked neither by wealth nor poverty. The common appreciation of equality obscured differences in talent, or, as Tocqueville wrote, "Although the capacities of men are different, as the Creator intended they should be, the means that Americans find for putting them to use are equal" (1945, 55).

The hegemony of the idea of equality in the twentieth century, disseminated through nationalism and modernization, means that its loss through globalization affects Morocco more than a century later and far from the early democracy of the United States. If Tocqueville is right, that democracy depends on the common goal of equality and the principle of equality underpins the formation of a middle class, then the middle class cannot survive under globalization, which exists without the legitimizing idea of equality. The end of the middle class does not mean, however, that we are left with a petite bourgeoisie rendered vacuous by consumer desire and destructive by the entropy of individualism (see Agamben 1993; Baudrillard 1988). Giorgio Agamben writes, "The petty bourgeoisie has inherited the world and is the form in which humanity has survived nihilism." For Agamben, this "planetary petty bourgeoisie . . . has taken over the aptitude of the proletariat to refuse any recognizable social identity" (1993, 62). In other words, like the petite bourgeoisie of Laroui, this global petite bourgeoisie pursues an ahistorical and immaterial ideal, thus denying any attachment to the present and, likewise, responsibility to others. Instead of sacrificing the *epanouissement* of the nation, as the older petite bourgeoisie did, the planetary petite bourgeoisie may, because of the futility of their search, produce the finality of all humanity (Agamben 1993).

In theorizing this new social formation sociologically, I suggest that what has replaced the national petite bourgeoisie or the modern middle class is more complex and more promising, perhaps closer to Agamben's own ideal of "singularity," of an individual who exists without the destructive attachment to identity. The global middle class has emerged through economic, political, and subsequently sociostructural change, rituals of social inclusion and labor relations that engender financial and job insecurity, political pressures that render the citizen more important and less engaged than ever before, and the emptiness of both the ideals of equality and the market actor. Theoretically, the global middle class has formed in that moment of passage between the nation-state and globalization, when the loss of the ideal of equality is the shadow that informs consciousness and the uncertain and unknowable world of globalization lays the ground for a new subjective position in the world.

Globalization across Disciplines

At the beginning of the chapter, I suggested that the theoretical approach developed here parallels the focus on liminality of cultural and postcolonial studies but from the perspective of economic and social organization. Whereas theorists of postcoloniality or globalization throw their theoretical weight behind a search for interstices, for the fractures between hegemonic discourses,[19] I study the emergence of social formation that challenges what we have regarded as conventional urban class structure (working class, middle class, upper class) in modern society. In researching the middle class in Morocco, I have examined the processes that produce material inequality and interpreted the transformation in subjectivity instigated by these material conditions. Methodologically, I have brought together changing political, material, and social conditions, conditions all measurable in their objectivity, with qualities of self-perception and collective discussion that at best can only infer the constitution of subjectivity and social consciousness.

By intersecting subjectivity with structure in a sociological study, I cross disciplinary boundaries in what I believe is a necessary effort today for students of development and of globalization. First, an interdisciplinary conception of class formation can add complexity to a political economy of development that concentrates on how groups either cooperate with the state or move against it in relation to their benefit from liberalization. This conception includes interpreting political alienation — and support for oppositional Islamist movements — as more than blocked mobility and political and economic disenfranchisement.[20] Second, an interdisciplinary conception can contribute to cultural and postcolonial theory when the middle class appears as a hollow inversion of the condition of marginality or as a natural social category and thus an actor responding to the new exogenous forces of globalization (Appadurai 1996). Alienation would represent more in this conception than a response to the disintegrating, although still hegemonic, discourse of national identity (Bhabha 1994; Harvey 1989; Jameson 1991; Appadurai 1996) or to the speed of a capitalism that supersedes national borders, destroys the linearity and stability of time and space, and mixes signs uprooted from a prior referential logic (Castells

1996). In short, bringing political economy and globalization and post-colonial studies together would imply approaching alienation not only as a generic reaction to abjection or as inherent to subaltern identity, but also as symptomatic of a substantive change in social consciousness itself.

Furthermore, bringing these two fields together within sociology does not preclude pushing cultural anthropology or cultural studies toward political economy or vice versa. Referring to an evocative subject located in obscure, far-flung terrains, outside nations and between histories and languages, Homi Bhabha (1994, 191) writes, "My concern is with other articulations of human togetherness, as they are related to cultural difference and discrimination." This other articulation is in that intersubjective space, the "temporal break" where signs lack a subject and symbols, their order. Stefania Pandolfo (1997), conducting research in the Drâ' Valley of Morocco, describes an old cemetery, "a rocky empty space, rippled by the movement of sand and the emerging tips of the *shuhud* [gravestones]," that is referred to in Arabic as *l-qber l-mensí* (the forgotten tomb) because it bears no memories or living attachments. It "carries the atopical and intemporal indifference of death, without name, place, or face — a signifier of disjunction, detachment, and break," and thus becomes "a dangerous physical place, and a zone of avoidance in discourse" (167). The cemetery is a "cognitive hole," unknowable, untranslatable, incomprehensible.

Although perhaps difficult to imagine, political economists can join in the discussion of liminality and in-betweens. The idea of where people go in their life experience should be important to students of development still concerned with direction, even if not toward an ideologically defined goal. Debates could go beyond the authority of the state over private actors or vice versa, or its role in economic growth and the amelioration of living conditions, and inversely, the efficiency and fairness of a free market. Political economists may not go wandering through the broken tombstones of an unused cemetery, but they can take notice of the people who seek in the forgotten dead a cure to the mourning of an irretrievable loss (see Pandolfo 1997, 167–68). Where have people gone to mourn the loss of agency in modernization, where the work of the individual held meaning in society? What are the implications of the new individual constituted at least in part by the dislocated act of consumption and the lonely condition of economic insecurity? Is it still possible to think about the concept of emancipation not only from cultural and social domination but also in the act of individual creation and production that sustains an economy?

Summary

The argument I have outlined here can be summarized in three points. First, market liberalization has led to the transformation of the role, structure, and consciousness of the middle class. For one, economic policy has fragmented the urban educated into groups separated by career trajectory within the white-collar labor market. In addition, the retreat of the state from its modern purveyor role has disrupted the link between self-identity through human fulfillment and developing the nation-state that characterized the post-Independence period. The end of the mutual dependence between self-actualization and state power has led to widespread alienation among graduates of the university or any school of advanced education. These graduates still represent a minority in Morocco, and thus still feel entrusted with a mission of "progress," but they perceive their position as between Morocco and the world, which becomes a counter-Morocco, the inverse of diminished possibility and unforgivable compromise.

Second, global social formation is a kind of challenge to the nation-state, if not through political opposition and violence, then through the doubt that the nation-state is the arena in which to act and through the melancholic, rather than positive, origins of identity. During the post-Independence era of the 1950s through 1970s, the monarchy confronted the opposition of angry and popular socialist and Marxist movements that sought the development of a different nationalist project. Today, rather than mobilize, the young, urban, educated fantasize about and plan for another future. They fantasize about migration and consumption, but not as a consequence of these trends, as most contemporary globalization studies would suggest. The origin of their collective and individual experience is always this loss of place and moment for the actualization of self-potential.

Third, an emerging global social formation in Morocco makes a statement about the study of globalization, which is that we cannot drop the question of class. This question, as I posed it above, does not have to imply that classes exist for us to find. It keeps focus on the issue that market liberalization can change the social structure of society by producing new social groups. These groups evolve in a particular position within the division of labor and in a particular position of weakness vis-à-vis political and economic elites. The fact that these groups, regardless of material and social differences, respond in the same way to the process of market reform suggests that we may be witnessing the birth of a class that does not take transformation of the state as its objective, but rather pushes for a role in the global economy. The success of this effort may remain doubtful, but the effort itself gives globalization a dimension of social and political "conflict" among tight circles of international elites, a politically and socially alienated middle class, and the more located, often more politically and socially organized workers in manufacturing and agriculture.

2

*National Development
and the Formation of the
Modern Middle Class*

Apart from such political and economic forces as totalitarianism and socialism, it was in particular the institutionalization of the two great social forces of mobility and equality that has steered class structure and conflicts in directions unforeseen by Marx. . . . Social mobility has become one of the crucial elements of the structure of industrial societies, and one would be tempted to predict its "breakdown" if the process of mobility were ever seriously impeded. — Ralf Dahrendorf, *Class and Class Conflict in Industrial Society*, 1959

In their biography of Mehdi ben Barka, the nationalist leader and undaunted socialist and champion of the Third World, Zakya Daoud and Maâti Monjib (1996) laud ben Barka for his precocity, his love of education, and his obstinate struggle to serve his country until his assassination in 1965.[1] The son of a *fqih* and tailor, one of seven children, ben Barka grew up without electricity or running water in a house shared by three families.[2] The authors write, "At nine, Mehdi is a stubborn child; he accompanies his older brother and insists upon entering with him into the class." Too young for school, Mehdi finds that "the door for him remains closed. Each day, he sits at the foot of the portal and waits. The weeks pass, one month, two months, three months. One of the older teachers at the *medersa*, Si Taibi Bel Maâti, takes pity upon him. He convinces the [wife of the school's director] to accept him as an auditor." Although placed at the back of the classroom, "his thirst for knowledge and his *vivacité d'esprit* impress the teacher so much that he finds himself in the first row. In less than a year, the small *nouveau* expresses himself well enough in French to participate in class with more aptness than the older students: these sons of the well-off [*nantis*], these unthinking privileged [*privilégiés inconscients*], he beats them on their own territory" (62). Ben Barka, of course, does not stop there. He goes on to attend an elite French *école* and then *college* (Moulay Youssef) and *lycée* (Gouraud), working during his vacations from the age of 11 in different government offices.

The manner in which the authors portray the maturation of their hero and the trajectory of ben Barka himself reflect the model of collective progress and individual success propagated by nationalists, whether socialist, like ben Barka, *salafiyya* (al-Fassi and the Istiqlal Party), or monarchist.[3] Individuals could "move up" (*yitl '/mônter*) through education and a post in either the colonial or Moroccan national administration at the same time that the state, Morocco as a nation, came into being and embarked on a course of economic and social development.

In other words, though ben Barka was an exceptional person, the steps he followed were not. Most of the students enrolled at lycées, universities, or *grandes écoles* in the 1950s, 1960s, or 1970s were children of illiterate or traditionally educated (in the *msíd,* or Quranic schools) parents who worked in manual trades, not modern professions. Arabic was spoken at home, not French, and education was regarded as the path to a completely different, yet very desirable, way of life. Discussing the differences between the educational system of today and the past, and the stages of his own life, the director of a private high school recounted to me how he grew up as part of a family of twelve living in a two-bedroom apartment in Casablanca. His father worked as a *sh 'ush* (courier) in the administration. Despite overcrowded living quarters and meager economic resources, the director and all of his siblings attended school and most now work as professionals, either in Morocco or overseas. "Will and poverty pushed us to do something. We were very poor. My father worked day and night for his children." A banker friend, a divorced woman in her mid- to late forties, told me how her parents pushed their five daughters and one son to study. Her father and mother spoke only Arabic; the father's education was at Quranic schools, but all of his children spoke French, and only one, the only child who does not work, had not passed the baccalaureate. My informant worked at the same state-owned bank for over twenty years (from the beginning of the 1970s), two of her sisters worked in government ministries, one sister as the manager of a restaurant, and her brother on a farm.

In this chapter, I describe the bankers, teachers, bureaucrats, and political activists who make up the modern middle class. I discuss why and how this modern middle class became so important politically, socially, and economically despite its relatively small size, and, conversely, why economic reform necessarily meant its decline. Organizationally, I first offer a very brief history of social change in Morocco from the nineteenth century until Independence in 1956, connecting the encroachment of European powers to the birth of different social groups. I then turn to the postcolonial period, from 1956 until the late 1970s, during which the middle class became an object of political gain as well as national modernization, and new space appeared in the structure of opportunity.

The notion of a modern middle class follows from the argument that an explicitly modern path of social mobility and a modern notion of individual emancipation were critical to the legitimacy of state power and to the ideology of an essential, unified Moroccan society. In the third section of the chapter I explore the unity among a national system, social structure (distribution of material and social assets), and social formation (collective subjective position that determines social action). The point is to demonstrate how critical was transformation of the latter two to strengthening the ideological and institutional foundations of the nation-state.

In the course of economic development in Morocco, social mobility did not mean significant redistribution of income. During the postcolonial period, from the 1950s through the 1970s, revenues from agricultural and phosphate exports allowed the state to invest in the economy and society. Despite a dramatic jump in phosphate prices in the 1970s and the nationalist economic policy of *marocanisation*, income remained concentrated among private and public sector elites. In the last section of the chapter, I suggest how the failure of the state to foster the rise of an economically and politically independent middle class, one not so dependent on state resources and, conversely, one able and motivated to engineer political and civil activity, hindered economic development both before and after market reform.

Social Formation in Precolonial and Colonial Morocco

Below, I outline social formation during the pre-Protectorate, Protectorate, and independent Morocco through the end of the 1970s. I skimp on historical detail to look specifically at how substantively different sets of relations with Europe engendered directly and indirectly the production of different social groups.[4] For example, European economic investment and commercial exchange led directly to the formation of a local merchant class and the rise of industrial labor. More indirectly, the lure of opportunity in urban areas fostered the rise of a "subproletariat." The shift from economic expansion to political domination under colonialism indirectly pushed Moroccan commercial partners to become a more politicized, cohesive elite allied with an organized working class and the Islamic establishment, the *'lim*s, who protested foreign presence. Finally, French motivation to modernize social and cultural life led to the birth of a small middle class created through new educational systems and the development of professions.

European Encroachment and the Motivation to Reform

Although anarchic and weak in the early to mid-nineteenth century, Morocco remained virtually closed to European influence. Fragmented internally into Berber, or *tamazirt* (pl. *timizarn*), and Arab tribes differentiated through lineage, divided by language into Berber (*tashelhit, tamazight, tarifit*) and Arab dialects, and by Judaism and Islam, Morocco endured as a collective entity through its insularity and the control of the *makhzen,* the traditional seat of government. Most of the population survived by subsistence agriculture, with Berber and Jewish merchants operating trade routes and commerce centered among a group of Fassi families. Above all of the diversity and competing political and economic interests reigned the sultan, who was legitimated through descendance from the Prophet (a *sharif* or *chérif,* hence the reference *l'Empire Chérifien* for Morocco), and Islamic law, which stresses the need to maintain order under central rule.

The *'ulema* (Islamic scholarly elite, plural of *'lim*) also enforced insularity and cohesion through criticizing contact with the non-Islamic world. Until the second half of the nineteenth century, they successfully limited, at least for Moroccan Muslims, interaction of any kind. Their condemnation of commercial exchange and diplomatic contact forced the makhzen to send Muslims as ambassadors to cities along the pilgrimage to Mecca, but not as commercial envoys to Europe. The injunction notwithstanding, the sultan derived considerable income from piracy and commercial treaties through the eighteenth century, justifying contact with the *mutanassirin* through *jihad* at sea.

The French occupation of Egypt in 1798, under the leadership of Napoleon, launched a series of military incursions and trade negotiations that chipped away at Arab independence until, by the beginning of the twentieth century, all of North Africa and the Middle East had fallen under European colonial influence.[5] European governments and businessmen became more interested in the region as their populations grew and made economic expansion necessary, and as advances in industry, internationalization of finance, and innovation in transportation, by sea and overland, made expansion possible. Governments likewise put more pressure on Arab rulers to change laws and encourage local merchants to engage in foreign investment and trade.

For example, through her representative, John Drummond Hay, England pushed for greater circulation of goods and people in Morocco, tax exemptions for Moroccans associated with Europeans (thus encouraging contact), and installation of consuls.[6] Each European state conducting trade with Morocco during the second half of the nineteenth century then consistently upped the ante.[7] They demanded lower customs duties, greater allowance for agricultural and beef exports, and other tax exemptions.

Socially, the growing exchange of goods between Europe and Morocco reinforced a privileged merchant class, particularly the protegés of European consulates. These protegés did not pay *mukus* (non-Islamic market taxes) because of extraterritorial status, and often, because of administrative disorganization, customs duties at ports (Schroeter 1999, 92). Exchange with Europeans also benefited Moroccan Jewish families who were excluded from the clerical injunction. Through connections to the sultan and networks of Muslim traders in the interior of Morocco and the Sahara, Jewish merchants gained extensive control over foreign trade.

Whereas commerce generated the rise of a merchant class, unfavorable trade treaties, war indemnities to Spain, and debts to England inspired a wave of reforms that influenced organization among rural populations, urban elites, and the 'ûlema. First, the imposition of free trade and the attempted reforms of the makhzen negatively affected the rural masses obliged to pay non-Islamic market taxes (mukus) to help the sultan pay off debts and to finance modernization and expansion of the administration and military (see Salāwī 1954–1956, vol. 9; see also A. Laroui 1977b, chap. 6). Second, the reforms facilitated the entrance of urban notables into the administration. Inversely, because they were justified as a defense against Europeans, the mutanassirīn, the reforms set a precedent for judicial interpretation among Islamic scholars concerning national transformation and resistance. These intepretations set in motion a process of self-critique and nationalist resistance that became organized in the *salafiyya* movement during the Protectorate.

Most important, Moroccan integration into European economies and the jockeying among Spain, England, Germany, and France over trade and economic influence led to the creation of a rudimentary modern state apparatus. The makhzen's taxes necessitated creating a modern system of tax collection, in which the tax collectors, or *amin-al-mustafad*, were drawn from the 'ûlema, established merchants, or notaries (A. Laroui 1977b, 285). But tax collection, as Laroui puts it, "acted as a simple change of rapport of forces at the interior of the old system: the traditional bourgeoisie assuming the advantage at the expense of the army, the city at the expense of the rural areas" (285). Reformism also induced the sultan to send Moroccans to Europe for military training, and those who returned to serve in the makhzen became a corps in the bureaucracy, "cultivated, upright, innovative, animated by a mystique of the state" (285). Confronted with meager financial resources, the disorganization and archaism of the administration, and the jealousy of the non-European educated members of the makhzen (who accused the returning Moroccans of only picking up the customs of the mutanassirīn; 287–89), these trainees were too few and too unsupported politically to accomplish much.[8]

The French Protectorate

To Abdellah Laroui (1977b), the French approach to colonialism was that of social Darwinism: "Cultural regression, the cleavage between urban and rural Islam, the contradiction between central authority and local liberties —all these factors betokened a structure of lasting decadence. Colonial violence merely severed the few remaining ties betwen the historical domain (states, cities, Islamic justice, and ritual) and the infrahistorical (zâwiyas, rural communities, customs, folklore and private life). Insinuating itself between the two and in the name of history, it condemned the one to decay and oblivion, the other to regression and death" (344).[9]

In fact, French industrial and commercial expansion fit well into a Marxist analysis of the effects of colonialism. The rise of Moroccan capitalist and working classes meant that a "modern" capitalist society evolved alongside a threatened traditional society organized through agnatic tribes and orders of sufi saints. Militarily and administratively, the French administration attempted to enforce their authority by subduing tribes and dissipating the strength of the local sufi brotherhoods (*zaouias*) that worked in tandem with tribal organization. The administration also set up schools to educate the children of commercial and landed elites and invested in agriculture and industry to develop the economy.

Economic modernization allowed Fassi entrepreneurs to become a dominant economic elite, although based in Casablanca and not Fez. Individual businessmen such as Mohammed Laghzaoui became multimillionaires. Laghzaoui made his fortune from a bus company he established in the 1930s to serve Moroccan clientele; Omar and Mohammed Sebti, the owners of a grain storage business, profited, like other investors in commodities, from scarcities created during World War II (Clément 1986). Social and cultural modernization, as well as the common goal of national independence, brought more coherence and structure to the elite as a social group. The older, prestigious families of Fez sent their children to the same elite French schools and used advantageous marriage alliances among themselves to promote political and business interests, setting up the kind of interlaced political and corporate networks that would govern independent Morocco (Waterbury 1970, chap. 5). Marginalized by the *Residence* in favor of French firms and investors, these families united in the Istiqlal Party to fight against French capital and for control of domestic industry and commerce.[10]

At the same time that Moroccan entrepreneurs asserted their leadership, rural migrants seeking work and a new life in the modern cities seized their share of the social landscape. Urban job opportunity escalated dramatically with French investment in public works, projects in infrastructure that created the most jobs. Between 1949 and 1956, two-thirds of capital went to construction and housing, particularly in European *quartiers*, and in the decade after the war, more than 400 billion francs were invested in public works as a whole (Ayache 1997, 37). Drawn to the security of a rapidly growing market in a population of about 7 million and the availability of inexpensive labor, large French companies rushed to establish branches in Morocco. European investors, most of whom were French, poured 220 billion francs into *sociétés chérifiennes* (the remainder, 150 billion francs, came from domestic investors). Food, metal, and textile industries attracted the most investment, as light industries where investors could rotate capital and pay off debts (*amortissements accélérés*) quickly (38–39).

As they became more politicized and unions became more acceptable to the Protectorate and Moroccans to French union leadership, Moroccan urban workers participated in strikes with the French union, Union des Syndicats Confederés (CGT), and in a particularly hot year, 1936 (at Com-

pagnie Sucrière Marocaine, or COSUMA, and Compagnie Phosphates), succeeded in synthesizing the labor code of Morocco with that of France
(through three *Dahirs* [the legal instrument exercised by the king] on June
18, 1936). After the war, Moroccan workers formed the majority of the
CGT, or 30,000 out of 45,000 members in December 1945, and two-thirds
of the overall membership of 70,000 in 1948 (Ayache 1997, 103–39).

In a qualitative study of the working class living in the *bidonvilles* (shanty-
towns) of Rabat and Casablanca, Robert Montagne (1948–50) and his
research team devised four general occupational categories: those in facto-
ries (the largest category); those in modern technical occupations, such as
a plumber or electrician (the fewest); artisans tied to the locale, or painters,
masons, water carriers, or professional beggars; and small property owners
or employees, namely shopkeepers, cheap restaurant owners, maids, soldiers, and, of course, the unemployed. From a total city population of
about 750,000, Montagne quantified the proletariat in Casablanca as
300,000 Muslims and 80,000 Jews and divided them into several categories
according to origin. The first group was composed of Berber migrants who
came to the city only for work and thus possessed of the intention to return.
These rural migrants were normally from sedentary tribes in the Draa Valley or the Souss and were "the workers most appreciated by employers and
who are also the most capable of adapting to the conditions of the modern
economic life. These are the cousins of the Kabyle (from the Kabyle—
Berber—region of Algeria) who colonize France" (268). The second
group, what Montagne refers to as nonsedentary Berber and Arab tribes,
was much more troublesome, presenting "a spectacle of alarming social
decomposition. These are those who represent in our eyes the true social
danger that threatens Morocco" (268–69).

The modern economy in Casablanca, Montagne insisted, could not provide employment for all would-be workers, who waited for factory jobs
and survived through petty labor or barely survived at all. Without resources, he asserted, divorce, prostitution, and pervasive disrespect for
social and religious order prevailed. In fact, the most unstable group was
born in Casablanca: "We remark that in modern businesses, the workers
born in Casablanca are the most unstable. Some among them are skilled
and have learned a trade, but the majority is without value and above all
incapable of being helped (*se fixer*). These children, left to their own de-
vices, are inferior, vulgar vagabonds not guided by any principle" (1948–
50, 270). How rare in comparison, he pointed out, were the few individuals who rose from this milieu, characterized by "the harshness of competi-

tion, the significance of parasitism, the shameless exploitation of the poor by the rich" (271) to become technicians, conscientious employees, and serious businessmen and shopkeepers.

Finally, the colonial power expanded education, although not considerably, developed urban centers, and increased substantially the size of the administration, laying the ground for the rise of a modern middle class after Independence.[11] During the period 1920–50, the urban population in Morocco grew from 10 percent of the total population to 25 percent.[12] In 1955, there were 240,944 students in *enseignement général*, 346,584 in 1956, and 504,719 in 1957. Although also increasing, the number of students enrolled in technical programs was far lower than the needs of the new country. In 1955, there were a total of 11,177 students enrolled in what was called *enseignement technique du premier degré et second degré*; in 1956, 11,309; and in 1957, 12,598. In the same years, respectively, 268, 341, and 384 Moroccans received a *certificat d'aptitude professionnelle*; 282, 269, and 369 the *baccalauréat 1re partie*; 155, 164, and 206, the *baccalauréat 2me partie* (*L'Evolution Economique du Maroc dans le Cadre du Deuxième Plan Quadriennal (1954–57)*, 1958, 71).

Modernization and the Changing Structure of Opportunity

As an independent nation of more than 11 million people, the Moroccan state became a tool for consolidating power, a site of contestation among leftist parties, the Istiqlal, and the monarch. Whereas French colonial business investors and policymakers had acted for the mother country, leadership of the independent state needed to manage domestic resources so as to affirm local support and maintain national economic solvency. Economic policy became a method of appeasing a small network of elites, wooing and quieting urban middle and working classes, and alternately rewarding and punishing rural tribes according to their seeming allegiance to the makhzen and the king.[13]

Both equity and the trajectory of economic development suffered from the control of the commercial and landed elite, who were relatively uninterested in and unmotivated by the potential of significant industrialization. However, the crises of legitimation that this favoritism caused, and overall growth and spending, benefited the modern middle class during the several decades after Independence. Furthermore, the mass departure of French professionals and administrators, from 350,000 to 400,000 between the 1940s and 1960, made training and education imperative (Hourani

1991, 373). For the state, the function of the new class was to serve as administrator and ally as well as indicator for the world of Moroccan development (which is still the case).

Interest in Building a New Class

In the late 1950s, after Independence, Mohammed V consolidated the power of the monarchy in spite of opposition calls for transforming the traditional court into a modern state system. The elites surrounding the monarch remained the same, as the commercial families from Fez and *shuwarfa* (descendants of the Prophet), particularly the former, attained high positions in the administration and state-owned enterprises. To avoid conflict and thus political weakness, these families continued to impose on themselves social contact through intermarriage, education, and commerce. Waterbury (1970, 110) describes the generation of elites that assumed responsibility for the country after 1956: "They have taken up the old defense of patrimony, not for their fathers but for their own account. Yet the result is the same. With a modern veneer they have adopted the tried and true techniques of building clientele groups and alliances with patronage, encouraging far-reaching systems of mutual obligation, and utilizing their power for defensive purposes."

During the formative postcolonial period, King Hassan II, who succeeded Mohammed V in the spring of 1961, accommodated military leaders and rural *notables* through the transfer of French properties, particularly in the fertile Gharb (center-west region of Morocco), and manipulation of tariffs, customs duties, and monopolies to reward loyalty. Residents of the Souss and other agricultural areas, who had already seen their land expropriated by French colonists, now became dependent on seasonal wage labor and, tangentially, the luck of annual rain. Following the political logic of the transfer of land, state economic strategy focused on the promotion of agricultural exports. Shortly after King Hassan declared a state of emergency rule in 1965, the state created the Office de Commercialisation et d'Exportation, which exercised a monopoly over the export of citrus fruits, unseasonal fruits and vegetables, wine, and vegetable conserves, 41 percent of all exports at that time. By 1964, the state had already established subsidies for the development of irrigation, unhappily replicating the same course of favoring a minority of landholders.

During the 1960s, Morocco enjoyed moderate growth, a minimal trade deficit, and greater agricultural production than population growth (a situation that was dramatically reversed in the following decade). Government spending was low and relatively efficient, instigating higher rates of growth (a GDP of 4.4 percent by the end of the decade) and restraining inflation (2.2 percent for the decade). During the 1970s, accrued national debt and revenues from phosphates allowed the state to invest in education and industry, create a civil service (at the beginning of the 1970s), establish requirements for pension and health insurance benefits and a minimum wage, to continue to hire in industry and the administration, and even to grant wage raises and subsidize food products.[14] Budgets swelled for the prime minister's office and the offices of the secretary of planning (8 million dhs in 1971 to 427 million dhs in 1977, dropping to 37 million dhs in 1978), finance (117 million dhs in 1971 to 3,089 million dhs in 1977, dropping to 1,240 million dhs in 1978), and public works (452 million dhs in 1971 to 1,711 million dhs in 1977, dropping to 1,684 million dhs in 1978; *Morocco: Economic and Social Development Report* 1991, table 5.5).

Responding in part to the political instability of the early 1970s, the state also decided to encourage middle-class ownership in the private sector through marocanisation of ownership in Moroccan companies and of company management.[15] Although the middle class profited from this decade of phosphate boom and debt accumulation, marocanisation itself reinforced the economic and political resources of the Moroccan bourgeoisie more than it promoted greater equity. High-level administrators and wealthy businessmen took advantage of international and domestic connections to secure access to capital and the sale of shares in the companies themselves (El Oufi 1990). The state had intended to support middle-class investors, or officially those persons with less than 500,000 dhs capital, through a state/bank loan program. Unfortunately, the investments of this population were significantly less (15 percent, or 50 million out of a total of 330 million dhs capital invested in marocanisation; El Oufi 1990, 144) than investments by those with greater personal resources (a disappointment in state-run loan programs to help small-scale entrepreneurs with limited means that repeated itself with the *jeunes promoteurs* program in the 1990s).[16] Yet, despite its limitations, marocanisation reflected the explicit address of the state to the middle class. The policies of the 1960s and 1970s, following on those of the colonial era, had irreparably changed the social structure and the social fabric of Morocco.

The Material Origins of the Modern Middle Class

The importance of the urban modern middle class lay in its symbolism, its weight within the social relations that fed into, that buttressed, the nation-state, and not in its size relative to the rest of the population. For one, by the early 1980s, most Moroccans still did not attend school. In 1960, 87 percent of the total population was illiterate, including 96 percent of women.[17] By 1982, at the beginning of the period of market reform, these figures had decreased only to 65 percent of the total population and 78 percent of all women. The urban rates were lower: 73 percent in 1960 in urban areas and 44 percent in 1982 (88 to 57 percent of women).[18]

In addition, income distribution remained concentrated at the top. In 1971, 18.8 percent of the population was responsible for almost 50 percent of national consumption, and the bottom 40 percent for 12 percent (Cherkaoui n.d., 219). Related problems of poverty, regional disparities, infant mortality, unemployment, and housing as well as access to adequate health facilities, potable water, and electricity persisted. In fact, they have persisted, as the World Bank repeatedly notes, to a degree that is sharply discordant with Morocco's level of economic growth.[19] Poverty rates did drop through the 1970s, if not in sheer numbers, at least in percentage of the population.[20]

Data on income distribution, measured in Morocco through household consumption surveys, offer the most succinct social measure of Morocco's course of economic development.[21] Statistics in Morocco are difficult to interpret, but they generally suggest the slow rise of a middle-income segment of the population. They also suggest, regardless of any qualifications of stages of economic growth and the reliability of statistics (which in fact may offer a dimmer picture than reality because they do not include hidden income overseas or unreported expenditures), widening separation between rich and poor.[22] While real wages rose, the path of economic development only aggravated economic imbalance.

The expenditure of the top 20 percent in urban areas rose from 42.7 in 1959–60 to 50.4 percent in 1970–71, while the lowest 40 percent income group declined from 18.8 to 12.5 percent, and the bottom 20 percent from 7.1 to 4.1 percent (*Economic and Social Development Report* 1981). Differences in expenditure were close to the regional average in 1978 of 21.4 percent of total expenditure from the top 5 percent and 5.3 percent from the bottom 20 percent. However, equity in Morocco compared negatively to countries of similar per capita income. According to the World Bank, the top 5 percent of the population of countries of per capita income between $281 and $550 spent 15.2 percent of overall expenditures, while the bottom 20 percent spent 6.3 percent and the bottom 40 percent spent 16.3 percent (*Economic and Social Development Report* 1981).

As the gap between those at the top and the majority of the population expanded in the years of nation building, expenditure levels for middle-income groups (below the top 10 percent to above the bottom 40 percent) rose steadily, an increase hinted at in the rise from 43 to 49 percent shown above. In *Indicateurs Socio-Economiques du Maroc,* Abdelmalek Cherkaoui (n.d.) offers more detailed figures on expenditures that suggest a larger middle-income bracket (versus the missing 40 percent that expends 39 percent, above). Here, based on 1971 consumption surveys, the 40 percent at middle-income levels (third and fourth quintiles) consumed 44.8 percent of total expenditures.[23]

Furthermore, all of the trends that allowed for the rise of a new social class accelerated in the 1960s and 1970s. The urban growth rate between 1960 and 1971 was 4.3 percent (Cherkaoui n.d., 217), and the urban population as a whole grew from 29.3 percent of the total population in 1960 (3.41 million) to 42.8 percent in 1982 (8.73 million; *Les Indicateurs Sociaux* 1993, 66). The standard of living, measured in household expenditures and consumption habits, improved significantly in urban areas in the 1960s, as the percentage of households spending more than 4,200 dhs (about $500 today) a year more than doubled between 1959–60 and 1970–71, reaching almost 50 percent of all households.[24] During the 1970s, concentration of income diminished (Morrisson 1991, 25–26), due in part to remittances from migrant workers in Europe and state subsidies on food. The gap between the top and bottom income groups never shrank dramatically, but the share of expenditure by middle-income groups widened. According to the 1984–85 survey on consumption, the wealthier 50 percent of the population spent 82.1 percent of total expenditures in 1970 and 77.35 percent in 1985, with the approximately 5 percent loss coming from the wealthiest 25 percent (*Consommation et Depenses des Menages 1984–1985,* 1987–1991, 42).

Finally, the public sector, including public health, education, and the administration, grew considerably after 1970, at which point there were 149,212 employees in *la fonction publique.* Together, supply and demand expanded, as school enrollment, and the need for teachers, shot up in the decades after Independence.[25] Between 1970 and 1977, secondary-level enrollment increased 10 percent a year and university enrollment more than tripled, exceeding the goals of the 1973–77 five-year plan (*Economic and*

Social Development Report 1981, 251). Casablanca and Rabat, unsurprisingly, claimed the highest rates of overall school enrollment. For all of the 1970s, the total number of *fonctionnaires* grew at an annual rate of 5.5 percent, or 10,251 employees a year, to reach a sum of 241,515 at the end of the decade. These figures decreased in the 1980s, to 3.3 percent annual growth or 7,988 employees a year, prefiguring the rise of unemployment among university graduates. In fact, annual growth reached its highest annual rate of 9.3 percent in 1977, and after 1980, this rate never surpassed 4 percent (*Population et Emploi* 1992, 264).

Though overshadowed by other figures of illiteracy and poverty, these numbers held more meaning than a straightforward portion of the population. They implied the existence of a minority clearly separated out from the majority, that was attached to and dependent on modern, developing institutions for their material welfare and social identity. The state reinforced this minority's favored status through imbalanced investments in higher education and public sector management and professions. More than expenditures, however, state efforts to normalize (homogenize) professional licensing, training, and employment benefits such as retirement and health insurance strengthened its authority over the life organization of its protegés.

The Promise and Possibility of Education

Writing in the early 1970s, John Waterbury mentions that perhaps the greatest threat to elite monopoly over economic and political power was the rapid expansion of education. He cites statistics on school enrollment between 1953 and 1970, showing that in *enseignement primaire*, enrollment increased by almost a million during this period; in *enseignement secondaire* from 4,648 to 287,438; and in *enseignement supérieur* from 2,800 to 12,770.[26] Investment in education almost doubled between 1960 and 1980, rising from 9.74 percent of the total state budget in 1960–64 to 17.33 percent in 1978–80 (Salmi 1985, 51–55). Salmi estimates that total public investment in education (including investment figures from all ministries and state-owned enterprises) rose from 3.12 percent of the GDP and 10.33 percent of the state budget in 1956 to 4.22 and 15.25 percent in 1970 to 8.45 and 28.54 percent in 1980. Following the overall pattern of state expansion in Morocco, the biggest jump occurred in the 1970s.

With greater investment in education and popular interest in social mobility, educational enrollment, particularly at the basic level, increased rapidly. In 1970, 52 percent of the total school-age population, and 36 percent of girls, were enrolled in primary education (grades 1–6). In the same year, 13 percent of the total school-age population, 7 percent of girls, were enrolled in secondary school (2 cycles, grades 7–12; *World Development Report* 1995, table 28). By 1974–75, there were 32,711 students in postsecondary education. The primary net enrollment, or the percentage of school-age students enrolled in school, was 47 in 1975 (*Les Indicateurs Sociaux* 1993, table 14).

By 1980, over 2 million children were enrolled in primary education. In his analysis of education in Morocco, Salmi (1985, 55) calculates this figure as six times more than enrollment in 1956 and more than double the figure of 1970: 1,175,277. Approximately 800,000 children were enrolled in secondary education, almost 8,000 times more than in 1956 and about three times more than in 1970, or 298,880. There were 93,851 students enrolled in higher education, about 2,000 times more than in 1956 and 8 times more than in 1970, or 16,097. Overall, according to Salmi's calculations, between 1956 and 1980, enrollment at the primary level increased an average of 8.32 percent a year, enrollment at the secondary level 19.77 percent, and enrollment in higher education 14.31 percent.[27]

Substantial investment in education, however, did not mean fulfilling the personnel needs mentioned above. A 1966 World Bank report states that in 1963–64, there were 8,000 students in higher education, 7,000 of whom were in Morocco and the rest abroad, mostly in France. The majority of students in Morocco, or 43.6 percent of the total of 6,975, were enrolled in law, economics, and social and political science. Of the remainder, about 21 percent were enrolled in arts, 8 percent in teacher training, 5.7 percent in science and mathematics, 5.5 percent in medicine, 4.5 percent in engineering, and 1.7 percent in commerce (*The Economic Development of Morocco* 1966). Eleven years later, 23.7 percent were majoring in the humanities, 53 percent in law, 12.8 percent in medicine, 1 percent in engineering, 9 percent in hard sciences, and .5 percent in other disciplines (Ministère de l'Enseignement Supérieur, from a table in Cherkaoui n.d., 132).[28]

A Surge in White-Collar Jobs

National development led not only to a surge in white-collar labor, but also to substantial changes in the organization of the workforce in general. First, because of population growth, industrialization, education, and urbanization, the percentage of workers in industry, professions, and administration almost doubled between 1960 and 1982. The percentage of the population employed in the public administration increased from 23.6 in 1971 to 26.5 in 1982. At the same time, the percentage of workers in commerce, the service sector, and agriculture and fishing either remained approximately the same or decreased (Centre Marocain de Conjoncture 1993, 15). The overall number of women in the urban workforce also increased during the same period. As the percentage of women working who were fifteen years of age or more rose consistently over the thirty-year period of 1960–90, contradicting trends of urban unemployment (although following the logic of cheaper, more exploitable labor), the percentage of the male population active in the workforce steadily declined.[29]

Second, with the modernization of industry and the expansion of the administration, the percentage in the total urban workforce of salaried workers grew considerably, although overall, noncontractual labor within families or as independents continued to amount to a slim majority.[30] With market liberalization, these figures dropped, particularly in the administration, whereas the number of salaried workers grew in commerce and services (Jaïdi 1995). Between 1982 and 1991, employment in commerce grew 45.8 percent and in services 57.7 percent, whereas employment in the public administration, la fonction publique, declined 41.1 percent (Centre Marocain de Conjoncture 1993, 15).

The Last Link: Policies of Economic Welfare

The modern trajectory of education and skilled labor included benefits ensuring economic security. The state established the national social security fund (La Caisse Nationale de Securité Sociale or *sandûq il-watni l-dmin il-igtim'i*) with the Dahir of December 31, 1959, modifying its management and fund organization and expanding its responsibilities through the 1970s (Dahir of July 27, 1972) to include more payment types and a system of *polyclinques*. With the massive investment in the economy and receipts from phosphates, the state also indirectly instigated a rise in real income, one of the few times this has occurred since Independence. Despite only slightly better (the top 20 percent) or worse (bottom 40 percent) positioning in the distribution of income, real incomes themselves rose in manufacturing and the public sector during the 1970s, along with GNP per capita. In the years 1970–75, real per capita GNP grew 2.2 percent, and through 1975–80, 3.6 percent (Diwan and Squire 1993, cited in Pfeifer 1999, 57).

The Steps to Build a Nation and Cultivate a New Class

Among the principal characteristics of the fight led by the Moroccan people under the Protectorate and after Independence, we note that they have not stopped showing interest in the problems of education due to the fact that they are perfectly conscious of the fundamental role that knowledge plays in eliminating the causes which were at the origin of colonial domination, and building a new society that responds to all material and moral needs of the population, and permits the individual to recover his dignity and to profit from modern civilization in participating in its progress. — 'Allal al-Fassi, from *Charte Nationale pour l'Enseignement*, Parti de l'Istiqlal, 20–21 February 1971

Regardless of party affiliation and ideological stance, intellectuals and political leaders agreed that the objective of state intervention into education and employment was to establish a model of individual fulfillment. This model would bind together all those who followed it, encouraging the "sameness" that Frantz Fanon (1967) found so abhorrent in middle-class culture but that nationalist politicians and intellectuals regarded as critical to the popularization of the modern conception of citizenship. Citizenship here meant not only, as in the dictionary definition, residence in a particular place, loyalty to a country, or right by naturalization or birth to the protection of a state. It also had a more positive connotation of participation in a common cause, the nation, with accruing benefits, such as social services, legal protection, and legitimized travel between countries, as well as obligations, such as military duty and taxes. For Moroccan as well as most intellectuals of the decolonized Third World and post–World War II Europe, homogeneity was fundamental to unquestioned belief in the validity of citizenship and the assumption of its duties. Propounding the ideology of unity that postcolonial theorists would decades later critique, nationalist thinkers like Allal al-Fassi never questioned the imperative of nondifference, explaining it in terms of the Muslim *umma*.

The argument that individual emancipation was possible only through the nation was, of course, nothing unique to Morocco. For example, Habib Bourguiba, the president of Tunisia from the year after Independence in 1956 to 1987 (when he was deposed by Zine el-Abidine Ben Ali), became in the postcolonial period the region's strongest proponent of Westernization and modernization. In his official *Discours* (1977) and policies toward women and economic development, he consistently spoke about the necessity of the nation for human equality and individual liberation. In one speech (1983), after the discovery of a plotted military coup d'etat, he denounced the "criminals" threatening "notre oeuvre d'edification." He added, "Every citizen, I repeat, must be persuaded that he has his place in the country insofar as, through his work, he contributes to his life, to his prosperity. As such, he has the right to the solicitude and protection of the Chef d'Etat."[31]

Hannah Arendt (1976, 301), warning of the dangers of creating a population of *apatrides* in postwar Europe, wrote, "Our political life rests on the assumption that we can produce equality through organization, because man can act in and change and build a common world, together with his equals and only with his equals." The modern middle class exemplified the production of equality. The institutions that supported social mobility, that manifested individual fulfillment, constituted the organization that produced the equality that gave the nation substance and humanity its light.[32] The argument below outlines three stages of the circular interchange between the modern individual and the modern nation-state. The three steps, from the ideal of individual emancipation to justification of the nation through this emancipation to the practice of emancipation within the nation, encompass the political conflicts and strategies of economic development that characterized post-Independence Morocco. In other words, it was not political conflict itself, between whichever parties or actors, that produced the modern middle class. Rather, this class emerged out of the accepted conceptual terrain of nation and citizen, the imperative of economic growth and social development, and the subsequent consolidation of authority in a state apparatus.

Step 1: Idealizing Emancipation of the Individual

Abdallah Laroui (1977a) ends his book *The History of the Maghrib*, which he published originally in French in 1970, with a list of three historical obstacles to economic growth and democratization in postcolonial North Africa. These problems, derived from archaic religion-based forms of power, popular disinterest in or fear of politics, and immature domestic political institutions contorted by colonialism, could be confronted if the greatest obstacle, that of mass faith and participation in national unity and development, could be overcome:[33]

> The true problem, as we have said, is cultural (i.e. to unify the country beginning with the youth and to build a single organization capable of dissolving the historic distinctions which only too often add up to

something very close to a caste system) and political (i.e. to encourage, beginning on the local level, the participation of all groups in public life, so putting an end to the negative attitudes inherited from the past and bringing about the long delayed fusion of the state and society). The future belongs to the cities. We must encourage urbanization rather than try to impede it . . . the new urban masses will have to be organized and work somehow found for them, which, even if not economically profitable, will be socially educational. (87)

An intellectual pursuing the promise of decolonization, Laroui wanted these urban masses to feel the will to participate, to desire to speak to each other and from there, strive for a "development" and a politics that belong to them, not to a colonial power or a distant ruling class. He wrote, eloquently, "In concrete terms, what must be done is to induce the victims of all the defeats and repressions of the centuries to come down from their mountains and in from their deserts. . . . Before the Maghribi can become reconciled with his time and his country, he must first be reconciled with himself and his brother" (1977a, 388).

Laroui is like al-Fassi, for whom he shows respect as a nationalist thinker, except that Laroui, with his predilection for Marxism and sociostructural analysis, shows his ambivalence toward the ahistoric notion of authenticity ("consciousness" without structure) espoused by a Muslim nationalist thinker like al-Fassi (see chapter 1). Al-Fassi, in *naqd a-dhati* (*autocritique*), defends the notion of a Moroccan society, downplaying the importance of the division between Jews and Muslims and dismissing differences among Moroccans of Berber, Arab, Israelite, and African origin.[34] For al-Fassi (1966, 255) the nationalist, the only issue is whether or not each individual feels "citizenship" and passion for Morocco in his soul (*ruĥ ilmuwatana*). For al-Fassi the Islamist reformer, policies that act like medicine for the ailments of a society cannot transform the society ("medicine alone is not enough to put us on the road to a cure"; 260). This transformation, urgent in the face of problems of illiteracy, ignorance, poverty, and health, can only come from the faith of the people and a revolution in their way of thinking. Like Laroui, he wants the Moroccan people to liberate themselves from "the mythologies of the past [*harafāt ilmādi*] and the trivialities of the present [*ibatīl ilĥadir*]" (264). Al-Fassi supports religious faith and assimilation of law, though, as he urges Moroccans to follow the path Islam has laid out for them and not historical, materialist analysis as the emancipatory method.

The differences among all of the ideologies of postcolonialism — namely, a monarchy claiming legitimacy through *baraka* (grace) and genealogy, nationalist socialism (Union National des Forces Populaires [UNFP] and its leader, Mehdi ben Barka), and the salafiyya (Istiqlal and Allal al-Fassi) movement — were in method, and not geography or intent. Each propounded a theory of individual emancipation bound up in the modernization of the nation.

Ben Barka was the secularist founder of UNFP and president de l'Assemblée Nationale Consultative du Maroc from 1959 to 1960, before his first period of exile in 1960–61. Laroui cited him as the most technocrat of technocrats, the voice of planification who argued that "it is indispensable that we have an economy freed from the ties of dependence . . . [a five-year plan in preparation] will mark a step ahead in the path of liberating our economy, in the path of the realization of this very long process toward progress and the true satisfaction of needs" (quoted from an interview with Raymond Jean in Ben Barka 1959).[35] So different in substance then from al-Fassi, he uses the same language of fulfillment (*s'epanouir*, or "to bloom"): "To give meaning to this term of 'building' [*edifier*], I would be able to say that it means constructing a new society, here in Morocco; this will permit a man to blossom, to benefit from scientific and technical contributions" (1959, 3). He also envisioned a population homogeneous in spirit, if not in ascriptive characteristics or religious practice. At the initial meeting of UNFP, whose leaders broke off from Istiqlal in 1959, ben Barka insisted that "there is no contradiction among the elements that constitute the Moroccan people. The Union alone is able to thwart covetous [*convoitises*] colonialists and realize national objectives" (quoted in Daoud and Monjib 1996, 230).

Step 2: Justifying the Nation through the Individual

It was obligatory to study. In the fifties and sixties, there were these images of famous European women, it was very close to the colonial period, and Mohammed V sent his daughter to school. The family believed in development, that education can help development. — Leila, a schoolteacher in her mid-forties

Partha Chatterjee (1993) argues that political segmentation enhanced state authority in India, as the state assumed the role of the neutral, rational force of development needed to assert authority in the face of the irrational, biased, contested terrain of politics. In Morocco, the state became, as in India, the guardian of modern industrial sectors and the purveyor of social mobility. Its function as an employer, regulator, and owner was not in question in the battles among political leaders, but rather how it would act in these roles. The modern middle class, a product of the "objective" logic of development, assumed neutral authority as its agent.

In the circularity of the modern nation-state, the inner workings of civil administration, the organization of state-owned enterprises, the evolution of human capital, and the modern identity of university graduates all became nationalist goals and academic science. This objectification spoke for the legitimacy of the nation-state, in that the state justified consolidation of power in the name of bettering the lives of individual citizens, who could reach personal fulfillment only within the organized rubric of a national collectivity.

The collective work and goal of individual evolution and freedom could come, in the Arab World, through secular education and cultural dialogue with the West. Taha Hussein (2001) in *Mustaqbal i-thuqafa fi-misr* urged Egyptians to find economic, political, and cultural greatness, to achieve glory not just in comparison to other Arab countries but to the West as well, through learning Western culture. He encouraged Egyptians to return to their position as mediator in the Mediterranean among Greek, Roman, and Arab civilizations, and through this position, realize Egypt's potential as a nation.

For those not desiring to reject the colonial civilizations, the alternative path lay in following the principles of comportment and belief outlined in the Quran. In his intellectual trek into a nationalism founded in Islam and the historical integrity of Morocco, Allal al-Fassi calls for unity through a belonging to the land, a self-model (*nimudhij nefsi*) from Islam, and the spirit of the age (*ruh il 'sr*). These are abstract concepts but for al-Fassi, also important personal sentiments and real historical moments that can, in a state of conflict, provoke revolution (he mentions as an example Russia in the early twentieth century), and when in synthesis, inspire "true nationalism."

The generation after al-Fassi, born during the height of the nationalist movement for independence, pursued a model of nation and self with as much or more fervor than al-Fassi himself. Their movements, predominantly Marxist and communist rather than Islamist, strove, as radical movements of this period did, to reduce poverty, eliminate elite privileges, and create a government of "the people." "Born," as one former leader I knew said of himself, "to do a service for Morocco," they became part of the lost generation of students and intellectuals of the entire Arab World. Hundreds of members of the two major Marxist movements as well as officers associated with the two attempted coup d'etats were imprisoned in the early 1970s for acts of treason. United in such complete identification between self and nation, this generation of the 1960s and 1970s has expressed a passion for national modernization and state accountability for oppression of the groups that sought it, namely leftist intellectuals, that sometimes mystifies the younger generations of globalization, who see this behavior as an outdated attachment to the past.[36]

In an article in *Jeune Afrique* (7–13 September 1999, p. 24) published after King Hassan's death, the writer Abdelhak Serhane, at the time 49 years old, wrote, "After the mourning period and the tears, the time has come for an account. Not to engage in polemics or put salt in the wound [*gratter la plaie*], but to ask and understand where we are going. The best proof of love and fidelity that we can demonstrate to the country is to tell the truth." He fights for, among other things, an overhaul of the educational system, of hiring qualified teachers, permitting instruction in Berber, modernizing Arabic, and placing emphasis on acquisition of foreign languages. In his declarations that "the time is no more for blind nationalism . . . We have to recognize, in all modesty, that we did not invent either the telephone or the fax or the Internet," he echoes the language of the nationalists of the colonial era. He fleshes out his not-unique conviction with a hyperbolic warning of Morocco's worst fate: "We have to refuse to remain the eternal consumers of foreign technologies, if not, we will tomorrow be the trash collectors of producing nations, the sewer cleaners of strong nations, the chimney sweeps of modern nations, the beggars of developed countries. . . . This is to say the slaves of the New World Order."

During the 1960s and 1970s, social scientists pasted the behavior and attitudes of this generation of Moroccans onto the "evolutionary" chart of the nation. An article written by Douglas Ashford (1973) for the U.S. State Department offers an assessment of how much progress the up-and-coming generation of the 1960s had made toward becoming national leaders. Ashford justifies "national values" as a method to understand the psychology of educated Maghribi youth by contending, "There may be some advantages in focusing on the most important and most familiar new variable in the lives of young elites. The new factor is the nation. It has become a focus of instability and uncertainty for millions of people in Africa and Asia, but it is also a structure fairly well known to more developed societies. In recent work on Africa, scholars have frequently underscored the novelty of the national economy, a national legal system, and national political institutions" (97). He searches for how youth identify the nation, for whether the nation acts as motivation for second- and third-generation lycée and university graduates to work for social change.

Just as critical as Laroui of political indifference, Ashford warns that training without political consciousness "brings security with irresponsibility. One just calculates, gives the best possible solution, and hopes for the best without individually associating himself with the consequences. . . . No matter what happens, he has the security of the entrenched civil servant" (1973, 99–100).[37] Younger men coming into white-collar jobs after Independence typically reject the older nationalists as their leaders, as these men stop fighting for change once they have won their struggle. They admire the younger generation of nationalist leaders, such as ben Barka, but these leaders "are more concerned with ways to associate the mass with the nation than with ways to constructively orient the talented youth to the nation." Ashford admits that progressive politicians recognize the need for skilled managers, "but their thinking often assumes that young people will simply not be able to resist the attraction of social revolution . . . but it is not so clear that a more privileged young person sees himself, in ben Barka's phrase, as a 'true militant citizen'" (98). A young man may preoccupy himself with conflicts occurring elsewhere in the world, or he may, echoing Laroui's analysis of the technocrat, ignore politics in favor of scientific analysis.

Social scientists took interest not only in analyzing and categorizing political identity and participation that favored the evolution of the nation-state, but also in the intellectual activity and self-reflection that promoted modernization and development.[38] Mohamed Lahbabi, in a 1970 book attempting to foresee the Morocco of 1985, cites Japan, as many others have, as a country that succeeded in orienting labor away from agriculture toward the industrial sectors where value added would be highest.[39] He looked to youth as the primary resource of Morocco as long as they are trained and respect the primacy of work. He wrote in the magazine *Lamalif* (1970, p. 13) that "There is nothing as consistently durable as the free man [*homme libre*], the active citizen, respected, esteemed, mobilized, and animated by a creative and conscious enthusiasm."

As in much of the developing world, post-Independence Moroccan governments strategized about improving the quality of human resources and referred to, at least in the theoretical sense, education and work as fundamental rights. The right to education is guaranteed along with work (regardless of actual practice) in Article 13 of the Moroccan Constitution ("Tous les citoyens ont également le droit à l'éducation et au travail"). Jamil

Salmi (1985, 45), in a book about education and social reproduction in Morocco, quotes the minister of education at the publication of the first five-year plan, who stated that the state "must offer to each child an education sensitive to helping him to raise his standard of living and to obtain as well his '*emancipation sociale.*'" King Hassan II himself declared in his 1962 annual *Discours du Trône*, "Our policy aims to emancipate the individual; this is a policy which protects him from ignorance . . . it is clear that all development and all progress depend on the extension of culture and the generalization of education."[40]

In their language of individual fulfillment, Moroccan officials borrowed from modernization theory, and Salmi (1985) compares the discourse of American sociology of modernization with the official ideology of the Moroccan government. He first quotes a sociologist who says that "our era demands years of qualified technicians and professional experts, and the educational system is more and more devoted to the task of preparing these men." Salmi then cites the five-year plan for 1960–64, which sounds eerily like the plan quoted above from the 1950s: "The entire economy suffers from a lack of qualifed personnel and technicians . . . this obstacle seems more serious than the insufficience of available capital . . . it constitutes a veritable bottleneck to which the development of all sectors of activity is submitted." The same plan also contends that "the search for high productivity in *le main d'oeuvre* constitutes an imperative for all countries that seek to industrialize and regain the distance from more developed countries. The constant improvement of techniques of production demand that la main d'oeuvre had received sufficient training to be able to adapt itself to new conditions of manufacturing" (45–55). In another clear example of the power of American theorists of development, Moroccan officials in the Ministry of the Economy claimed in 1961 that "an analysis of the potential of Moroccan economic development over the course of the next decade shows that she has attained, according to [Eugene] Rostow, the stage of '*decollage*'" (quoted in Salmi 1985, 49).

The modernization imperative of education was accompanied by economic necessity. In the 1968–72 plan, an argument follows the logic that "the politics of education must, while responding to the legitimate desire of each individual to cultivate himself and to educate himself in order to progress and to satisfy his aspirations, aim to bestow the country with the fundamental instruments for economic development that constitutes a qualified worker and competent [*valable*] management" (quoted in Salmi 1985, 46). The second four-year plan (1954–57) includes a section called

"Les Hommes" that reports the shortage of skilled technicians, engineers, and administrators after the departure of foreigners. The plan complains woefully that "there are not enough engineers in Public Works or in Rural Engineering [*Génie Rural*] or engineers in Agronomy and the existing structures do not allow a lot of them to face at the same time the tasks of management and conception" (70).

Weighing the advantages of recruiting foreign personnel, the plan dictates: "Suitably chosen, bearing on key sectors, foreign technical aid can invest an important determinant in the current circumstances, greater without a doubt than financial aid. This solution, in any case, will not be but provisional. The penury of technicians and qualified managers constitutes a critical bottleneck; this is the reason for the importance and the continuity of effort of professional and technical training at all stages upon which depends the success of every plan of economic development" (quoted in Salmi 1985, 70). Obviously, local training and productivity were ways of achieving independence from the former, still powerful, colonial state. They also acted as proxies, knowable and measurable in knowledge and work, of the fuzzy and untranslatable notion of the realization of human potential. Education and refining of skills and productive capacity would allow men to, as Hannah Arendt (1958, 208) wrote, "actualize the sheer passive givenness of their being, not in order to change it but in order to make articulate and call into full existence what otherwise they would have to suffer passively anyhow."

Step 3: The Practice of Emancipation and the Ritual of Social Conceit

Finally, the discourse of emancipation, whether in the sense of self-fulfillment or national development, was more than a technique used by those anxious to place Morocco and Moroccans in a linear diagram of progress among nations of the world. An ideological justification of the modern organization of power, emancipation became a method of social differentiation in popular practices and shared symbols within the population.

Bourdieu (1984) argues that social class should be constructed as an "objective class." Class for him consists of "the set of agents who are placed in homogeneous conditions of existence imposing homogeneous conditionings and producing homogeneous systems of dispositions capable of generating similar practices; and who possess a set of common properties, objectified properties, sometimes legally guaranteed (as possession of goods and power) or properties embodied in class habitus (and, in particular, systems of classificatory schemes)" (101). Social class should not be defined, as is sometimes the case in sociology, by a single characteristic such as income, but by a combination of characteristics of behavior, presentation, and taste that are inseparable from the factors that we consciously describe as being primary to social division. Following this theoretical argument, we can look at the assembly (systems of classificatory schemes) of opinions, tastes, and practices among the modern middle class not as an effect of education and work, but as a property of the class itself.

The production of a modern society (through the trajectory of social mobility) was fundamental to inclusion in the system of nations. The effort to follow the ideology of modernization and participate in "modernity," whatever its variant, weighed on the legitimation and evolution of education, white-collar employment, and Westernized comportment. In short, the modern middle class manifested social power in a society that, at the time, depended partly in its unification on the validation of the particular practices of the modern middle class. Men and women in professions or the administration, boasting of education and civilization, buying European rather than Moroccan furniture, drinking tea at one of the hotels along *la corniche* in Casablanca, or dressing in inexpensive copies of European clothes, served as a national model and thus a glue for everyone desiring to change the status of their children. This model was full of conceit, however, both from the pain of separation, of distinction and difference in Morocco, and from self-admiration if not always self-love.

An architect, on the border of the modern middle class and the global middle class, articulated an effective and stark perception of distance, a child's alienation that hinted at a generational plight and condition. He had studied in France, the only university-educated son among eight children. His father used to work as a dog trimmer. Three of his brothers (younger) were unemployed when I met him, and his four sisters were married and not employed. He had enrolled his own children in a private primary school, which is now fashionable and significant for opportunity in the private sector. This architect explained that he helps his immediate family, although he thought his father, apart from affection, offered him nothing because of his lack of education. "Without education, one is little more than an animal." About his siblings, who have some education, he said, "It is not much better." When I first sat down, in an office filled, naturally, with graphic supplies, prints, and paintings, he commented, "I am sure that art saved me."

From the inverse perspective, Leila Abouzeid (1989, 9) writes in *'M ilfil*, a well-known book in Morocco, of a woman being divorced on the eve of Independence:

> But why? he asks [about the divorce].
> Fury rises up inside me and I exclaim bitterly: I don't eat with a fork. I don't speak French. I don't sit with men. I don't go out to fancy dinners. Is that enough or shall I continue?
> Those are their standards?
> I am nothing but an old coin fit only for the museum shelf. Their positions in society now call for modern women.
> He looks as if he were listening to someone who has just returned from Mars.
> Principles are the most fragile of man's possessions, he murmers. How easily people forget!
> Everyone forgets. The nation itself forgets.

Obviously sympathetic to her protagonist, Leila Abouzeid criticized the condescension of the young, educated generation devoted to the dress, manners, and language of Europe. Driss Chraïbi, on the other hand, perceived as insurmountable the gulf between the older generation that matured in the colonial era and their own, the generation born during the struggle for Independence.

Dozens of articles and dissertations have been written on Chraïbi's most notable work, *Le passé simple* (1954), and almost any passage from the novel reveals a tormented, French-educated young man clashing with his father, the tyrant who controls the past yet also represents, in the form of national liberty, the object of return, from France and from self-alienation.[41] Although I present a vulgar and unfair condensation of complicated themes, scenes that frame the novel show what I interpret as a new class consciousness, of a modern middle class separated from what was Morocco and bound up in what the country was to be, as a nation. The principal character, also named Driss, has more resources than most of the people to whom I am referring, but his attitude, his approach to life, is little different. We first meet him, an immature, cocky, rebellious young man, smoking a cigarette at *maghrib* during Ramadan. He determines his identity against that of his beloved mother, whom he perceives as weak and submissive, and that of his father, le Seigneur, whom he dislikes and fears as a despot:

> This man in the tarbouche is so sure of himself: a fly will not take flight unless he gives it permission. He knows that every word that falls from

his mouth will be engraved on my mind. On his mask-like face, there is not a shudder. I removed this mask and read: he is illiterate and consequently proud of maintaining any kind of conversation in whatever subject matter. I would willingly compare him to those little old men who know everything and who have experienced everything: children, grandchildren, diplomas, fortune, reverses of fortune, mistresses, fornication, chances . . . if not for the hatred because of that illiteracy. He knows that the Occident towards which he has propelled me is outside his sphere. Therefore he hates it. And out of fear that there be in me an enthusiasm for this new world, he flails, shatters, cuts off, and dissects everything I learn. Cheapens it.[42]

Le Seigneur wants him to return from France prepared to assume responsibility for family business affairs. Driss imagines his father, who seeks a blessing from the sultan for his departure, relishing his control over his son's fate: "That boy, Satan and damnation, almost went over to the enemy's camp. . . . Now he is docile, reflective, armed for combat. We are sending him to Paris. He will return from there, increase tenfold the estate we will bequeath to him, and will become one of the leaders of the governing class. Come what may, whether our country becomes a colony, or a republic, or your head falls off, of no importance. Driss will not suffer" (156). Driss leaves for France after his mother, unable to resist the disdain and cold authority of her husband or the misery of her life, commits suicide. On the plane, he speaks to himself and his absent father:

I unsnap my seatbelt. I am going to the toilet. I see Casablanca slipping away and growing smaller. Now it's my turn to exhalt.

Not an ounce of my past escapes me, it parades in front of me. Quite simply, I gambled and I won.

I the indigent had revolted, the revolt of an indigent, and when one is indigent, one does not revolt. Despite being indigent, shabby, something worthless a penniless student would have cast aside, face to face with the feudalism that even the French Residency could not shake — and face to face with indifference. Or I could have ended up by going back to the Julius-Caesar-marionettes-the-rebels-of-the-gullet-on-the-lips, and going no further. Or becoming a vagrant? Or bring down the curtain, living a quiet little life in a foreign country, in turn becoming indifferent. I don't think so. I am a Moroccan, and in a way, Morocco belongs to me. . . .

By being docile and repentant, I was able to get him to send me to

France. First, count it on your fingers. Then he subsidizes me, will lead me to a degree and to a position. I will return, will gratefully accept the fortune reserved for me that he holds out in his open hand. Then, but only then, will I revolt, suitably, and with certainty. (157)

Emancipation, the rebellion and brashness of a Driss exploring ideas and possibilities, became for the emerging class an anthem and a figurative line of demarcation. Today, these men and women wax nostalgic when comparing their own faith and politics to that of the seemingly apathetic and materialistic younger global middle class. A friend of mine, a woman who grew up in Fez and is now a teacher in Casablanca, offered a comparison of generations, drawing on her own experience and that of her husband. She compared her choices and desires to that of her stepdaughters in their teens, who will become part of the new social formation that I describe in the following chapters. Her rhetoric sounds patronizing except that she echoes the complaints of many and repeats the same idealization of the past. She hints at the transition Morocco has made from overwhelming illiteracy to expanding education in the model of emancipation to now making it within market reform:

There is a problem of values. Before [in the era of the modern middle class], there was a mentality of values. These were values of personal enhancement. Now, it is the choice between an Italian brand and a French brand. Our mothers [the generation of Independence] told themselves that they did not want us to suffer like they did. We struggled. It was not easy to be a girl twenty years ago. After school we had to help our mothers with the housekeeping and to run errands. Fine, if I had work, she left me alone. When I did not have work — I adored comic strips and *romans à photos* and I put them in my books. As she was illiterate, she could not recognize the difference except that she knew well the comic strips and she told me, you do not have work, go do errands. Today, the girls watch television and movies and series from the U.S. But they have no idea what the U.S. is. My mentality is traditional. Even if I think my daughters should marry, I do not dare say that in front of my friends [who are leftist intellectuals]. I have said to my daughters to help me in the kitchen so they can learn. But, they do not want to. They do not think that they are going to get married. But, I say, even if you are single, you have to cook. Before, it was clear what we wanted. We wanted to study, go to France, not to marry. Now, young women do not want to marry but [shrugging] . . .

Teachers reminiscing fondly over the profession and students of the past reveal how much the manifestation in comportment of "advancement" affected social judgment.[43] Amira, a teacher in her early forties from a Fassi family, described how she had fought for her job and position, as a single woman living alone in Casablanca, and how strenuous teaching had become as a job. Her father worked as a notary and then as a secretary in the Ministry of Habous. He studied at Quranic schools and Qurawiyyin, the great Islamic teaching mosque founded by the Idrissids. His daughter describes him as "not ignorant." Married to four wives, he had more than twenty children, some of whom died young. His wives lived in separate homes, but they saw each other constantly.

Amira rebelled against his conservatism, against the limitations he felt his daughters needed. Finally, he relented, but the barriers he imposed, and her resistance against them, marked the way she leads her life. At sixteen, she said, "we [the daughters] were afraid to go out [of the house by themselves]. But I truly fought to leave at sixteen years. . . . I broke the barrier. I did not want us to hide. There was nothing to hide. I had the audacity to dialogue with my father. Slowly, he understood that I reason well. He saw that he had children who reasoned well."

She pointed out that in the past, "teachers gave an example to students in their dress and comportment. Now, no. They are respected today but also pitied for their salaries. People don't want to rent an apartment to a teacher with their salaries." Moreover, Amira noted, the students have changed: "We are for the emancipation of girls, to fulfill themselves. I went to a café the other day with another teacher. We saw a student from our school who started singing. She was with a friend and man around thirty [she is about fifteen]. She was flirting with him, but he has the means to take her out. But we were shocked that she could act that way in front of us. This is emancipation in the *mauvaise sens* [the wrong way]."

She is a member of the Socialist Union of Popular Forces (USFP) and a leader of the local section of the party. She participates in the teachers union and sympathizes with human rights organizations and civil society leaders pushing for more freedom of expression and the political and legal acceptance of a public space for debate and critique. Idealizing her generation, she insisted that "before, we were not afraid. In the seventies, the system was more repressive, but we were not afraid. Today, the state lets you talk, but the government is stubborn."

Summary: Economic Development and the Middle Class

By the end of the 1970s, the expansion of investment had produced a much higher rate of inflation (9.1 percent for the decade; *L'Annuaire Statistique* 1996) and bound the state in a vise common to developing countries, that of enormous debt, declining revenue from natural resources, and sluggish industrial advancement due both to mistakes in government management and weak private investment and international competitive advantage. The 1960s and particularly the 1970s had irreparably altered the social structure of Morocco, but the middle class that arose from this period now faced an altered future in the 1980s and 1990s. This was a life in which state intervention was no longer possible and the private sector could not grow fast enough, one in which pensions decreased in real value and unemployed children lived at home.

Real incomes started to fall in the 1980s, instigating the deterioration of the status, based on profession and consumption, and political importance of the modern middle class. Real GNP per capita fell to .4 percent growth between 1980 and 1985, 2.0 percent between 1985 and 1990, 2.9 percent in 1990, 2.2 percent in 1991, and −4.6 percent in 1992 (*L'Annuaire Statistique* 1996). In terms of relative income as well, salaries for workers in manufacturing and the administration began to drop in the 1980s. In 1980, the average salary in industry was slightly more than 3 times the minimum hourly wage (SMIG), and the average salary in public administrations was 4.5 times the SMIG. By 1993, the average salary in industry was 2 times the SMIG, due to an increase in the SMIG and a decline in real salaries in the manufacturing sector, and the average salary in the administration represented only 2.5 times the SMIG.[44]

Furthermore, although the ideal of individual emancipation within the nation had lent legitimacy to the state as an institution, as a source of authority and power, in the postcolonial period the state itself did not lead a course of economic development that would give the modern middle class, or other groups, for that matter, the foundation to become a source of transformation. The modern middle class was created as a necessity of nation building, induced by the imperative of development as well as the departure of the French and the personnel needs for implementation of economy and social policy. When the king perceived this class as an area of political support, its formation also became a political objective.[45] Morocco was unlike other countries, for example, Taiwan and South Korea, where land reform (although supported by UNFP and other leftist parties) gave rise to a rural middle class, or where, as in post-Independence Egypt, military leadership seized control. King Hassan occupied the army with the war in Western Sahara from the mid-1970s onward. He also ensured that an intertwined network of business and political elites continued to dominate the economy, a substantive and functional closeness that made it difficult for either to become independent actors in the 1980s.

Circumscribed in its capacity for collective action and political influence, the modern middle class therefore did not help push Morocco into a more advanced stage of industrialization or a different political system. If, using a Marxist analysis of class and economic transformation (see Brenner 1976), the modern middle class had gained some autonomy from the state through material investment and greater access to power, then they possibly would have pushed elites into greater economic and political reform. Without this ability, like the Eastern European peasants of Robert Brenner's comparison of economic transformation in Europe, they and the following generation have landed in a precarious economic position and become a headache for both the regime and business elites eager for foreign investment drawn by human resources and an inviting consumer market.

The next chapter relates how different the present is, in that now the young, urban, educated generation has become fragmented into groups connected in different ways to the global economy. Chapter 4 draws on the similarity between generations, or the imprint of personal fulfillment so indicative of the modern middle class. Individual emancipation, the cry of the older generation, has not lost its underlying appeal. However, the unity between the rise of a middle class whose project and purpose was modernization and the strength of the nation-state now stands in dramatic relief to the contemporary rupture between the nation and the alienated, restless younger generation of globalization.

3

New Social Groups for

a New Era

In a series of articles discussing Morocco of the twenty-first century, *La Vie Economique* featured a profile of the "new elite," the men and women under 40 who have succeeded in business. In an effort to emphasize the flash, aggressiveness, and self-confidence of this elite, the article ran the following subtitle: "They have no shame at proclaiming their attachment to money, to success. They claim equality of opportunity. *La specificité marocaine,* alibi of all bizarre political behavior, holds no grace in their eyes. They are the Morocco of tomorrow."[1] The article continued with such proclamatory description: "They are young, good-looking, intelligent, taking a bite out of life and advertising their ambitions without false modesty. These are the potential leaders of 21st century Morocco. This 'new race' which imposes itself as the elite of tomorrow has a profile type which differs from that which directs the country now and which carries in it the seeds of certain ruptures." This "profile type" consists of an American versus a French education, an MBA over the *doctorat,* affiliation with American culture, and support for democracy not based on socialist, Marxist, or liberal principles, but on free exchange and easy access to credit. "Democracy demands a financial system which permits social mobility, in offering to savers different products and to entrepreneurs the financial resources responding to their needs."

They are brash, these young men and women in business. They seek only a level playing field so that they can prove themselves. "The only value which is a social concern is this notion of mobility. They claim only equality of opportunity and the possibility for the better 'competitors' to climb the rungs of the hierarchy. . . . At thirty years old, they have full CVs and do not hesitate to seize every new opportunity to improve their salary. The stability of employment dear to their parents is not their thing." If these men and women do not simply quit at the mention of higher remuneration elsewhere, then they attempt to alter the organization of the company in which they work. "In the structures which take the risk of hiring them, they are the agents of rupture. Instead of adapting to the environment, they take the initiative, make proposals, formulate critiques, and take to heart their work." They do not appreciate the nepotism and obscure accounting of older Moroccan *patrons*, and certainly, they dislike the small circle of established businessmen, landowners, and intellectuals that govern political parties and exclude them from political power.

If the "new elite" consists of small-scale entrepreneurs and corporate managers in multinationals or Moroccan firms in the process of revamping for the free trade agreement with the European Union, then the ben Barkas of today, the teachers and intellectuals of middle- and lower-income origins, are among the hundreds of thousands of unemployed and provisionally employed who dominate the national political and social landscape. They are Driss, who came home after completing a doctorate at the Sorbonne to face unemployment for a year and a half. After participating in several sit-ins held by unemployed doctorates, he secured one of the administrative posts created at the initial impetus of the late King Hassan himself, who supposedly regarded jobless doctorates as a national embarrassment.[2]

Those Moroccans fortunate enough to graduate from elite Moroccan business schools or foreign business programs enjoy the benefits of an income high enough to afford luxury items, travel abroad, and financial investment. In contrast, graduates from public universities and most private professional schools typically accept positions in the administration or a private company that, in the worst case, do not compensate for minimum costs of room and board and, in the best, allow for a comfortable but limited lifestyle with extended family assistance. Meanwhile, these graduates wait for the job they feel they deserve because of their education, capacity, and ambition.

In this chapter I discuss both of these populations, suggesting that global market integration has produced among the generation of young, urban, educated two relatively coherent social groups and a broad, mixed group brought together through diminishing status and security. Changes in the division of labor and the rules of competition for jobs have interacted with forces of social reproduction to reconfigure the organization of social differentiation and social status. Separated by their connection to the global market economy, the three groups include consultants and managers guiding the process of integration; service professionals and administrators struggling in sectors still largely regulated by the state; and the unemployed, the nonparticipants, and those clerical or managerial workers employed in unstable, often noncontractual positions. Without political organization or networks and substantial material resources, the young, urban, educated have become, in the case of public sector employees and the unemployed, the victims of economic transition, and for entrepreneurs and managers, opportunists waiting to fill the niches in services and management created largely through foreign investment and trade.

I first discuss how the retreat of the state from market and social intervention and the simultaneous expansion of liberal market capitalism have produced similar consequences for labor markets and economic and social inequality in both the Organization for Economic Cooperation and Development (OECD) and middle-income countries. I then look at how the specific political economy of Morocco, meaning the decisions and larger positions of political and business elites, has affected control over political, economic, and social resources among young graduates and their families. While Morocco has maintained stable progress implementing IMF-prescribed macroeconomic policy, economic growth has never achieved consistently high enough levels (5 to 6 percent annually, according to IMF and World Bank estimates) to decrease unemployment and poverty. The global middle class has thus formed between the sanctions on state investment into a middle class, namely, into sectors like education and public works, and the absence of sufficient foreign and domestic investment to replace job opportunity and income.

Finally, I analyze the rise of new social groups out of changing labor markets and resources. These social groups reflect the new structure of opportunity and manifest a new system of social differentiation derived from this very organization. In the evolving system of social evaluation and distinction, local properties of educational, cultural, social, political, and economic capital interact with the ideology and structure of global market capitalism. The consequence is a new method of distinguishing and justifying social inequality, this time within market capitalism and not within the nation-state. In other words, a proclivity for success in the global market economy is not a mystical quality that graces certain individuals. Rather,

what Bourdieu (1984) calls a scheme of social classification of human character determines individual success by labeling qualities to be of economic
merit and worthy of market demand.

Inequality in Global Market Capitalism

Much of academic analysis of globalization and development has centered
on specific relations between factors, namely, the correlation between trade
liberalization and economic development (e.g., Ben-David 1993; Rodrik
2000, 2002), between labor market flexibility and employment (e.g., di
Tella and MacCulloch forthcoming), and between liberalization and inequality among and within nations (see Bowles 2002; Firebaugh 1999;
Stewart 2000; Jones 1997). More general debates, conducted by academics
and nonacademics alike, have focused on the positive and negative social
and economic impacts of market integration and the relation among inequality, democracy and human rights, and globalization.[3] The volume of
debates around globalization, however, obscures the paucity of research
into both direct cause-effect relations and broader connections in social
historical change.

Both high- and middle-income countries have experienced rising inequality in income distribution due, among other factors, to state retrench-
ment from redistribution policies, deregulation or devolving regulation of
labor markets, and widening differences between occupational prestige and
benefits. Comparative analysis reveals that 15 out of 18 OECD countries, 8
out of 13 countries from Latin America, and 7 out of 10 Asian countries
experienced rising inequality during the 1980s and 1990s (Stewart 2000,
15). Research on income distribution in the United States has indicated
that the earnings of the top 20 percent of the population increased 15
percent during the 1990s, whereas earnings for the bottom 20 percent
increased less than 1 percent and for the middle 20 percent, less than 2
percent. By the end of the decade, surveys showed that the average income
of the top 20 percent of income distribution was, at $137,500, ten times
more than that of the bottom 20 percent (Economic Policy Institute 2000).
Likewise, research conducted on income distribution between 1993 and
1998 in Argentina suggests a widening gap between workers and owners
despite greater labor productivity and an increase in real GDP (Economic
Policy Institute 2001).

Despite inequality in income distribution, conservative economists and
politicians have typically argued that increases in overall growth related to

deregulation and global market liberalization have helped all segments of society, even if income levels have remained widely disparate. Men and women, particularly men, with limited skills have not reaped the rewards of growth as much as higher-skilled populations, but during the 1990s, they still benefited from a tight labor market and an adjustment to the minimum wage. The most conservative argument traces inequality to a high concentration of immigrants, a larger share of employment in service sector rather than manufacturing jobs, and urbanization (see Cox and Alm 1999). Statistics on inequality supposedly also hide mobility into a higher income bracket. Ultimately, these economists turn around the justification unions give for investing more in manufacturing and protecting American workers. They admit that the transition to a dominant service economy and knowledge-based growth may necessitate greater inequality and provoke short-term job loss, but they also contend that, more important, "creative destruction" during the transition sparks momentum and maintains growth.

The critical argument, buttressed by the evidence of, among other trends, increasing disparity in income and wage stagnation for most of the 1970s through the 1990s for middle-income families, is that only a minority truly benefited from the economic boom of the 1990s.[4] Services, the dominant source of employment in the United States, created a large number of bad jobs, with low pay and low possibility.[5] James K. Galbraith (2000), contending forcefully that we consider raising wages rather than simply promoting education and retraining, repeats the contention of other liberal intellectuals and labor unions that we are witnessing the "decline of the middle class" of midcentury America: "The haves are on the march. With growing inequality, so grows their power. And so also diminish the voices of solidarity and mutual reinforcement, the voices of civil society, the voices of a democratic and egalitarian middle class" (265). The division is between the haves and have-nots, with society increasingly polarized between top management and knowledge workers on one end (in what Galbraith calls the K-sector, or capital goods), and production and service sector workers (in what Galbraith calls the C-sector for consumption goods, and the S-sector, now 80 percent of the working population, for in-person services) on the other.[6]

Despite the vast differences in economic growth and industrial development, trends in the Moroccan labor market for educated workers mimic those in the United States, Europe, and Southeast Asia. Jobs in industry and the public sector, sheltered for decades through unions and political interest, have deteriorated in quality. There are a small number of good, high-skill jobs appearing in financial and management services as well as information technology, and some jobs in traditional middle-class occupations such as teaching and other professions, but with inferior working conditions and stagnant or lower pay. Most jobs created, those requiring less training and education, are in in-person services typically associated with female labor, for example, in tourism, office management, and clerical work. Noneducated or lower-educated workers in Morocco can look for jobs in chemical and mining industries, low value-added manufacturing, particularly in textiles and clothing and food processing, as well as in the low-paying, long hours of retail, domestic work, salons, dry cleaners, and so on.[7]

Income distribution in Morocco during the 1990s remained approximately the same, at least for the poorest and wealthiest segments of the population. Between 1990–91 and 1998–99, the percentage of total consumption of the poorest 10 percent of the population declined from 2.8 to 2.6 and rose for the wealthiest 10 percent from 30.8 to 31 (*Les Indicateurs Sociaux* 2000). However, the numbers of Moroccans living in poverty jumped during the decade, increasing from 3.4 million individuals in 1990–91 to 5.3 million in 1998–99, or from 13.1 to 19 percent of the total population (Khadija Masmoudi, "Pourquoi la pauvreté a explosé depuis 1993," *La Vie Economique*, November 2001, 10).

Variation in earnings over time suggests the relative economic position of middle-income groups. Net salary compensation for midlevel administrators grew at a slightly higher rate between the 1980s and 1990s than for upper-level administrators in the public sector, at 4.3 versus 3.8 percent annually between 1983 and 1996 ("1999–2000 Stagnation" 2000, 96). By 1998–99, the third 20 percent consumed 14.8 percent of overall consumption, the fourth consumed 21.3 percent, and the fifth consumed 46.6 percent (*World Development Report* 2000–2001).

Gross figures of compensation perhaps offer a more telling picture of relative inequality. According to a study conducted in the mid-1990s by the Moroccan human resources firm LMS Conseil (1997), a *directeur général* in the private sector earns an average salary of 1,067,989 dhs annually, and a *president directeur général* 1,142,720 dhs. A machinist earns 44,703 dhs annually; a mechanic 64,344 dhs; a skilled worker 47,197 dhs; a secretary 61,357 dhs; a salesperson 100,638 dhs; a programmer 66,894 dhs; a more skilled programmer 120,295 dhs; and an accountant 85,489 dhs. These are reported salaries, which might be lower than real salaries for executives and management (not including perquisites or under-the-table money), and they reflect for the most part wages in medium-size and large (more than one hundred employees), well-established companies (76 percent of companies surveyed; 68 percent of the companies were either entirely foreign-owned or of mixed capital).

The Production of Social Inequality in Morocco

The transformation of the middle class in Morocco reflects the changing interests and behavior of political and economic elites and, likewise, choices about the policies of economic transition — from retaining control over natural resources to altering labor codes — that have propelled global market integration. Formerly implicated in national development as the directors of public sector enterprises or as government administrators, political and economic elites must now reflect on their own connection to the global market and to global social networks.

Beyond budget restrictions, the retreat from state-led investment reflects this creeping distance between younger middle-income populations and the business and political elites that govern the country. First, unlike their concern for low-income rural and urban families still reliant on public subsidies of basic goods, the late Hassan II and Mohammed VI have unabashedly pushed the young, urban, educated to assume individual responsibility and look for positions in the private sector. Mohammed VI has reiterated that *les jeunes diplômés* should not look to la fonction publique as the only source of employment but "explore the private sector *sans complexes*" ("Les Cent Jours de Mohammed VI" 1999).

Second, rather than participate formally in politics through joining a party, younger generations of elite families as well as older businessmen prefer increasingly to participate in civil society organizations that focus on lobbying specific issues at a national level or local projects of development. A survey commissioned by *La Vie Economique* of high-level managers in Morocco found that only 3.2 percent of five hundred cadres belonged to a political party, whereas 25 percent belonged to an *association*. Although these organizations contribute to a climate of political *ouverture*, they reflect the segmentation of interests and division between personal and public behavior. For example, as in the United States and elsewhere in the Arab World, parents with adequate resources prefer to send their children to private schools and, for higher education, abroad, rather than pay attention to reforming the public educational system. In the survey commissioned by *La Vie Economique*, 55 percent of parents sent their children to private elementary schools and 27 percent to *missions étrangères*; 50 percent sent their children overseas for higher education versus 23 percent to the public system in Morocco ("Styles de vie et salaires des cadres," *La Vie Economique*, 1 June 2001, 14).

European and American critics of state divestiture of responsibility warn of the repercussions of this distance between the haves and the overwhelmingly more numerous have-nots (see Skocpol 2000). For instance, Robert Reich (1992) talks about symbolic analysts living in their gated communities, separated in work and leisure from other segments of the population. This separation does not mean, however, that no relation exists, but rather, that relations have taken on a more directly material and less political dimension. Those businessmen who do not grasp the new materiality of social relations, who do not restructure their companies to attract capital and remain competitive, will in all likelihood lose their companies after the Uruguay Round and the EU accord are fully phased in.

Business owners and financiers in Morocco, faced with free trade agreements and erratic economic growth, need consumers willing to purchase goods rather than save, creditors locked into loan payments, and workers attracting through wage levels and, inversely, consumption habits, the inflow of foreign capital and investment. Consumer credit offered by banks and *sociétés de crédit* to individuals and to enterprises almost doubled between December 1995 and December 1997, increasing from 8.36 billion dhs to 14.73 billion dhs (Centre Marocain de Conjoncture 1998, 11).

Market Reform in Morocco and the Bases for Social Transformation

Morocco won praise during the 1990s for its structural adjustment and privatization program, not for explosive economic growth but for steady and stable movement forward with what the IMF calls "sound macroeconomic management."

Following IMF prescriptions, the government restrained inflation (under 3 percent between 1996 and 1998), kept the external current account deficit below 1 percent of GDP, and shored up official reserves.[8] In keeping with the intended consequences of these policies, low inflation allowed the government to reduce interest rates (from 6 percent in February 1998 to 5.5 percent in March 1999). Central government debt, although still at 75.6 percent of GDP in 1998, decreased in percentage of external debt (down more than 13 percentage points between 1994 and 1998) and in debt service ratio (from 32.9 percent in 1994 to 25.2 percent in 1998). By 2003, preliminary estimates had central government debt continuing to decrease to below 70 percent and external debt service ratio down below 16 percent (IMF 1999, 2001, and 2003 Article IV Consultations).

Finally, to create a more appealing and supportive infrastructure for business, the state established six commercial courts and simplified and modernized customs procedures (IMF 1998). By 2002, the government had created one-stop windows to facilitate creating businesses and eliminated reference prices in customs valuation to comply with World Trade Organization rules, causing Morocco's rating in IMF trade restrictiveness to drop (IMF 2003).

To attract investment and trade, Morocco joined the WTO at its inception and signed a free trade agreement with the European Union to be phased in until 2010. Responding to the privatization of state-owned enterprises (SOEs) in utilities, infrastructure, telecommunications, and derivative industries of natural resources, foreign investment reached a total of $1.2 billion in 1997, four times the total of 1996 and 3.5 percent of GDP (IMF 1998). Foreign direct investment doubled overall between 1990 and 1998, rising from $165 million to $322 million (*World Development Report* 2000–2001). By 2003, the IMF and economic analysts were commending Morocco on the privatization of Maroc Telecom (2000–01) and the sale of a cellular telephone licence in 1999, the intention to privatize the tobacco sector, and continued liberalization and restructuring of national companies.

The IMF and World Bank have also expressed concern over rates of economic growth that generally have remained lower than in other countries of the region. During the mid-1990s, economic growth, particularly nonagricultural growth, seemed to be improving. Change in real GDP rose from a low of −6.6 percent in 1995 to 6.3 percent in 1998, and in nonagricultural GDP from a low of 1.9 percent in 1995 to above 3 percent from 1996 to 1998 (IMF 1999). Overall, though, average annual growth in GDP between 1990 and 2001 was 2.5 percent, below lower- and middle-income countries in the Middle East and North Africa, which averaged a 3 percent annual growth rate, and lower-middle-income countries globally, which averaged a 3.7 percent growth rate (*World Development Report* 2003).[9]

Morocco's continued economic dependence on agriculture, which makes up about 15 percent of GDP, has led to wild fluctuations in economic growth, depressing the average growth rate over time and inhibiting institutions like Moody's and Standard & Poor's from giving the country investment-grade ratings.[10] The IMF and World Bank have also criticized the Moroccan state for labor management, from the perspective of neglecting investment in education and training and not reforming sufficiently the labor code and more dramatically reducing the wage cost in the civil service. The IMF calculated that Morocco's change in average GDP growth per laborer was −1.23 percent between the 1980s and 1990, the second-lowest rate in the region.[11] The World Bank has gone further by criticizing slow progress on rural electrification and potable water distribution as well as continued corruption and inefficiency in the administration.[12]

Yet, the slow but relatively consistent effort to adjust macroeconomic policy and privatize SOEs may have allowed Morocco to escape the general crises of legitimacy that have unseated leaders as theoretically unassailable as Suharto. Unlike the other countries of the region, the Moroccan state, with the exception of "bread riots" in 1981 and 1984 and protests against the Gulf War in 1991, has managed economic transition without significant political challenge (Algeria, Egypt, and, to lesser extent, Jordan) or increased authoritarian rule (most notably Tunisia). Furthermore, over the past several decades, the Moroccan state has either tried to control the political legitimacy of Moroccan Islamists through limited inclusion (namely, *al-aslah wattajdid*, the party of Abdelilah Benkirane) or their activity through security measures and political exclusion (*'dl wal-ihsan*, the party of Sheikh Yacine).[13] King Hassan also allowed a coalition of opposition parties (the Koutla), led by Socialist Party (USFP) leader Abderrahmane Youssoufi, to come to power in the fall of 1997, pushing these more popular parties to assume responsibility for economic and social policy rather than parties and political figures closer to the Palace.[14]

In the eyes of the United States, France, and other European countries, Morocco thus offers the hope of North Africa and the Arab World for political liberalization.[15] Morocco does face the same explosive dilemma as states in the Arab World and Indonesia of finding jobs for a young population, particularly lycée and university graduates, while reversing a decline in relative income.[16] In Morocco, the annual population growth rate averaged 2.2 percent between 1970 and 1995, and real earnings per employee were −2.5 percent between 1980 and 1992 (*Human Development Report 1998*, 2002). Urban unemployment rates in Morocco have averaged above 12 percent, and often as high as 60 percent for recent university graduates, since the mid-1980s. Overall urban unemployment in 2000 for men and women ages 15–24 was 37.6 percent; ages 25–34, 30 percent; and ages 35–44, 10.4 percent. Urban unemployment for men was 37.8 percent for ages

25–34 and 9.7 percent for ages 35–44, and for women in comparable age groups, 36.8 and 12.5 percent. The unemployment rate for Casablanca was 23.1 percent, and for Rabat 22.4 percent (*Annuaire Statistique* 2001).

The most important phenomena in unemployment that market liberalization has produced are weakly documented national trends in long-duration unemployment and underemployment and fairly well-examined unemployment among university and lycée graduates. In 1999, the average duration of unemployment was 38.6 months and 71.4 percent of the unemployed had been without a job longer than 12 months (*Les Indicateurs Sociaux* 2000). The qualification to these statistics is that we have little idea as to the nature of jobs found or the security of tenure, so that we cannot evaluate the role of turnover in employment trends.

For university graduates, the unemployment rate in 1984 was 6.5 percent, and for graduates of grandes écoles and institutes, 1.2 percent. By 1990, the unemployment rate for university graduates was 23.3 percent; for graduates of grandes écoles and institutes it was 1.1 percent (*Population et Emploi* 1992). In 2000, 22.7 percent of the active urban population (age 15 or older) with a baccalaureate was unemployed, 45.7 percent with a university diploma, 2 percent with a diploma from a grande école or institut, and 29.6 percent with a technical degree. The overall unemployment rate for university graduates was 28.9 percent; the rate for graduates of professional school was 32 percent. By comparison, the unemployment rate among men and women without a diploma was 7.1 percent and for men and women with a basic education (six years), 25.8 percent (*Les Indicateurs Sociaux* 2000).

The Course of Liberalization

Progress on economic reform has remained consistent and steady in Morocco because, first, historically, the makhzen has functioned as a broker and manipulator of decisions in a pluralistic context. Second, all of the actors implicated in the decision-making process over economic reform support the continued legitimacy of the monarch. Third, Morocco has never fully implemented a state-planned economy, allowing the private sector, with the king often at its center, to grow even during the most state-centered economic periods.

King Hassan took advantage of his triple role of broker, supreme leader, and businessman to push not only economic transition in general, but also the marginalization of political figures and business leaders reluctant to follow along. On the other side, acting as the representation for business leaders, the Confederation Générale des Entrepreneurs Marocains (CGEM) has proven to be prepared and organized for debates over policy. CGEM has worked to propel reform forward without dismissing the power-sharing arrangement maintained among leftist opposition parties and unions, the Palace, and large landowners, and thus potentially inciting political instability.

I do not elaborate on the political economy of structural adjustment in Morocco because other students of the region have done this work (e.g., Zartman 1987; White 1998; Deneoux and Maghroui 1998). Political scientists have analyzed structural adjustment and market reform with much more sophisticated models of decision making than I present here. Rather than examine the interplay among different elite political, agricultural, and business leaders over the pace and scope of reform, I focus on how adoption of a particular model of economic growth and development becomes the catalyst for social division and social formation.

First, market liberalization has created incentives for global alliances and self-perception and thereby diminished local political interest in local social formation. Structurally, whereas the Protectorate led to the rise of a working class and national elite and the modern state fostered the evolution of a modern middle class, business and political elites within market reform have sought to become partners of international capital while workers have joined the global competition for cheap labor. The absence of state support for middle-class participation in the market economy and skewed distribution of resources has also given an advantage to children of wealthy families, meaning that some of the most successful participants in market reform are also among the youngest. For example, the two most prominent Moroccan-owned investment banks, Casablanca Finance Group and Upline Securities, were founded by 30-year-olds, Amyn Alami and Hassan Ait Ali. The most successful conversion was conducted by King Hassan II, who bought a majority stake in Omnium Nord Afrique (ONA) in 1980 and pushed it to become a Moroccan goliath in industries from media to fishing to the import of consumer goods.[17]

In contrast to the transnational relations of elites, Moroccan workers, whether in agriculture, the informal sector, manufacturing, or industry, identify, at least to some extent, with neighborhood leadership, the local *caïd,* unions, and potential association among workers on the factory or shop floor. In other words, their resources may extend beyond their immediate income and work benefits to family and more conventional political hierarchies. Moroccan unions, which represent about 10 percent of Morocco's approximately 5 million urban workers and are concentrated in the public sector, have conducted regular strikes during liberalization. These strikes are typically confined to public sector occupations, such as teaching, and meet with resistance, even repression, in the private sector.[18]

The three unions of Morocco, Confederation Democratique du Travail (CDT), Union Marocaine du Travail (UMT), and Union Générale du Travail Marocain (UGTM), have participated in a *dialogue sociale* with the state and the CGEM since 1996. The unions have also had little recourse, except single factory strikes, to protest nonimplementation of the existing Code du Travail, although they have maintained the SMIG (minimum hourly wage, for urban areas) close to average wage and much higher than the SMAG (minimum daily wage, for rural areas).[19] Expectedly, the IMF has insisted on implementing labor market flexibility measures — freezing civil service employment and reducing or eliminating the minimum hourly and daily wage and benefits — to slow down rural-urban migration and decrease labor costs to employers.

The slow movement forward to avoid radical departure or isolation of important political actors has not helped the fate of most of the younger generations of lycée and university graduates. State actors, constrained by political pressures, are unable to regulate the private sector or to offer incentives to reduce unemployment, enforce meritocractic rather than nepotistic hiring practices, or improve training and education rapidly enough to match the needs of the job market. The state cannot even assist the model entrepreneurs, who need intervention to compete with corporate elites buttressed by political connections and the material resources to pay rents when necessary.[20]

The state has not ignored unemployment completely, a politically untenable position at best. Although insisting that they look in the private sector, King Hassan repeatedly promised to help create jobs for university graduates, particularly unemployed doctorates, in government ministries. For example, in a 1998 discours for *La Fête de la Jeunesse,* the king called on Parliament, the government, and "les partenaires sociaux" to guarantee the creation of 25,000 jobs a year for jeunes diplômés having a doctorate or *le bac* + 2 (two years of education beyond the baccalaureate exam).

Under the king's leadership, the state encouraged the private sector to hire *stagaires*, or interns, for no or minimal wage. The state created CIDOPE, an employment service for young graduates that runs workshops and posts job listings, the Conseil National de la Jeunesse et de l'Avenir (CNJA), and the program of *jeunes promoteurs* that offers loans to young (under age 45) entrepreneurs. However well-intentioned, the loan program was not well-designed. Entrepreneurs with typically little training or experience were forced to carry a debt of 90 percent of their start-up capital, which itself, at 1 million dhs to 3 million dhs, was not enough. The state and bank each provide 45 percent of the loan, to be paid back over twelve to fifteen years at a rate of 5 percent interest. Unfortunately, even with a three-year grace period to begin repayment, many of the awarded entrepreneurs defaulted on payments, unable to sustain both profits for reinvestment and personal survival as well as the loan.

Furthermore, these loans were mostly granted to young doctors and lawyers seeking to open an office or entrepreneurs from families tapped into the right social networks, through which the young man or woman can find a sympathetic ear in a cooperating bank. Eventually, banks, aware that the loans were structurally flawed and nonproductive economically, offered few loans or quit offering them altogether. According to a report by La Banque Centrale Populaire (2000), the national bank that provided 60 percent of the loans, between 1988 and 1998, only 10,000 loans were granted for a total investment of 5.26 billion dhs and a total credit of 4.3 billion dhs. These loans created 37,000 jobs, or 3,700 positions a year. La Banque Populaire itself granted 6,450 loans between 1988 and June 30, 2000, generating indirectly the creation of 26,500 jobs. Of these posts, 53 percent belonged to medical professions, 13 percent to other professions, and 27 percent to industry and services. At least 41 percent of borrowers either defaulted on their loans or faced difficulty with payments, either to the state or to the bank.

The Nagging Question of Jobs

For younger generations of graduates, liberalization of regulations regarding trade and foreign investment, privatization of SOEs, and reduced state presence in the economy has led both to niches of entrepreneurial opportunity in the private sector and a drastically diminished labor market for white-collar jobs. For young entrepreneurs searching for low-risk investment opportunity that requires little start-up capital, greater importation of foreign goods and foreign and domestic production of consumer goods have created demand for market research, advertising (design, printing, copying, and the media forum, such as magazines, to expose products), information systems, and management consulting. Imports of consumer goods, although well below countries like Indonesia or the Philippines in total value and growth, almost doubled in value between 1986 and 1992, rising from 3.47 billion dhs to 7.09 billion dhs (*Resilience and Growth through Sustained Adjustment* 1995, table A16). Clearly reflecting changing taste for consumer goods, average annual expenditure per capita on secondary goods grew at a slightly slower pace than expenditure on basic goods between 1970 and 1985, or 10.9 versus 9.4 percent, but grew at a much faster comparative rate, 8.8 versus 17.5 percent, between 1985 and 1991 (Centre Marocain de Conjoncture 1996, 32).[21]

On the other hand, university, professional school, and lycée graduates have for the most part seen shrinking opportunity. Companies eyeing unstable rates of economic growth and increasing competition tend to prefer temporary employees and, despite complaints of a paucity of talented middle managers, seem to regard managerial staff (educated white-collar labor) as a luxury. Although successive governments have pressured the private sector to hire more university graduates, the private sector, crying economic pressure and unqualified labor, has resisted successfully. Morocco's trajectory of economic growth certainly has not favored liberal arts or science graduates, or even graduates of the now plenitude of private professional schools. Annual growth in services, the most likely sector for university graduates to enter, averaged 2.8 percent between 1990 and 1995, a decrease from 4.2 percent between 1980 and 1990 (*World Development Report* 1997). The value added of the service sector to GDP remained around 50 percent through the 1990s (*World Development Report* 2000–2001).

Sluggish in terms of jump-starting overall economic growth, new investments in industries like textiles and chemicals produce tens of thousands of jobs annually, whereas new investments in services related to industry rarely produce over five hundred jobs a year (*Resilience and Growth through Sustained Adjustment* 1995, table A15). The state has encouraged the private sector to hire stagaires, or interns, who work for no or little pay. However, companies as well as the administration itself profit from this system by simply renewing internships rather than hiring full-time workers.[22]

The Moroccan state began to cut jobs after 1984, halting an upward trend in job creation that the state started in 1975. Government consumption did not shrink significantly in terms of percentage of GDP after the adoption of a structural adjustment program, declining from 18 to 15 percent of GDP between 1980 and 1995.[23] However, comparatively speaking, government growth dropped off considerably after the mid-1980s. Between 1971 and 1975, the government grew at an average of 6 percent a year; between 1976 and 1980, 13.4 percent; and between 1984 and 1993, never more than 7 percent, falling to rates under 3 percent by the beginning of the 1990s (*Resilience and Growth through Sustained Adjustment* 1995).

Statistics on job growth between 1970 and 1989 reveal how much hiring itself fell off in the public sector. As mentioned in chapter 2, from the early 1970s, annual job growth in the administration reached figures as high as 8.8 percent in 1974, 7.8 percent in 1976, and 9.3 percent in 1977. The last year that showed this level of growth was 1980, at a rate of 6.1 percent. Afterward, job creation in the administration never surpassed the 1988 rate of 3.5 percent (*Population et Emploi* 1992, 264). The number of jobs created in the administration ranged between 10,000 and 15,000 from 1983 to 1994, a drop from 45,267 posts in 1982, the last year before the adoption of a structural adjustment program. The numbers decreased or increased by several thousand during the 1990s, reaching 25,000 in 1999 (el Oufi 2000). However, the Jettou government in 2003 committed to not hiring in the civil service and to encouraging early retirement and a review of the remuneration and advancement system.

Of the professionals and bureaucrats I interviewed, only two had found permanent positions in the administration, and two as teachers in the public system, although these two women obtained their posts in the early 1980s, before unemployment rates among university graduates soared.[24] Most of the men and women I interviewed work for private companies in clerical or low-level staff positions that pay by the hour or month and offer no health or pension benefits.

Responding to instability and weak remuneration in the private sector, young university graduates prefer public sector posts, which offer job security. In a survey conducted among five hundred students at the Facultés of Letters, Sciences, Law, and Medicine, as well as INSEA (the national business school), 36 percent of the students expressed a desire to work in the public sector, versus 16.8 in professions and 21.8 in the private sector; 9 percent responded that they wanted to become jeune promoteurs (Bourquia, El Harras, and Bensaïd 1995).

Yet, beyond analysts at the IMF and World Bank, political figures and intellectuals in Morocco believe the labor market regulations that maintain security and higher wages hinder employment growth. They also perceive the attitude and behavior of unemployed university graduates as distorting demand. *La Nouvelle Tribune*, a paper run by the son of Ali Yata, the long-time head of the Socialist Party (PPS), argues that labor law in Morocco "organizes unemployment more than it encourages employment" (April 3–

9, 1997, p. 13). A *Vie Economique* article states without compunction, "Ask an unemployed person if he accepts working for just the SMIG, or even less . . . and he would be delighted, indeed happy. His frustration will be immediately replaced by hope, his dignity comforted. Consequently, his penchant for revolt and striking will be dulled greatly" (March 14, 1997, p. 36).

The Effect on Education

With the reorganization of the labor market has come a reorganization of education, as private education becomes more prestigious and more students elect to pursue professional training over a general scientific or liberal arts education in the public universities. Education, though, has continued to claim a sizable portion of government budgets, remaining above 17 percent since 1981. Numbers of students enrolled have also continued to climb. Secondary school enrollment reached 28 percent of the total school-age (12–17) population by 1992; postsecondary (ages 20–24) enrollment reached 10 percent (*World Development Report* 1995). By 2000, there were 452,365 students enrolled in public secondary schools out of a population of approximately 3.2 million ages 15–19 and 261,629 enrolled at universities out of a population of 2.9 million ages 20–24 (*Annuaire Statistique* 2001).

Entrepreneurs and businesspeople have usually attended private school from kindergarten to elementary to postbaccalaureate, perhaps switching only for public lycées, which are still considered to be of higher quality than most private lycées, or considered at least sufficient after acquiring learning skills at private elementary schools.[25] Instead of studies in France, for instance at the Sorbonne or at the national French school of administration (ENA), they go to les grandes écoles, the national management school, Institut Supérieur de Commerce et d'Administration des Enterprises (ISCAE), elite *écoles de commerce et gestion*, such as Ecole Supérieure de Gestion (ESG) or Institut des Hautes Etudes de Management (HEM). They may also attend an *école supérieure d'informatique et d'electronique*, the most prestigious of which is Ecole Supérieure d'Informatique et de Gestion (ESIG). When they study overseas, they attend business programs, preferably in the United States rather than France. Several of the men and women I interviewed had pursued an MBA in the United States, and others who had studied in Morocco had visited the United States on training tours or business. They also study at the English-language university, al-Akhawayn, created in a partnership between the Saudi and Moroccan governments, with personal financing from King Hassan II.

The material and educational resources offered by the private and the public grandes écoles and ISCAE attended by future entrepreneurs and managers allow greater access than *les facultés* or the less expensive private schools to the areas of knowledge critical to economic globalization, such as software technology and international finance, and even opportunity to study in France. The quality of instruction, from class size itself, and physical differences between the campuses can also be striking. For example, ISCAE boasts a swimming pool and new buildings and HEM, among others, its own building, whereas the much larger, overcrowded facultés of law and humanities provide minimal facilities, transport, and funding for the students. The less expensive écoles de commerce offer older computers and basic sparse classrooms that occupy the single floor of an office building.

The lives of the teachers themselves reflect the contrasts in resources. I heard more than once in the gossip about their declining standard of living that there are professors at public universities and schools living in the bidonvilles outside of Casablanca and that teachers now want positions in rural areas where they can afford a car and an apartment, or what they could expect in the past. More than a few teachers I knew or knew of teach both in the public system and the private, and both students and teachers complained that these teachers would shirk their duties at the secure public job for the hourly wage they earned on the side.

The students from the *fac*, described in more detail below, become one among the masses if they study liberal arts and unemployable because of little commercial or state research and development if they study physical and natural sciences. Of course, neither type of education, despite the prejudices of those in the more practical disciplines of economics and business, implies inferior capacity. A top-level banker once told me that rather than be impressed with the graduates of one of these elite schools, who should possess all of the skills and savoir-faire companies want, he admires the university graduates for their survival skills and drive. "If someone survives the fac, I say *Chapeau* [hat's off]." Despite his confidence, however, an increasing number of students at the fac who want to optimize their opportunities are opting to quit for vocational or professional training or one of the less expensive écoles de commerce.

The Appearance of New Social Groups

Before, there were very few very wealthy families. There was another social structure. These were the families that were *très bien eduqués*, they had a certain culture. There were members of the families that were well educated, when we say educated for this time, we mean religious education, often because they were at the religious university [Quaraoui-yine], etcetera, so they possessed a philosophy, morale, ethics, *un savoir-vivre*. But very few were the great landowners or *commerçants*. There were very few families like this in Morocco, at least in my milieu. In Fez, it was the people from the Souss, the families from the Souss. But above all, it was the people who were eduquée, civilized, etcetera.

After Independence, people made money because everything had to be redone. There were people who made money who had not gone very far in their schooling. They began with commerce and industry and things worked. It was very easy. Others went overseas for their education and then they came back. Like my father, he is a doctor. He studied medicine in France and then he came back. He lives well but he is not rich here. He lives well, he has given his kids a good education. He was one of the first doctors in Morocco, okay, not one of the first, but they were very rare during that period. He preferred to set himself up in a *quartier populaire* because of his ethics, because he was a little bit to the left. In the beginning, he made a lot of money because there were very few doctors, but that's it, he doesn't make anything anymore. There are so many doctors that he, he is lost in the masses. It is over. He does it for pleasure now. He is too old [68 at the time]. — Myriam

It is necessary to have ambitions, above all in a country like Morocco. It is necessary to guard these ambitions. If I were in the USA, I would be able to take a position and be content. Here, you should have your business to earn enough money for an ordinary lifestyle. You have to give kids private education, etcetera. I don't know how people who earn 2,000 dhs a month survive. They must wear torn clothes and eat simply. In my family, and we are not many, my father can spend 600 dhs a week just on meat. But Moroccans, you know, they get by despite everything. They have their televisions, video players, the satellite dish. They earn 2,000 dhs a month but they get by nevertheless. — An agent at a consumer credit company

Entrepreneurs, private sector managers, professionals, stagaires, low-paid service workers, and the unemployed claim in common the immediate effect of economic reform on their lives, whether through the emergence of economic demands such as marketing or the disappearance of jobs. However, in terms of the imbalanced struggle over resources that underlies the organization of social inequality, these are different groups with different interests, polarized, as Erik Olin Wright (1997) would argue, between those possessing authority and skill in the marketplace and those whose skills fail to acquire authority.[26] Their locations within a class structure outlined by Wright would be at opposite ends of the middle class. They are the hustling young entrepreneurs claiming far more economic power than the unemployed, the *meskīn,* meaning "poor, miserable, submissive, servile."

I draw a distinction among the three groups on the basis of economic activity and symbolic success in a more general atmosphere of globalization. Their formation into social groups is based on larger processes of social and economic closure that depend on what Bourdieu (1984, 172) describes as "the distribution of capital, the balance-sheet of a power relation." Bourdieu proposes that actors draw on different forms of capital when they participate in particular fields of activity — political, social, cultural, or otherwise. Drawing on this capital takes objective form in the systems of classification through which actors act and think, systems of social classification that perpetuate in turn social hierarchies based on distribution of capital. In other words, capital is objectified cognitively in characteristics such as manner of articulation and posture that imply confidence, intelligence, and sophistication, qualities that mark social differentiation and social class.

I suggest that we can conceive of new social groups because trajectories of social mobility and the very types of actors they produce have changed with the imposition of global market capitalism. Distribution of capital now separates individuals into career paths that support market reform and legitimize a new system of social classification based on evaluation of economic ability. Here, analytic capacity, intelligence in business, and initiative serve as reference points for social distinction and, thus, employability in the new marketplace. Value in fact depends less on the needs of an autonomous market than on the imperative of social reproduction. Entrepreneurs and managers claim the intellectual and analytic capacity to put together a spread sheet, design an advertising campaign, update software, and even reorganize a company, and thus find employment, acquire resources, and achieve status more easily than their peers. However, the value of their abilities depends not simply on function within market capitalism but also on social translation of capital into ability. A secretary, an accountant, and a teacher may work just as hard or harder than an entrepreneur and demonstrate relatively equal creativity. Yet, they confront in what they produce the lower value that their social, economic, and educational capital assigns to their individual talents.

Channeled into specific trajectories, identified with certain qualities, young men and women form sociospatial networks and claim physical spaces as their own, whether nightclubs, parks, or homes, and cultivate lifestyles that mark social affiliation. The sections that follow discuss first the distribution of social, economic, and educational capital that underpins the structural formation of each social group and determines its boundaries. For instance, although the unemployed could become bureaucrats, the inevitability of this depends on the specific individual. Both the unemployed and the bureaucrat could not, at least in my research, go on to become managers in a multinational or Moroccan company.

The biographies of the men and women I met in Morocco suggest that among the institutional relations, or what Bourdieu calls "class of conditionings" and "structuring structures," within which they engage, educational capital appears more critical than social and economic capital to determining career trajectory. Economic and social capital, as well as gender, have more influence than education on the particular position of the individual within the division of labor. For example, the men (mostly) and women who become entrepreneurs can draw on family financial resources and social contacts in the administration or other companies, whereas men and women from less well-off families tend to look for jobs in established firms, breaking out on their own only after years of experience. In addition, women tend to dominate in service industries like media and advertising, and men go into market research, graphic design and printing, and consulting.

After laying out the structural formation of social groups, I analyze how media, the discourse of market liberalization in general, and the men and women themselves explain social differentiation within market reform. More specifically, how do they justify their own success or struggles? Do they cite individual merit, privilege, or external handicaps? I try to explain how social separation, self-identity vis-à-vis one's peers, reflects the production of new social categories and ideological influence. The process resembles the emergence of the category of middle class during the period of modernization and nationalism but this time, focuses more narrowly, and this is significant sociologically, on labels of entrepreneur or unemployed during economic transition.

Entrepreneurs and Managers in the Global Economy

These men and women could be called Morocco's symbolic-analysts, the category of workers Robert Reich (1992) defines as problem identifiers and problem solvers.[27] They are the smallest group, measured perhaps most accurately by the thousands of students studying at ISCAE, the four or five elite business schools, and the grandes écoles and institutes.[28] According to Reich, symbolic-analysts in the United States typically work outside of a corporate structure and earn their reputation and income more through demonstrations of creativity than sheer quantity of work hours. They congregate in particular geographic areas and neighborhoods, such as Silicon Valley, feeding off their social networks and exchange of knowledge to further their careers.

Of the men and women I interviewed in this group, all except one, an engineering supervisor in a manufacturing firm, worked in the service sector. They either owned their own business in marketing, consulting, or printing, or they worked for an advertising agency, media organization, or one of the investment banks that conduct initial public offerings. If married, they lived in a middle-income area near the center of Casablanca, and if still single, often in the villa of their parents. With the exception of one woman who dropped out of the university to attend a less prestigious private business school, all of these men and women attended an elite business school, an MBA program, or a foreign engineering/applied technical school. About half came from Fassi families, and their fathers worked as professionals, high-level administrators, or business managers. The fathers of the other half were teachers or illiterate laborers.

Whether running their own business or working for a company, entrepreneurs and managers typically earned at least 10,000 dh ($1,000–$1,250) a month with benefits. Employees in Moroccan and multinational companies also often earned money on top of the official salary declared to the government, "black money," or a supplement given under the table. Myriam, who eventually quit the advertising agency to open a restaurant, told me that she earned 15,600 dhs ($1,560–$1,950) a month before taxes and 10,500 dhs ($1,050–$1,313) a month after, with 2,000 ($200–$250) added monthly through *frais de representation*, or, as she called it, the "2,000 that comes from dust," to total a salary of 12,500 dhs ($1,250–$1,563) per month. Each month she paid 33 percent of her income in taxes and 160 dhs ($16–$20) to social security. For her, the salary was not high enough. Before she quit, she complained, "I do not think I earn a good living. I am the director of a department and there is a lot of stress."

The entrepreneurs were typically saddled with debt, paying off jeunes promoteurs or other forms of loans. As mentioned above, the jeunes promoteurs loans, at 90 percent of the start-up capital of a young entrepreneur, were financially infeasible, burdening a 20- or 30-year-old, relatively inexperienced businessperson with insurmountable financial obligation. I asked Myriam about starting a fast-food restaurant in a downtown space her father owns.

Myriam: I have been so discouraged by everyone. I mean, administratively it is unbearable. There are too many problems. The people who start their own businesses are not able to stabilize because there are so many taxes, so much corruption, so many things. We cannot do it honestly. It is very embarrassing morally. Me, I am not someone who is extremely ambitious. It is very problematic for me to not be honest. Also, I do not have specific training. I have an education that is very general. Ultimately, an MBA is very general. It is not a specific thing that I do. I can work in the restaurant business, design, all that I can do, but it is not a particular expertise. I am not an engineer, I do not have a *cabinet d'étude*. It is not a trade that I do.

Author: Don't you think that you have succeeded very well here?

Myriam: No, yes, I have succeeded in what I do. But this does not please me. I am going to change. But I don't know were to go. I do not like marketing at all. It is not that I don't like it but that what I do is just part of a processing line of marketing. Marketing is a tool. I absolutely do not want to be the tool of another person. I want to use others to succeed myself.

However, despite debts and complaints of unfair salaries, this group still earned sufficient income and received enough family support to subsidize a particular lifestyle. They drove their cars, went out to eat, and surfed the Net. They traveled in Morocco and less often overseas, and took business trips within and outside the country. When I asked Myriam what she did for fun, she replied, "I go out with my friends, most of the time just girls, not with boys, except a brother or a cousin. I drink a lot in Morocco, more than in the U.S. [where she studied business as an undergraduate for two years]. I go to Fandango, Barberouz [night clubs along the boardwalk of Casablanca]." Myriam also pointed out how much social capital can influence lifestyle: "Lifestyle depends upon family contacts. If you know people in other countries you can stay with them. Other people with the same salary who do not have the contacts have to pay [for a hotel]."

Unlike Reich's symbolic-analysts, who knew during the 1990s that their labor was in high demand and therefore claimed social status in the United States and elsewhere, entrepreneurs and managers in the service sector contended that they are not adequately appreciated, financially or socially, for their abilities. Daoud, married to an art teacher who also studied in France, certainly earned above 10,000 dhs/a month, drove one of his father's cars, and lived in his grandfather's old apartment. Despite the relative privilege of his material life and the luxury of being able to marry in his twenties and live in his own place, for Daoud, his possessions were hand-me-downs, and his dependence, as a salaried and therefore taxable employee, a position of weakness vis-à-vis the state. The cultivation and worldliness he believed he demonstrated was for him a cause for social marginality, not higher positioning in the Moroccan social hierarchy.

Daoud's disgruntlement, which receives fuller treatment in the next chapter, reflects how financial analysts and managers, the most elite group among the new global middle class, are also the first group to disconnect, to float between the nation-state and a half-imaginary, half-real global arena. This contention of marginality underscores the orientation and binding mentality of the group itself. These are men and women educated at the same institutions, sharing the same social networks (through marriage and friendship), and speaking the same language of global market capitalism. The ambition, analytical skills, and knowledge of market capitalism that this group feels so proud to claim as their own also isolates them from other groups that they perceive — because of education, background, and manner of self-presentation — as less ambitious, less capable, and less deserving of professional reward.

When Youssef, the owner of a computer graphics firm, and I began to discuss his two sons, he told me that he had given a Macintosh to his older son when he was 4.

> Youssef: I think that the *éducation* of the parents is more important than the school. At least, fifty-fifty . . . After, the children will find their voice themselves. The problem of the future is that there will be two classes. One, the people who know, who have access to knowledge, or the class which progresses. Two, the people who do not follow, or the class which is dragged along, [where] unemployment is going to become more pronounced. It will no longer be a problem of means but of knowledge. Children who have access to a computer are going to be very curious.
>
> Author: What will be the consequence of this division?
>
> Youssef: [Society] will crack. This is not to say there will be a revolution but a crisis in the society. It is very difficult to evaluate how this is going to evolve. If everyone was like me, perhaps it would be better. You do your work, you follow your rhythm like me. I created value added, I am able to employ [in the future] twenty people.
>
> Author: What percentage of the population do you think acts this way?

Youssef: There are some young people who make this effort. They work a lot. They create. There are people like this.

The Traditional Occupations: Professions and the Bureaucracy

A bureaucrat may have originally been the unemployed graduate and, therefore, someone whose social identity passed from one stage to another. On finding work, the formerly unemployed university graduate can take on the self-protective, confident air of someone who has overcome what is now the misfortune of others. I asked the co-owner of a small music taping business if he sympathized with the hunger strikes and sit-ins unemployed doctorates organize to protest for government jobs. Although Rachid, the owner, had been unemployed for more than a year before he started the business with his cousin, he replied matter-of-factly, "I do not know. I am not unemployed." Yet, whether six months or six years from graduation, membership in a particular group still depends on the distribution of capital and thus assumes a structural dimension.

The men and women in this group all earned a *licence* and often pursued a *3ème cycle*, or Master's-level graduate, course of studies. A few attended a public or private professional school, such as the national school for tourism in Tangiers or one of the second-tier private écoles de commerce. The men tended to work in the professions of the older modern middle class, as state bureaucrats, professionals, and teachers. Many of the women worked as accountants, clerical staff, or secretaries in private enterprises or in government ministries.[29]

Typically born outside of Casablanca, the parents of professionals and bureaucrats as well as the unemployed moved into densely populated residential areas away from the center of Casablanca, such as Hay Mohammadi, or into older areas, such as 'n Shuq. Professionally, the fathers of the men and women in this group, like the fathers of the unemployed, fell into two groups: middle- and lower-level state employees and professionals who belong to the modern middle class, and largely illiterate factory workers and tradesmen.

For example, Rachid is the son of a retired administrator who also owned a few pieces of property. Rachid's older cousin and business partner, Habib, is the son of an architect and a schoolteacher who live in El Jadida. However, the father of Ibrahim, a teacher of English at a private language center and two private lycées, was an illiterate factory worker. The father of Khadija, a secretary at a private company, drove trucks from Morocco to northern France six times a year and taught himself to read.

Such stark contrasts in literacy, parental education, and profession actually had little impact on career trajectory. Administrators and factory workers alike pushed their children to attend school and to pursue a stable office job, in other words, to follow the path of social mobility enjoyed by the modern middle class.[30] In fact, only financial contribution distinguished parental intervention into mobility. Those children who could borrow money from their parents had the possibility to launch a business, no matter how small. They could also remain in school, even if they had to repeat a year or go to work in public hospitals or private clinics that often pay very little. In contrast, those students whose parents could not help financially often quit their studies if the program required too much time or if they encountered problems, such as failing an exam or needing to make an expensive, time-consuming commute.

For instance, Mounir was born in Casablanca to a family originally from Ourzazate, in the south of Morocco. His father worked at customs in the airport for more than thirty years, and his mother worked in an office of a government insurance program that reimburses bureaucrats for medical expenses. Of Berber origin, he did not speak Tashlahit, though his parents do (his family speaks Arabic at home). When I spoke to him, his two sisters were 24 and 19. The older started out at la Faculté de Droit in Casablanca but then switched to a private training institute to become a *prothèse dentaire*. The program lasted for three years, at the end of which she wanted to open her own office. Her family lacked the means to pay for this and she was considering taking a *credit jeune promoteur* (although, as her brother commented, "Ce n'est pas evident"). The school cost 4,000 dhs/month and Mounir told me to mark down that it is too expensive: "You put down that it is too expensive. The school is really for the children of the rich. We do not have the resources to put three kids in a private school."

The younger sister also attended the university, but the conditions of the fac overwhelmed her. She was thinking of going to work with Moroccan artisana or to open a caftan store. Of her studies, he said, "It is not serious. Everyone just has a good time. Because she has no transportation, she takes eight buses a day. She is obliged to be the first student there because if she is not directly in front of the professor, she cannot follow the lesson."

During the conversation, Mounir told me that he wanted to be a psychiatrist, although if he decided to pursue this goal, he would have to continue his studies for five more years. "I cannot continue, though, if I do not earn a salary." At the time, he received 900 dhs/month from the government as an intern (seventh year). He worked at a hospital as a generalist, changing specialities every two months. There are not a lot of psychiatrists in Morocco, he explained, and "fewer that are good." There is a "shame of going to a psychiatrist. This signifies that you are crazy. There is much more of a custom of using traditional methods." Describing his options, he protested his inability to leave Morocco for better opportunity elsewhere:

> I have the right to go abroad [even if he cannot practically]. France accepts beggars and refuses doctors. I find it not logical that a Moroccan who does dishes and marries a French woman [in order to get his papers], while me, a doctor, am not welcome. Studying abroad is an expectation of human rights. Everyone has the right to learn. This is to say that, for example, the U.S. declares itself to be the freest country but not in this way. Everyone has the right to learn and then return to their country to serve. [Yet] France accepts only those who have the means. If I had the money, I would go even to the U.S. I tell you, if Morocco does not grow, that is not our fault, it is the fault of the Americans, of France. Swiss banks accept Moroccan money and then tell their clients to come to them [to live] if they have a political problem [because of high unemployment rates, and so on]. I find that dishonest.

I asked him what he intended to do in order to go abroad and he replied that he was applying to take a job in Morocco and forget about his studies. He said nonchalantly, "My personal solution is to work in a laboratory. I did an interview, they like my CV, what I have done."

Distant from the elites and even the minimal family clout enjoyed by entrepreneurs and managers, bureaucrats, temporary employees, and the unemployed depend on contacts through extended family, friends, and intermediaries, and luck or reward through merit.[31] Ibrahim, a teacher, studied English at the fac and went on for graduate study, but quit after a year. He cited the expense and fatigue of the commute from Casablanca to Rabat as the primary reasons for dropping out. He also remarked bitterly on several occasions that the students who passed the tough qualifying exam for the succeeding year were the worst students and the best connected. Beyond their living at home, among the men and women I interviewed only Rachid and Habib benefited from the resources of their families. They remodeled a vacant store space that Rachid's father owned, furnishing it with stereo equipment and CD covers, as well as posters of Arab, European, and American bands. Habib's father also helped him pay the tuition at a private business school after he studied English literature at the university.

More often, men and women with a stable income assisted younger siblings, who might themselves be unemployed or temporarily employed, and their parents with expenses for education and the home.[32] Ibrahim, who is a middle child, explained that he relied on his older brothers and sister when he was at the university and that now he must provide for the sister, who just finished her degree in economics and is contemplating another at a private business school. When I knew him in the late 1990s, Ibrahim still lived in a two-room apartment with his unmarried brothers and sisters (all in their twenties and thirties). He denied his interest in marriage, preferring to save money to buy a car or to accumulate savings for the future. After I left, he found a job with a language institute and started to travel, taking groups of English-language students to places like London to practice their skills.

The few entrepreneurs and managers who did not come from upper-middle-income families contributed as well to the family income. One of this small group, a 34-year-old, French-educated engineer, resented his role as the eldest: "I work for a family of ten. The day that I marry and establish my own *foyer*, my family will have problems." Unlike him, with his French education and his entrance into the job market when possibilities were more numerous, his brothers and sisters will graduate from the fac and face greater competition for jobs.

Professionals and bureaucrats who are situated between financial success and the ennui of unemployment typically demonstrated the most resignation toward the power structure in Morocco and the least conviction that they could alter their circumstances by moving elsewhere. They get by on their one to several jobs, they separate themselves from the larger group of unemployed, and they make plans for the future. Parallel to classic notions of petite bourgeoisie and middle class, they reach a fragile ground and occupy their time maintaining control over it.

For instance, despite low profits and the risk of not surviving, Rachid's small business tempered his frustration and granted him a modicum of social respect not allowed the unemployed. When I asked Habib, his partner and cousin, what he though of a nationwide strike conducted by the labor unions, he responded, "Why do it when it will bring nothing?" Habib and Rachid probably earned less than an average of 200 dhs / day, which they shared with Habib's younger brother, and they themselves saw little guarantee that their business would succeed in the long or medium term. Yet, Rachid was the one person I interviewed confident that he was going to become rich. Rather than wait to inherit the property his father owns, he wanted to create his own fortune, become wealthier than his father, and then ensure that his own son will become the wealthiest of all. He told me that in Morocco, "There are people with a lot of money and there are a lot of people who do not have money." Conveying in his tone his disrespect for the former, he insisted that "it is better to work on your own, to prove yourself and fulfill yourself." Before I left, the two cousins invested with a third partner in a second music/video store, although it was unclear how profitable this venture would become.

The Unemployed and Insecurely Employed

I like teaching. I teach not because I am interested in money. I teach because I like teaching. You deal with the students and the landlords [school owners]. I teach the future victims of our country because they do their education and find themselves without a job. What do you call a victim? — A teacher in a private lycée

The third group is distinguished more by their process of waiting, by their frustration at finding jobs that offer little security and low wages, than by their education or family origin. Of the unemployed, stagaires, and underpaid service workers I spoke with, four had completed doctorates and three the university. All had studied overseas, three in the humanities (one, a woman, studied journalism) and one in engineering. The university graduates studied Arabic, English, and sociology. Graduates of certain departments, such as Arabic and philosophy, faced more trouble in the job market than graduates of economics departments. The unemployed who had not finished dropped out for the same reasons as professionals who had not finished advanced studies: a parent was sick, the commute was too expensive and the cost of not working too high, or, most often, they did not pass an exam and quit. Those who did not finish the university in all likelihood stayed in insecure jobs.

Unemployment and provisional employment imply more, however, than job status. In Morocco, as in France, Spain, and other countries with high unemployment rates, they represent a way of living. Filled with ennui, anxiety, restlessness, and despair, this way of living demarcates a social group, a population consisting of hundreds of thousands of unemployed or temporarily employed university graduates clamoring for, demanding, and abandoning the possibility of finding a job. An unemployed doctorate in engineering in his late twenties who had studied in Ukraine gave me his schedule so that I would know when to contact him. "I stay at home in the morning, until after lunch. Then, for a change, I go to the café in the afternoon. Sometimes I do come into Casa to see my [extended] family." One of his other friends sitting at the table with us, also unemployed, laughed and concurred that he follows the same agenda. A man I met who was unemployed for six years and now works in a government ministry told me that he had been able to read quite a lot during those years, and that he sees his younger brother, a recent graduate and unemployed, following suit.

Toward the end of the time I lived in Morocco, I visited Driss in the apartment of his parents in Hay Mohammadi. He had lived in this apartment since he was born. It was well-maintained, with a nice kitchen and master bedroom for the parents, two bedrooms for the sons, and a central salon. Driss had his own television (unplugged), stereo, and hundreds and hundreds of books of philosophy and science fiction (mainly the former). Before eating lunch, he showed me around his book collection, of which he had read an impressive amount.

He was angry and very frustrated. He spoke in an impatient, semidesperate tone. He had studied for years in France, felt nostalgic for his country and his family, and returned definitively to Morocco. He told me that he had come back once in four years for a week. He claimed that he was receiving guests during that week, that he did not leave his house, and thus had no idea what was happening outside. A friend who lived in France joined us, a friend who at the time was married and earned a "decent" salary. This friend had insisted Driss stay in France, even without papers, because he was aware of the difficulties in Morocco. Driss ignored him, only to have the *gauche* under Jospin come to power with the strategy to help resolve the problem of *sans-papier* and foreign students. Toward the end of the conversation, Driss remarked that he had "la mal chance, et pourtant mon nom signifie chance."[33]

He flipped back and forth during the conversation between the decisions he had made and the options he thought he might have in the future. He began the conversation with the comment that he regretted his studies and returning to Morocco, that he should have gone through with a *marriage blanc* with a friend of his in France. Later however, he said he did not regret the studies and the development of his consciousness and knowledge. He had read extensively this year, up until the strike at UMT headquarters, where he claims he had not been able to read.[34]

Then he showed hope that the state might intervene, particularly in his situation, as an unemployed doctorate. "Do you know what I heard? You are going to miss something. After the elections [of 1997], the *licenciés-chômeurs* [unemployed university graduates, who he claimed numbered 130,000] are going to give the new government five days to resolve the problems or they are going to create a scandal [as they did when President Carlos Menem of Argentina visited Morocco in 1996]. Of course, it is impossible, but they are sick and tired of being unemployed. At least, they can resolve our [the doctorates'] problem. We are not too many. Basri [the former Minister of Interior under Hassan II] has given work to 2,500 doctorates. He looked in the ministries even when he did not have the budget."[35]

On the other hand, he was searching for possibilities to leave the country, hoping to avoid waiting for what his friend described as a job in the administration, where "people study a lot to file papers and open dossiers." Driss told me, "I promise that if I leave, I will never return. I regret being born in Morocco. I don't care about the Moroccan nationality. I will come back to see my family and that is all." His friend looked at him with mixed sympathy and fear. "Our country does not want us," he continued, "and so we are going to emigrate. We wanted to sign a petition to immigrate to Israel but we have the Muslim Brothers [the opposition Islamist movement originating in Egypt] with us. We were afraid that would come back to us. Me, I don't care. I will go to Tel Aviv."

Media coverage of the unemployed often describes dramas of hunger strikes, sit-ins, personal depression, despair, and suicide. Despite inadequate toilet facilities and police barricades, over a thousand unemployed university graduates, including pregnant women and women with children, crowd into UMT headquarters in Rabat to protest for jobs. An unemployed young man participating in a sit-in throws himself from a window. Another man, married with four children, a graduate of an agriculture institute and unemployed for almost ten years, finds himself in prison after he protests corrupt hiring practices (demanding payoffs for jobs or employing relatives) by local government officials.

A weekly magazine, *Maroc Hebdo* (26 April–2 May 1997), described a young man with a degree in economics who, along with his two brothers, had to support himself through selling contraband lingerie and cosmetics in northern Morocco. With his savings from three years' worth of work, he bought a few sheep that died from a virus during Morocco's long drought: "On the edge of depression, he returns to his hometown, and gives himself over to 'drags of *kif.*' He who had worked so hard to aid his parents, finds himself, with his four younger brothers, dependent upon them. A situation that becomes all the more precarious as his father, retired from the public sector, receives monthly the modest sum of 900 dhs. Just enough to cover the medical expenses of his diabetic mother" (17). The young man decided to return to school. Living off the generosity of friends, he obtained a Certificat d'Etudes Scientifiques (CES) in econometrics. Yet, at 39½, he still could not find a job, and the maximum age for entering the public sector is 40. He decided to join a possible hunger strike, explaining, "I am ready to do it to the finish. To quit is to let go of my life [*Quitte a y laisser ma vie*]."

For the provisionally employed who work as stagaires or in jobs that pay just above the minimum hourly wage (SMIG) and offer no security, work can offer constancy but only in openly exploitative conditions.[36] Low-paying and often stressful, these types of jobs can, but often do not, unfold into more permanent, higher-paying employment.

A man who had studied English literature recounted for me all of his jobs. He had worked for a dressmaker as manager of production and at a major department store on the outskirts of Casablanca. He quit the latter job because he considered himself to be a manager, that he was hired to be a manager, and instead was working on an aisle selling goods. He then went to work in a pipe factory and then as a marketer for a computer store, where he earned 2,000 dhs/month, or just above the minimum wage. He did not care for the owner, and at the time I met him, was looking to do something else. When I asked about his job instability, he agreed that employers generally prefer not to hire someone who has changed jobs so often, but he also added that it is the employers who are truly unstable: "If they paid better . . . they hire you for a low salary and you take it because you think in six months it will be better. But after six months, a year, two years, it is still the same. And then after three years, they decide they do not want you anymore. I also studied English literature and not management. I had to learn a lot of new things [he attended a management school at night while working at the irrigation pipe factory]. Now, I have a lot of experience."

Classifying New Social Groups

In *Distinction*, Bourdieu (1984) denies "true" objectivity in any system of classification, be it of social classes or aesthetic tastes. He remarks at one point that "interest in the aspect observed is never completely independent of the advantage of observing it" (475). Illustrating the struggle between groups fighting for control over the social order, and thus over social classification, Bourdieu explains how social groups take shape: "Principles of division, inextricably logical and sociological, function within and for the purposes of the struggle between social groups; in producing concepts, they produce groups, the very groups which produce the principles and the groups against which they are produced. What is at stake in the struggles about the meaning of the social world is power over the classificatory schemes and systems which are the basis of the representations of the groups and therefore of their mobilization and demobilization" (479).

In Morocco, among the questions media, businesses, intellectuals, and government officials pose about the social consequences of economic reform are Who are the unemployed? Who has a job, even if it not a good job? and Who is successful in business? How, in turn, do these men and women perceive themselves and each other, and, as Bourdieu is telling us, not just as a function of educational degree or the ability to find a job, but as what they supposedly represent as human beings?

According to Bourdieu, social classification of innovation, motivation, and sophistication (knowledge, appearance, diction, composure), qualities needed to attain a high-powered job in Morocco, is bound up in the economic and social capital of the classifier, in this case, foreign officials, politicians, intellectuals, and businesspeople. Conversely, the unemployed and provisionally employed, or the majority of the global middle class, supposedly lack the economic intelligence, or the intellectual creativity and analytic capacity, and the initiative and self-motivation to succeed professionally. They become, if not helped, part of a troubling mass lacking force and destiny. No one in Morocco would divorce self-initiative, personal ambition, and the capacity to articulate, analyze, and solve problems, characteristics so validated in the process of market liberalization, from educational, economic, and social capital. Yet, these characteristics, as in any market economy, also assume value on their own, as intrinsic human qualities that enable survival. The unemployed university graduate, the teacher, and the financial consultant have become, in the course of market liberalization, different types of people in the social landscape: those who can and do succeed and those who should and must compromise in their life trajectories.

In this social landscape, entrepreneurs and managers in the global economy view themselves much in the same way intellectuals saw themselves in the aftermath of colonialism, as dynamic and forward-thinking. This time, however, young entrepreneurs are the potential saviors of economic rationalization and global market capitalism and not the lieutenants of national modernization and development.

The editor of what might be called the Moroccan version of *Glamour*, who was in her early thirties and a graduate of ISCAE, told me that the employees at the magazine regard themselves as "a small group within society. We understand each other very well here, but we cannot become integrated into the rest of society. Perhaps we would feel more integrated in the U.S., where there are groups, discussions, different cultures." Hicham, the 40-year-old owner of a design agency, explained, "There are two types of youth: the more motivated *techniciens* and the university students, who go into planning and the administration. It is the techniciens who are going to employ the university students, who are going to put them to work." Describing his generation of businesspeople, he remarked, "There is another mentality now . . . everyone wants to do something of value. Twenty years ago, people earned much more without doing anything. Now they are criticized: 'Ça ne va pas.' They [wealthy businessmen] benefited from not paying workers and overcharging—now there is a critique of this behavior." Like other small-scale entrepreneurs, he defended economic rationalization for it allegedly injects meritocracy into a nepotistic, clannish economic structure: "For someone who has the will, who is serious, and who has the knowledge, he has his place, even with the problems with banks and the state. Now, we work like birds in a river, the state is the river. I am not [holds his hands beside his head to signify narrow-mindedness] . . . I am sure that I am on the right path and that this path brings you to a positive point. You have to be concrete, pragmatic, you are there, you always think straight. You have confidence that you are on the right path and you do not think too much about tomorrow. You are apt to become lost if not."

Repeating the sentiments of his peers, Hicham, in his discourse and self-perception, furthers a system of value judgment, explicitly or implicitly condemning university students and their like to second-tier status in terms of talent, knowledge, and ambition. As one friend, a woman who ended up working in the administration, told me, "They don't even know geography. It would shock me if they knew geography." A banker at a state-owned bank referred to the public university as "*la pagaille* [a mess] . . . if I had never enrolled at [his private school], I would not have tolerated enrolling at the fac. The people come from a low milieu. They are not *éduquées*. They do not reflect. It would astonish me if they reflect."

The media, corporate leaders, and public officials, supportive of the entrepreneurial spirit that shores up market reform and reduces the need for government jobs, shower praise on young businesspeople. The state, through its program of jeunes promoteurs, created a social category in and of itself, as newspapers like *La Vie Economique* ran profiles of managers and owners of small and medium-size enterprises. *La Vie Economique* (26 June 1996) wrote of the commercial director of a five-star hotel: "Devoted body and soul to the hotel industry, this young Jdidi [from El Jadida] is the archetype of the new wave of Moroccan executives, very *bon chic bon goût* and with his head on straight. . . . He did not have to fall apart through existential quests dissecting the help wanted ads in the newspapers. His sense of adventure and entrepreneurism, served by good looks and flowing diction, permitted him to 'sell himself' in France and then Saudi Arabia." First employed at an international chain, this director had little patience for their tradition of hiring only Europeans, Asians, and Americans for top-level management positions, and he quit to take his current job at a major hotel. He also enrolled himself at ISCAE in a *cycle supérieur* to study account-ing and learned new languages. "I arrived at a critical turning point in my career: make an immediate turnaround or stagnate to the end. I chose obviously the future and the renewed challenge that it implies" (39).

In a special section on women, *La Vie Economique* (7 March 1997) pro-filed a 29-year-old woman currently working for an NGO that sponsors rural development. After she finished her degree in agricultural economics, she remained unemployed for seven months. She found a post in the Min-istry of Agriculture, but "it was bureaucratic. I wanted to act directly, to resolve the problems of the community." The article referred to her as a representative of "a new race in Morocco, that of young people of post-structural adjustment who are obliged to innovate to exist." She herself adds, "The other generations were not born with the threat from birth of unemployment. I was already interested as a student in associations, and being myself the daughter of emigrants [to the city], I was always obsessed by rural areas. The poverty is extreme and the NGO more flexible than the administration" (40).

In the same section, *La Vie Economique* profiled a 26-year-old woman who heads the corporate finance division at a finance firm. She passed her bac, studied at the Ecole Supérieure des Sciences Economiques et Com-merciales (ESSEC) in Paris, acquired experience through three banking internships in Casablanca, New York, and London, and then returned to Morocco to her current job, where she met her husband. She claimed that she does not face prejudice on account of being a woman because "there is a certain cultural homogeneity that facilitates communication between the sexes. In this very competitive sector, competence is the key factor of success." Her long hours and stressful work did not affect her private life because, as she explained, "I came to realize that the most important thing was to make one's entourage correspond with one's choice of lifestyle. My husband works himself a lot, and his support eases things" (43).

Among the unemployed and insecurely employed, however, entrepreneurs and even bureaucrats possess a negative image, the inverse of the glory propagated in the press and by public officials. Once, I asked a taxi driver who was 34 and had never finished his degree in English literature at the university if he had ever tried to switch jobs. He replied affirmatively, that he had taken the *concours* for several administrative posts, but that he had never passed selection, except for the police, which he decided not to take because of their "bad reputation." "The exams are competitive," he explained to me, and "it helps to have *shwiya* [a little] contact." He continued by telling me that graduates of private business schools find jobs. I added, "Only the graduates of the most prestigious schools." "True, always you need shwiya contact." I asked Abdelkrim, who earns barely above the SMIG working as a day manager at a two-star hotel, what he thought of someone his age who owns his own company. He answered, shaking his finger, "I think that their parents have land or money . . . there are people who work hard. I work hard. You saw how I worked for Stephen [an American who wanted to set up an export business in Morocco]. I could have made money, 35,000 dhs off of one container [of the wood they would have exported]. When I see those people, I think inheritance."

In a suggestive moment for me, Abdelkrim introduced me to his friend Nourredine, who worked for years in Saudi Arabia. When Nourredine returned to Morocco, he joined his cousin to sell telephone equipment. At one point, Abdelkrim asked him to start a business together so that Abdelkrim could escape his dead-end job at the hotel. Nourredine refused. During the conversation between them at the café where Abdelkrim and I normally met, Nourredine dominated the conversation. He interrupted Abdelkrim and finished his sentences for him, particularly when Abdelkrim referred to traveling or working overseas. Nourredine then mentioned that he had been interviewed for the position of restaurant manager with a Lebanese-owned restaurant in Saudi Arabia. Nourredine addressed me, for Abdelkrim looked away for most of this part of the conversation, seemingly half-immersed in self-pity, half in self-doubt. Nourredine went on. He envisioned becoming an executive with this company, that one day he would be transferred to their office in Brussels and that if that were the case, he was not returning to Morocco. Later, as he was driving me home, I asked him about the salary. "Oh, I won't go for less than a thousand dollars a month. It would not be worth my time."

This division between a manager like Nourredine and someone in a low-paid job like Abdelkrim does not prevent them from being friends, but it does set up what might likely be the story of their lives. Driss, who was not alone among unemployed doctorates, studied at one of the most prestigious universities in France on a fellowship from the Moroccan government. He read philosophy and literature with extraordinary attention. Yet, on returning to Morocco, he found himself with no job possibility and dependent financially on his father, a retired technician who worked for an American company. In contrast, Myriam, who attended the French mission and admitted that she speaks Arabic with an elitist *chatié* accent, returned home to find a job in an advertising agency. From a Fassi family and the daughter of a doctor, Myriam felt that she distinguished herself from her colleagues at the agency through her manner of social interaction and her capacity to think and articulate quickly and succinctly, or her *esprit de synthèse*. Among her colleagues, who she claims are intimidated by (French) mission students, "the only person who learned this esprit de synthèse learned it from their parents. Their overall 'look' is not correct. I do not like to say this, it is ugly, but it is true." Myriam, who also says she can recognize a fellow mission student at a party through his or her "manner of speaking and discussing," was not expressing new codes and categories of social critique, but investing modes of distinction with new economic value.

The director of a CIDOPE office, the government agency responsible for helping unemployed graduates find jobs, commented to me that university graduates have little notion of self-responsibility and initiative:

> Director: We notice that people have no idea about employment. We try to make young people responsible for themselves. Young people think when they come that they are taken in hand and that CIDOPE is a service of the state. We try to instill responsibility, to give them weapons so that they can take themselves in hand at the same time that CIDOPE works . . . young people must take a hold of themselves instead of thinking that the state should find them a job.
>
> Author: They want stability and security?
>
> Director: It is more than that. A manager in the private sector with good training has perhaps more security than someone in the administration. A good portion of the young people who are unemployed have specialized training. They just do not know how to look.

Summary: Social Structure, Social Dislocation, and Alienation

The reorganization of the middle class into social groups divided by life opportunity has had expectedly negative effects on social stability and the general social climate. I discuss how the behavior of the young, urban, educated forces us to reinterpret our notions of society and political participation and identity in the next chapter. In this chapter, I have explored the trends that create social fragmentation and differentiation among the young, urban, educated, trends that occur against a backdrop of continued sharp disparity in income and increasingly vocal expression of frustration with current politics and policy strategy.

Moroccans are acutely aware of the social disruption the turbulent labor market and declining income have created, and not just for lycée and university graduates but for everyone. Marriage rates have dropped significantly over the past fifteen years. In 1982, 40.5 percent of the population ages 20–24 was single, 17 percent of the population 25–29, and 6.4 percent of the population 30–34. In 1994, the percentages of single people in the 25–29 and 30–34 age groups had increased to 48.5 and 25.3, respectively; in 1998, the percentages had increased again, to 57.8 and 33. Moreover, the general trend in marrying later may be carrying over to not marrying at all, or marrying well into childbearing years. Between 1994 and 1998, fertility rates dropped among all childbearing groups except those ages 35 or older (to 49), which increased by as much as 10 percent.[37]

Fragmentation among the young, urban, educated has perhaps socially simpler, but no less destabilizing, ramifications than the boats across Gibraltar or repressed labor strikes.[38] The exclusion of the majority of university graduates from career trajectories that are promising and materially rewarding implies both a socially rigid division of labor and an unstable system of professions. Blessed with economically valuable skills, degrees, and personal qualities, as well as respectable social status, entrepreneurs and business managers strive to legitimize their position in the domestic and global division of labor. However, bureaucrats, teachers, and secretaries are unable to defend the value of their labor on the basis of their own personal qualities and degrees and against the backdrop of widespread unemployment. Their inability to defend their capacity as workers deters them from cooperation, planning, or any other activity that would suggest the kind of occupational organization and solidarity that sociologists (see Abbott 1988; Grusky and Sorenson 1998) have long argued is a fruitful approach to class theory and analysis of professions.

Moreover, the structural distinction among these groups overlies a common alienation and a common subjective position in the world, forcing us to consider how much professional segmentation alone tells us about behavior and identity. The steps of market liberalization that lead to the rise of social differentiation and stratification within the labor market can also yield a common existential experience. Having divided the young, urban, educated population, I put them together again in the next chapter, attempting to interpret their alienation as symptomatic of the transformation of the national middle class of modernization to the middle class of the global market.

4

A Generation of Fuyards

We have always been taught that democracy is a government of the people for the people, that authority in democracy belongs to the people. We have been taught that it is impossible, in practice, that a people governs itself and that it is necessary to delegate this power to our representative through the ballot.

First distortion, because election signifies selection. In fact, the choice of representatives only comes from among five categories of the elite: the nantis, whose power is from money; intellectuals, whose power is from their white collars; politicians, whose power is from their organizations; dignitaries, whose power is in their caste; bureaucrats, whose power is in the administration. The commune of mortals, having no chance at winning, will be condemned to vote, most often by necessity, by routine but without great conviction in one of five categories.

With economic setbacks, social bankruptcy, deterioration of the environment, complexity of the budget, macro-economic betting, high illiteracy, the persistence and the increase of unemployment; in brief, with daily concerns, we witness a depoliticization of civil society or more or less a demotivation. The citizen lives from day to day and only believes what he sees.

We were also taught that democracy is synonymous with liberty: liberty to circulate, to organize, to join a union, and to discuss, and to speak.

Take the case of a teacher, like myself, with a salary of 3,300 dh, a rent of 1,600 dh and a family of four. Can I truly travel when I know that an ordinary hotel costs more than my daily salary? I am in a union but my salary has not moved in ten years, while the leaders of my union — the elite lives more than very well — receive compensation to represent me.

We were, in the end, taught, that democracy, it is human rights, right to culture, to education, to housing, to health, right to a passport, right to strike. It is great, it is formidable to have these rights. We can see how in my case I am able to use them. The right to housing is a dream, a utopia or more or less a miraculous exception for my social category. The right to health, a simple visit to the hospital of the quartier, to the emergency room, makes us realize the limits of this primordial right. The right to the passport, if it permits an individual to feel good in his skin, to give him airs and importance and a little hope, hope that is very quickly weakened by the visa and above all financial means. The right to education, for the luckiest, access to faculties without future possibility and in disciplines that are accepted only philosophically.

We see well that the ensemble of these rights that constitute the favorite theme of all political organizations and unions of right, center, or left are pious vows for my generation and my social category.

Very happily, the right to breathe, to marry, to pick a wife, of entering into marriage to have perhaps a descendant, of listening to the radio or turning it off, of choosing a television channel or the program that suits me, escapes still, for the moment at least, politics.

Be serious, messieurs politicians, the chosen of democracy, eligible for different rights and liberties, the elite: the average citizen, to think more rationally, the deprived citizen, has other preoccupations, preoccupations that concern very simply daily life.

I invite you to try, messieurs, the true alternatives [open up to opposition]: you come down here and you let us rise. Buses at rush hour, emergencies at every hour, the streets of garbage in Salé, Youssoufia or Yacoub Al Mansour, without speaking of the medina; tax collection and the Treasury the thirtieth of the month with small salaries and pensions; the vacant terrains where barefoot children continue to play ball. — "Vivre à quatre avec 3300 dh," letter from a teacher to *La Vie Economique*, 1 November 1996

The challenge in this letter is to situate the exstential experience of its author within a stage of capitalism, or global market integration, and within a moment of social change, in which identification between human potential and the political and social context of the nation-state shifts fundamentally. This chapter returns to one of the principal questions of the book: How do we understand the relations among the organization of economic and political power, social differentiation and structural inequality, and a condition of political and social alienation produced in market reform? How do we interpret what happens to subjectivity with the retreat of state power over individual well-being and the imposition of participation in the global market economy? And what is, from a sociological perspective, the theoretical significance of the economic insecurity that now plagues a younger generation pushed to become market actors in the global economy? The

transformation of a subjective position in the world and social consciousness may be as important to understanding the substance of class as materialist categorizations based on relative control over property and capital
(Wright 1997).

This chapter attempts to develop a preliminary, exploratory approach to
these questions. The three groups described in the previous chapter each
occupy a social space framed around education, occupation, and relative
knowledge of the referents and techniques of participation in the market
economy. These groups form social networks among themselves and assess
risk based on distinctive sets of opportunities within the private and public
sectors. They scramble for rights over capital and jobs, but their actions do
not reify the importance of a located social order (Bourdieu 1984). Rather,
their understanding of social differentiation and relative social value has
meaning only against the backdrop of negotiating the contours of a non-
fixed social space. In their alienation and disconnection from Morocco the
nation-state, these social groups together contest the frontiers that the
political elite and the national bourgeoisie traverse themselves but need
intact for political support and social validation. This chapter investigates
the alienation and disconnection of the global middle class from the nation-
state and political and economic elites and likewise analyzes the new orientation toward the nonlocated social space of the globe.

The Retreat of the State and the Coming of Melancholy

In theorizing the impact of the retreat of the state on subjectivity and
consciousness, I am questioning how the ambivalence of young, urban,
educated men and women toward collective and self-identity affects our
conceptions of social formation, society, and nation-state. In the postcolonial era, the connection among self-identification in society, emotion toward the self and the external world, and occupation originated in the pact
between governments and citizens that they both derived meaning through
the expansion of human capacity to its fullest degree. King Hassan II emphasized that Moroccan society "must know a harmonious evolution, as
much in the conditions of existence as in its modes of thinking so that cities
and the countryside can progress at the same rhythm toward one goal, a
common ideal" (*Discours du Trône,* 3 March 1964, from *Citations de Hassan
II* 1981).

Politically, the formation of a modern middle class in postcolonial Morocco corresponded with state discourse and popular discussion about Arab

rebirth, social development, and national power and greatness. Idealization of an autonomous form of modernization, and subsequent international power and prestige, centered on such issues as Arabization, improvement of education, and, for the political opposition, always political reform, whether toward democratization, communism, or *salafism*.

Some of the political issues, such as raising the quality of the educational system, are still focal points of discussion today, but the emotion among the middle class, the supposed up-and-coming leadership and citizenship of Morocco, is different. Prima facie, this middle class lacks the heroes (no Nasser) and the experience of massive positive change (nationalism, industrialization, education, and social mobility versus high unemployment rates) of the modern middle class or the generation of Independence.

In other words, the maxim suggested by the king, that the state will shape better individuals for a better society, has fallen apart, so that the state is still held responsible internationally and domestically for economic growth and joblessness, but individuals must manage their own advancement distinct from any notion of society. In this moment of historical transition between the nation-state and globalization, melancholia — the loss of an ideal, a past object of identification, and the subsequent internalization of this loss[1] — becomes the psychic unifier of a seemingly disparate group of people and the basis for social action. We can say, in fact, that social consciousness arises in the moment of loss, as young men and women maturing with market integration become reflexive socially or conceive of their social position only as a consequence of the withdrawal of state investment in the modern individual.

Born at the beginning of the twentieth century, Naguib Mahfouz assesses generational differences: "We did not have to worry about what life would bring us the following day. Our economic situation was far better, and we had more democratic rights. We could choose any political party, and we could choose our government. . . . We had the hope to rule, and to have a chance. But the young men of today don't have our hopes, or our opportunities. They also don't have our dreams" (quoted in Ajami 1998, 225).

I suggest that this generation does have dreams, but only in relation to the historic loss that constitutes their consciousness. This loss and the subsequent reflexive position it produces in the social world underscore more superficial political and economic differences. One young journalist complained to me that unemployed Islamists, leftists, the unaffiliated, could join together at a sit-in taking place at Union Marocain des Travailleurs (UMT) by submerging differences in favor of the most important objective for all, a job. He went there after the minister of the interior at the time, Driss Basri, had hired seventy of them, challenging the movement's cohesion and robbing it of its leaders. He found, though, "the day after, there were people with the microphone, saying we will go on." It annoyed this journalist, an ambitious and active man in his early twenties, that "there were Islamists, leftists — you know that these movements are normally associated with the left. But the leaders were saying: You, Islamists, and you, leftists, we are not here for politics, we are here to get a job. This is not right, this bothered me." He then repeated over and over again, "This is a mad [insane] country" (the conversation was in English, thus "mad" not *folie, m'bul*, or *majnun*) as he emphasized that these diplômés should find a job in the private sector, which "they don't know exists." He continued: "They starve, they are beaten by the police, but they will not start with 1,000 dh [for a salary], they do not innovate, they do not search to create their own businesses. They say, we cannot, that is for the rich, not here in Morocco. They do not think that even if they begin with 1,000 dh, they can earn 10,000 dh in five years. It is the makhzen. . . . I earn 10,000 dh in the private sector and not even for 20,000 dh a month would I work in the public sector with that mentality." Khalid Jamaï, the journalist I mentioned in the first chapter, also criticized the *association des diplômés chômeurs* for conducting a sit-in to demand the state find them jobs. "I don't like that," he said.

The protest for a job, though, only reflects immediate reaction to a lack of opportunity. Ultimately, the fact that they protest together for a job is more important for interpreting consciousness, for understanding the *mentalité* that the young journalist longs to change. These protestors have experienced the same loss of identification between individual practical and intellectual activity and a determined political economic system and social space, enabling them to communicate across political ideologies.

However, their protest does not reflect a positive Marxist for-itself. Rather, social formation within global market integration results from absence, from a void without immediate solution in attachment to another ideal. The lack of a new relation of identification leads to the same process Freud outlines in his analysis of melancholia: withdrawal from outward identification with the object only to save the love of the object through its becoming part of consciousness. For the young, urban, educated this process of taking on a lost ideal and the social status that it once symbolized provides the critique (the critical agency) and objectification of social position (the ego) that frame new social ("class") consciousness.

For example, in the letter at the beginning of the chapter, the author outlines what he perceives as the inherent qualities of his social and self-identity but admits that he knows these qualities only through their lack of realization. He writes the following:

> We were in the end taught that democracy, it is human rights, right to culture, to education, to housing, to health, right to a passport, right to strike. It is great, it is formidable to have these rights. We can see how in my case I am able to use them. The right to housing is a dream, a utopia or more or less a miraculous exception for my social category. . . . The right to health, a simple visit to the hospital of the quartier, to the emergency room, makes us realize the limits of this primordial right. The right to the passport, if it permits an individual to feel good in his skin, to give him airs and importance and a little hope, hope that is very quickly weakened by the visa and above all financial means. The right to education, for the luckiest, access to universities without future possibility and in disciplines that are accepted only philosophically.
>
> We see well that the ensemble of these rights that constitute the favorite theme of all political organizations and unions of right, center, or left are pious vows for my generation and my social category.
>
> Very happily, the right to breathe, to marry, to pick a wife, of conceiving to have perhaps a descendant, of listening to the radio or turning it off, of choosing a television channel or the program that suits me, escapes still, for the moment at least, politics.

The expression of the consciousness of the global middle class occurs both in this cynical, antagonistic critique of conventional politics and the utility of modern institutions and the discussion of leaving Morocco, of searching for that imaginary alternative. It was Samia, a private language tutor, who told me that her generation, men and women in their twenties and thirties, were flee-ers, *fuyards*. "Young people complain and I say 'open your mouth,' 'do something.'" When I first started getting to know her, Samia claimed she wanted to stay in Morocco to witness imminent political and social change. By the time I was leaving for the first time, in 1997, she was hoping to immigrate to Australia. "This country is not changing fast enough. I need to leave," she said during our last meeting together.

The government and the king have pushed for transparency in the electoral process and supported extensive advertising campaigns to encourage voters, particularly younger voters, to vote.[2] Yet, perhaps change in national politics either appears too irrelevant in comparison to globalization or too unlikely given the social distance of elites to allow for widespread participation. In addition, younger generations of Moroccans still shy away from joining political parties or participating in political movements outside of the diplomés-chômeurs because of the lingering stigma of corruption and co-optation afflicting political elites. A management consultant once mentioned to me that he had a friend who was very involved in politics but then spent some time in prison. "That does not inspire us to participate [*Ça ne donne pas le goût à participer*]," he said. He also joked with me that he and his friends vote no on referendums just to see if the votes count (i.e., appear in the final percentages).

The Implications of a Global Middle Class for a National State

Giorgio Agamben (1995) claims in *Homo Sacer* that organized power has become biopolitical, that the critical characteristic of the modern nation-state is "the absolute in-distinction between law and fact, juridical rule and biological life." He writes, "Every attempt to rethink the political space of the West must begin with the clear awareness that we no longer know anything of the classical distinction between zoe and bios, between private life and political existence . . . we are not only, in Foucault's words, animals whose life as living beings is at issue in their politics, but also — inversely — citizens whose very politics is at issue in their natural body" (187). Agamben, as well as Foucault, interpret control of the body as integral to modern selfhood within the modern state. What they do not address directly is how critical the individual notion of self-fulfillment, spiritually, intellectually, and materially, has been to political and social order.[3] Legitimation of state power has been inseparable from the promise to cultivate the genius of the nation.

In Judith Butler's (1997) interpretation of melancholy, loss of social power becomes part of the ego and power of the subject. In Morocco, the state does not escape censure in the "act of melancholic incorporation" and the subject turning on itself. Having created the modern individual, the modern nation-state remains integral to self-identity. Thus, society and regime become part of self-reflection, that the failure of the individual to achieve is inseparable from the failure of the nation-state to provide, and thus both become objects of deprecation and anger. Self-reflection functions as a mourning for lost life promise, a mourning that cannot end while still at the site of this loss, Morocco.

Khadija, who stressed how difficult unemployment was for her psychologically, supposedly married and moved to Canada. For her, for the airport attendant who gave me a piece of paper looking for a woman to marry so he could leave the country, and the butcher who disliked the pollution and garbage in the streets of Casablanca, elsewhere represents more promise than Morocco. Daoud, who worked with the stock market and privatization of state-owned enterprises, once gave me a list of what he does not like in Moroccan society: the way people drive, that they make too much noise in their apartments, the bureaucratic paperwork, and taxes that salaried employees like him are forced to pay. The two primary advantages to staying in Morocco were his family and the weather. If the economic, as well as, it seemed, the social situation remained the same, he was going to return to the United States, where he had earned an MBA.

The political implications for the state of an attitude such as Daoud's are, first, ambivalence about a popular, national enterprise that gives credence to state power; second, alienation from local elite power and the notion of social cohesion under elite leadership; third and more specifically, skepticism and ambivalence about participation in state-led market reform and among model young entrepreneurs as well as bureaucrats and the unemployed; and fourth, replacement of state legitimacy by transnational authorities and ideologies and heterogeneous, transnational social relations.

Hussein, an entrepreneur, could be the darling of neoliberal policymakers and state officials alike. Born in Côte d'Ivoire to a Fassi family, Hussein moved to Morocco in his late teens. He attended one of the most prestigious private business schools in Casablanca and worked for a newspaper directly after finishing. He and a friend from school also tried for several years to start a company in market research. They obtained a credit jeune promoteur with the help of a contact in the bank in order to rent their office space and buy computer equipment. They then became part of a USAID project to promote small enterprise, and Hussein traveled to the United States for the training seminar. The USAID project failed, but Hussein and his partner, ambitious and hard-working in a still underdeveloped field in Morocco, succeeded in building their company. They attracted important domestic and international clients and they grew large enough as a company to hire a staff.

Although relatively successful professionally and financially, Hussein openly criticizes management of the government and business elites. He engages himself in this conversation, not relenting and never bored. When he complains, he talks about high taxes for middle-income employees like himself, the absence of a meritocracy, potholes in roads, underfunded hospitals where patients must buy their own needles and pay under the table for better service, poor rates of illiteracy, electrification, and potable water distribution, and the fabulous incomes of the rich. For him, Moroccans and Morocco could make it with different leadership and a different set of social rules because they are *debrouillardeurs*, because they are smart and know how to maneuver to reach their objectives: "Someone criticizes someone in power and when this person takes the position, they do the same thing. We are young. We have the time and we wait. The country is directed by old people. But who is going to replace them? The families of the wealthy who have one or two children. Their children cannot do everything. It is the middle classes who make some money who produce decent and intelligent people. But these people leave. The good quality leaves and it is the bad quality which stays, the bad quality."

Another model of social mobility and achievement, Aïcha worked for a government agency responsible for promoting trade in one of Morocco's most significant export-oriented sectors. Yet, she felt irritated at being overworked and underappreciated, and she distanced herself from association with any institution, party, or organization. She was also an astute and occasionally virulent social and political critic, who directed her anger at political elites while remaining ambivalent about her own identity in Moroccan society. Laughing, she told me that a respected leftist political leader and economics professor did not declare the salaries of his employees to the CNSS, the social security fund. He accepted a large order during Ramadan, and brought *harira* (soup served for breakfast during Ramadan) to the factory rather than allow the workers to go home. The so-called *gauchistes*, the opposition leaders, are for her "very good actors. I think that MGM should come here to recruit."

Even government employees, an obvious source of support for state power, expressed fading sympathy for a national project under the guidance of political and economic elites. Perhaps as much as any person I interviewed, Hassan reflected in his self-perception and attitudes toward the "rest" of society the *traditionalisme* of the petite bourgeoisie that Abdellah Laroui criticized. When I first met him, he worked in stock market investment in one of Morocco's largest state-owned banks and earned approximately $550 a month. His mother worked as a secretary in the same bank. His father was an engineer who worked for many years in the upper echelons of one of Morocco's most prominent state-owned enterprises. Hassan claimed his mother had no influence in securing him the job, which he stated he obtained as the result of exams and the relationship his prestigious école de commerce carried with the bank. He explained to me, "I want to rise by my own means. When I do my work, I want to know that I arrived myself. . . . I don't like *pistons* [contacts]. I am in horror of that."

Consumer-oriented and ambitious, he said that he wanted money. "Money does not bestow honor [*l'argent ne fait pas l'honneur*], but even so, it gives a little. I want to rise quickly in the hierarchy of the bank if I stay there [*escaler les echelons*]. I consider that I have risen more quickly than other young [employees]." In fact, as we discussed his ambitions, he drew a diagram of Maslow's pyramid of needs. He wanted to arrive at the top level of self-esteem. Like other children of high-level administrators and successful businessmen, Hassan saw himself as globally savvy, as oriented toward European culture while remaining part of a select population of young, ambitious businesspeople at home. To emphasize his difference in cultivation, he told me that he would not date a student at the university. "What could she add?" he asked. "What could we talk about? Not politics, not religion, for both of us they are the same. What could we talk about? How she makes couscous on Friday? . . . if I go out with European women, they add something. I can see both cultures. With Moroccan women, on the other hand, it is me who adds."

When he exclaims his frustration with the postcolonial petite bourgeoisie, Laroui judges the group in power at the time, those who declared themselves Lenin-style to be the needed leadership of the nation, of the backward masses, in the twentieth century. Men and women in the global middle class still conceive of themselves as an educated minority, but first, they lack power, and this is their problem, and second, they are the growing minority, expanding with the expansion of education. The culture of modernity that Laroui bitterly remarks is the tool of the petite bourgeoisie to differentiate itself from and govern over the rest of the population is now the tool of differentiation from the state, society, and culture, or the nation-state that is becoming increasingly anachronistic in the plans and ideas of the younger generations.

Hassan, who claimed in our first conversation that he wanted to stay in Morocco to participate in market reform, called me up after several months of not seeing each other. He told me that he wanted to discuss his plans for the future. Despite the fact that he held a good position at the bank, he felt there was little opportunity for mobility. I met him at the bank and we drove in his new Peugeot to a café on the outskirts of the city. It was fall, and he told me that over the summer he had made some decisions. He had gone to France for almost a month to attend the wedding of a Moroccan

Jewish friend. The friend, someone from his neighborhood who had immigrated to France years earlier, sat him down and told him to leave Morocco. His friend asked him what he made at the bank: "What are you going to do if you want to get married? Even if your wife works and makes at most 5,000 dh/month, that is not enough money. . . . if I thought there would be economic opportunity in Morocco, I too would have stayed." Hassan replied that he would take a loan from the bank to buy an apartment. "But that," he now explained to me, "would tie me to the bank for twenty years. If I left the bank for another job, I would have to pay back the loan." He continued:

> Hassan: My friend, he came from nothing. He studied here, at the Jewish School. After, he attended a technical school for two years and then he left for France. He studied there and now he has a job at IBM. He is assistant to a director in Tel-Aviv and he truly came from nothing. He is also a true go-getter [*bosseur*]. He has a mobile with him and he works. . . . I received an offer from a Saudi-Moroccan company. The Saudis provide funds in order to invest in Morocco. But, I do not want to work for them. First, I do not like their mentality. They could care less about Morocco. They can put their money in the U.S. and have no problems [*être tranquils*].
>
> Author: They want to make money [*profiter*]?
>
> Hassan: *Voilà*. Secondly, they treat their employees as slaves. They wanted to work with the stock market and privatization but I refused.

Hassan then changed topics.

> Hassan: The young, they want to move [*bouger*]. Ethnicity, religion, race, they do not count now. This is backward thinking. All that counts is money and business.

I once told Hussein, the co-owner of the small market research firm, about everyone I knew who wanted to leave because they do not earn enough and perceive little possibility of improving their situation. At one point, I asked him why he had returned to Morocco for his studies.

> I was accepted for medicine in France but I knew that if I went there, I would never live in Morocco. France has everything. I wanted to know the country. But now, if I did not have the company, I would leave. If there is the least problem, I am leaving. Everything is corrupt here. We pay at all levels. We do not know even whom to pay. One says

me and the other says me [pointing with hands crossed in front of his chest to emphasize entanglement]. What is more, if you do not have contacts, there is not a chance at mobility. In the U.S., Bill Gates at 19 started a company and now he is the richest man in the country. This is a meritocracy. I have friends who work for ONA who are not motivated.[4] They work a lot but ONA puts someone above them who has contacts but does not know what to do. How are you able to be motivated if you work for someone who is not competent? In an American center where we worked, the head discovered that the consultant was better paid than he was. He said, How is it that he is better paid? This consultant sold himself as someone but he is incompetent, a false consultant. Plus, he had false diplomas.

Discussing salaries, I told him about an engineer who earns a little over $1,000/month.

Ten thousand dh/month, this is a manager. But what do you want with someone who earns 10,000 dh/month? The young woman I know at ONA has been working there four years and she earns 10,000 gross and 7,000 net. You imagine that she earns only 7,000 out of 10,000? She sees that the owner or director earns much more. Take the example of a manager in a bank who works the cashbox at a bank. He earns 3,000 dh/month. He sees millionaires who come for their money. You see the Ministry. The building is new and big and the bureaucrat lives in the bidonvilles. At least give him the money to buy a small apartment.

He talked about his own apartment situation: his father owned an apartment building but could not evict a nonpaying tenant to give Hussein and his fiancée the apartment after they married. He also told me that he earned a decent income, but had accrued heavy debts: "You know, there is an enormous Moroccan community in Canada. Even if you have only a small job, you live in a state of law, you have your rights. Here, the rich don't pay their taxes, it is the poor, the middle classes who pay. The youth are burnt out. Just a match will make everything explode."

He ended the conversation by talking about the reappearance of foreign companies in Morocco with market liberalization: "Lyonnaise is taking control of [the electric company] in Casablanca and the Spanish and the Portuguese in Rabat. The biggest spenders do not pay [and thus the state wants to sell to disinterested foreigners]. We are returning to the past. You know, we should rent the country to the Americans for thirty years. . . . You know, Morocco is the greatest country in the world and the worst."

Alienation, Labor, and Exploitation in Market Reform

Each day, I think of creating my own business with someone or another while guarding my position. If the company grows, then I will quit. — Rochdi, a manager in a factory

State divestiture from social mobility has logically affected the social meaning of work and allowed for a real rise in the exploitation of labor. For the young, urban, educated, this exploitation has both exacerbated the sense of loss of social identity in white-collar work and made this loss an even more fundamental factor in the constitution of subjectivity and social consciousness. At a moment in my research when I was still stumbling around and poorly phrasing my questions, I asked Khadija, a secretary who speaks English, French, and Arabic, if she noticed her position in society: "If I understand the question, I am frustrated. Have you ever worked as a secretary?" I said yes, and that I thought the work was often not very stimulating. "We are frustrated. We want to pursue our studies but we do not have the money to do it. I am a secretary because there is no other way. I want to go back to school to get my *doctorat d'etat.*" I asked her if she had ever been unemployed and she said yes, for about a year after finishing the licence and beginning the 3me cycle. "I thought of suicide. A job has a psychological role in the life of a human being. Before it is materially important, it is a psychological need."

I met Abdelkrim, the day manager at a two-star hotel, when I first arrived in Morocco and eventually saw him almost every week. As we got to know each other, he started talking about how much he resented his affluent boss at the hotel and his low wages (approximately $200–$220/ month) and his difficulty switching jobs. He was my age, or in his late twenties. He lived with his grandmother (on his father's side), who had raised him in Hay Mohammadi, a lower-middle-income quartier in Casablanca. His mother worked as a maid for a wealthy family and his father had held a variety of jobs, the last I knew about being a security guard at the Hassan II Mosque. Abdelkrim had studied English literature, in fact, with Khadija, and told me occasionally how he was known in his courses for his comments and his work. He also told me that he had failed an exam and, rather than retake it, decided to drop out altogether. I asked him why he did not want to return to complete his degree. "Look at Khadija. She has one year in Rabat [of a master's program], and she works as a secretary."

Although discouraged by entrepreneurial ventures in the export of Moroccan handicrafts, Abdelkrim was in fact confident and positive about his performance as a day manager. When he arrived, Abdelkrim states, the hotel lacked air-conditioning, television sets in the rooms, adequate decor, and a fax machine. Eventually, he convinced his boss to install air-conditioning, put in television sets, redo the interior of the hotel, and buy a fax machine. "I told the boss that other hotels have televisions so we needed to get them. And he did. I also told him that we have business clients and so we need a fax installed. I installed a third plug for the credit card machine, but the boss has refused to buy one. He is in love with cash."

Abdelkrim despised his boss, who refused to grant pay raises, reimburse expenses, or provide adequate benefits, such as health insurance. Abdelkrim called his boss "the fat boy" because of his obesity. An unfortunate caricature of the spoiled, greedy, ignorant son of a wealthy family, the boss wore thick glasses and stumbled when he tried to be articulate. To resist his low wages and lack of appreciation, Abdelkrim had started to turn away guests. Once, someone from a ministry telephoned him to reserve rooms, and Abdelkrim warned her to place the guests in another hotel the next time. At the end of one conversation, Abdelkrim insisted, "One day I am going to show my boss how useful I am. Maybe I will go away for a month, and he will realize how much he needs me." He pinched his fingers together to show how he will reach that moment when the tables will turn, when he will be able to put the pressure on his boss, instead of the other way around.

During a conversation with Abdelkrim and his friend Noureddine, the two men derided the fat boy, and Noureddine, well-off himself from his family and years working at a hotel in the Gulf, concurred that Abdelkrim had changed the hotel. Nourredine claimed that Abdelkrim's boss owes the hotel's improvements and thus its rating to Abdelkrim's suggestions. "The fat boy is not capable of thinking of such things," he said. Abdelkrim then added, "The fat boy spends in five minutes on a girl what I earn in a month. He just goes to these girls now to let him kiss them." Noureddine chimed in that the boss does not even give Abdelkrim money to go to tourism conferences. Once, they both explained, Abdelkrim had to go to Rabat to collect 200 dh and information about a government booking at the hotel. He took a bus with his own money and when he returned, his boss pocketed the 200 dh. "At least he could have given Abdelkrim 100 dh and kept 100 dh for himself," Noureddine remarked. Abdelkrim responded, "I brought several Italian guests, lawyers. I had told him that they were coming, but he went ahead and gave the rooms away. I had to put them in a friend of mine's apartment. . . . The fat boy never gives me a commission for bringing guests and he never thanks me. Just once, I would like him to show that he appreciates me, just a little [gesturing with his fingers to show a pinch]." Noureddine shook his head, "He never could and he never will." Abdelkrim ended, "I do not have the courage to quit. This is my first job and I have worked hard to improve the hotel. But sometimes I think that just for a raise of 50 dh, I will quit."

Alienation of labor for Marx (1988, 74) occurs because "labor is *external* to the worker, i.e., it does not belong to his essential being . . . in his work, therefore, he does not affirm himself but denies himself, does not feel content but unhappy, does not develop freely his physical and mental energy but mortifies his body and ruins his mind." Abdelkrim does experience pride and self-affirmation through the changes he has made in the hotel, but this labor is inevitably usurped by another, and therefore Abdelkrim can never truly incorporate it as part of his self. His form of alienation is at the crux of the sentiments of his generation. These men and women have been trained and educated precisely to maximize potential and rise in society. They are alienated from the objects they produce, in that what they make does not, in a manner far more psychological in nature than the objective deprivation of nineteenth-century factory workers, belong to them. In Marxist terms (Marx himself an intellectual of bourgeois origins),[5] they experience the "loss of the object" through exploitative employment conditions and limitations on mobility precisely because they are socialized as human beings with the ideology of "conscious life-activity," that they as individuals in modern Morocco are formed through their practical and intellectual contribution to the production of the larger collectivity. This activity is lost to them because they lack the power to control the contribution of the object. Whatever is produced in these conditions is therefore perceived as never enough for self-affirmation, and self-formation is always a blocked becoming.

Abdelkrim answered a question I asked on self-confidence among his peers:

> Abdelkrim: I would never have imagined that at my age [then 29] to have nothing in my pocket, no insurance, nothing. People when they reach 30, 31, 32, here they start to race with time and take any job. They know that behind them are all the people in their twenties.

Author: Do you think that you are normal in your attitude?

Abdelkrim: I wish that I were normal, that people did not throw garbage in the street or hassle a young woman when she is alone on a bus or somewhere.

Author: Do you think that people your age think about confidence and being fulfilled?

Abdelkrim: You know, someone who comes to Casa from the village, the rural areas, is realistic. He will sell cigarettes on the street to make money. Someone born in Casa wants to do something he thinks is at his level. You can find jobs in construction here [pointing to a building under construction across the street], but people do not want to take them. I worked in packaging before I took the job at the hotel. I was paid 3 dh/hr and the people there were all illiterate. I could not communicate with them. They could communicate among themselves, they all spoke the same language. . . . The problem was that I knew I was being exploited. I told him, "Tu m'a usé." He replied with "Do you want the job or not?" You know, he was like a brother, I knew him. But I could not do that. I worked there for two weeks.

I asked Abdelkrim why, as he dislikes his boss, he does not search harder for another job. He replied that three to four unemployed university graduates come each day during the summer to look for a job, as they know it is tourist season and the hotel may need more help. "I do not want to be one of those four."

Of course, as Abdelkrim points out above, if they sacrificed their expectations and their ideals, they could sell shoes on the street or go to work in a factory sewing clothes. Here, among the unemployed, the withdrawal of the state from life potential that has led to the emergence of a new subjective position is counterposed by a lack of opportunity in the new economy. The unemployed man or woman cannot just break with an attachment to the "suitable" job and income (and take the McDonald's option) that the processes of education and cultivation are supposed to yield to them. As Butler (1997, 195) puts it, "Survival does not take place because an autonomous ego exercises autonomy in confrontation with a countervailing world; on the contrary, no ego can emerge except through animating reference to such a world. . . . To make of melancholia a simple 'refusal' to grieve its losses conjures a subject who might already be something without its losses, that is, one who voluntarily extends and retracts his or her will." The unemployed could take any job, but in fact they live not to relinquish, in circular fashion, identification with the characteristics they have been recognized and rejected for in the first place. The unemployed, as well as entrepreneurs and bureaucrats, live with an attachment to what they have been denied, the material and symbolic reward commensurate with social and cultural capital. They most likely can never obtain this reward and therefore remain emotionally and behaviorally ambivalent, identified with an internal ideal and dissatisfied with its lack of realization.

Excluding a brief six-week internship as a secretary in government administration, Fowzia was unemployed for all of the three years I knew her in Morocco. She studied Spanish literature in Rabat and preferred a job working in the language. As far as I could tell, her primary effort at finding a job was to ask friends for help. When I first met her, she had recently married the director of a private lycée who doubled as an English teacher. They were cousins from the eastern part of Morocco, and it was she who pushed for the marriage. Both she and her husband wanted children. After trying for at least a year, they both underwent a series of medical tests, but according to the doctor, everything was fine. Her "stress" was his explanation. She thus became more fixated on finding a job, not only as a solution to the boredom of staying at home every day but to have a child for herself and for her marriage.

Before she found the internship through a friend, her husband wanted her to enroll in a secretarial training course. It would have cost more than $100/month plus a $50 inscription fee, and they ultimately decided, in light of the costs of fertility exams and shots, that she should wait. They had little idea how they were going to pay for the exams themselves, as Fowzia's parents still supported several children and could contribute only minimally. Her husband, out of pride, refused to ask his wealthy brother. During one conversation at her apartment, Fowzia repeated how frustrated she was with her situation:

> Fowzia: Now, we have to study for work. If we study at the university, we do this in order to know, but this is all.
> Author: It is important to know the world.
> Fowzia: But it is also important to study for work. [My husband] pushed me to find an internship in order to work with kids for a month. But I did not want to do it. It would be very boring. All those seven years of study in Spanish literature for nothing. You know that I took two buses in order to go to the university. I am not able. I am not lucky. I do not have work or kids. We had a friend at the university

who had a child at the same time she received her licence. All came at the same time, the husband, the child, and the licence. We said, me and my friends, that she was very lucky.

Fowzia looked to motherhood, a job, and a lifestyle as part of a middle-class family with an apartment, a car, a satellite dish, and various household appliances. A university student for seven years, her best opportunities seemed to be as a secretary. Whatever rationalization one could offer — that she studied Spanish because she made a certain score on the bac, that of course she should expect not to do something in Spanish because of limited job possibilities — she did situate herself within the social symbolic landscape in Morocco. She became the object of rejection rather than a positive agent, a figure marked socially by the absence of activity with normative meaning. Her pursuit of different activities to give herself a sense of fulfillment is emblematic of her generation of urban educated. None of these efforts completely worked or even worked at all, leaving her swaying between how de facto she perceived herself and was socially identified.[6]

The dissatisfaction and alienation of the young, urban, educated is in some part due to the fact that the state provided jobs for years and now the next generation expects the same service, as many older Moroccans and frustrated foreign officials claim. These men and women also tend to agree with the support of the IMF for economic rationalization and for obvious reasons dislike the nepotism that characterizes business and politics in Morocco. One of the tenets of *l'association des diplômés chômeurs* is support for transparency in hiring practices and civil service exams as well as fair wages and benefits.[7]

An entrepreneur I knew once expressed how much he envied the son of Driss Basri, the former minister of the interior. He admired the minister because he took advantage of his power to accomplish goals, an ability particularly evident in the development of his home town, Settat. About his son, the entrepreneur commented, "I would love to have the contacts that he has. I have a lot of ideas. But if it was me, I would try to build it [an investment of the son], and I would have to pay people and wait for twenty years. He is able to telephone his father to solve problems with [the electric company] and he builds in five years . . . if I pay all these people this, this is not *bakshish*, but associates as they take one or two centimes [out of every dirham]. Why do it?" The problem for the state, in Morocco and in general, is that these entrepreneurs focus more attention on the possibilities and abuses of power than on their own capacity to change its management.

As this entrepreneur told me after September 11, "We thought we could figure things out, that we knew what was going on or that we could guess. Now, we don't know anything. We just go about our lives." After the revelation of illegal accounting by Enron and other U.S. companies, Hussein admitted that "corruption is everywhere. The U.S. was trying to tell us how to run things and look, they are no better."

The Individual in Globalization

In explaining the importance of marginalized and oppressed groups to understanding culture, nationality, and identity, Homi Bhabha (1994, 172) invests culture with new anthropological and existential concerns:

> Culture reaches out to create a symbolic textuality, to give the alienating everyday an aura of selfhood. . . . Culture as a strategy of survival is both transnational and translational. It is transnational because contemporary postcolonial discourses are rooted in specific histories of cultural displacement, whether they are the "middle passage" of slavery and indenture, the "voyage out" of the civilizing mission, the fraught accommodation of the Third World migration to the West after the Second World War, or the traffic of economic and political refugees within and outside the Third World. Culture is translational because such spatial histories of displacement—now accompanied by the territorial ambitions of "global" media technologies—make the question of how culture signifies, or what is signified by culture, a rather complex issue.

For Bhabha, as well as others in postcolonial studies, it is migrants, as well as homosexuals, women, and other members of groups on the margins of society who show the false holism of nationalism and subjectivity. Subjectivity differs sociospatially for a member of the majority grounded in nation and locality and for the illiterate living under oppressive conditions or the migrant living between cultures and between nations. It is difference and contingency that force self-alienation in the postcolonial society, where multiple groups, with multiple ways of recounting who they are and why they do what they do, disrupt the teleology and historical unity inherent in an idea of national identity.

However, if identification with the state remains a critical part of identity, this time as the object of alienation and anger, then we must argue that culture is not the only site of existential tension and sociospatial dislocation. Exploitation, economic insecurity through consumption and debt, and job instability lend to a subjectivity that refers neither to the social space of the nation nor to a social space framed around the global market (which would imply, if the basis for a society, free flow of labor and non-constriction of movement), but somewhere in between.

Ismaïl, who owns a printing company, criticized the Moroccan government for its negligence of what he considers to be basic development issues: "The key to success is information. I know that I need to conduct a market study before I launch a product . . . we are going to return to slavery if we do not have access to technology, if we lack knowledge. . . . The leaders of Morocco are putting our children into slavery. The most important thing is savoir-faire. Unfortunately, we have nothing like that here. This is something that is very obvious. It is necessary to make the connection between today and tomorrow."

After critiquing corruption in the state and the family-oriented, exclusive hierarchy of many Moroccan companies, Ismaïl commented, "Every time I go overseas and I see how things work there, I think to make my life overseas. In Europe, the owner and the employee both have a car and a home and take vacations. [In Morocco] if one does not have a lot of money, he cannot have the car or the house or invest in the kids . . . this contrast pushes people to want money. This thirst of money is in order to own goods." In searching for money, opportunity, and freedom with deliberate disregard to borders, this generation contributes to the evolution, to the future, of globalization. First, these men and women look for opportunity and social recognition in relations that may traverse nationality, language, and culture, giving social depth to the process of globalization. Second, they measure positive individual change through participation in globalization at the same time that they romanticize and historicize the past of the nation-state. In effect, they articulate a break in social life in Morocco that allows for a present and future not connected to historically confined borders.

With these two acts, looking outward through social relations and enclosing historically the nation-state, the global middle class becomes a potentially powerful political and social actor. As individuals who no longer function within a system of collective representation, but rather are alone, facing the amorphous context of the globe, they become free to build social cohesion external to a vertical imposition of power. The politics of a global middle class then becomes creating social meaning through linking ideas and symbols, communities, and immediate environment and circumstances.

The romanticization of the past becomes all too apparent when young, urban, educated men and women talk of current economic and social conditions. The disc jockey and music store owner mentioned in the previous chapter told me once, "My grandfather, he could just walk out into the street and get a job." Karim, the owner of a new and very modern dry cleaners, compared the troubles he and his father have had in business with the nostalgic image his father had of the efficiency of the French companies invested in Morocco during the colonial and postcolonial period. His father told him that the French companies were much more disciplined than Moroccan ones. "He says that people lived well, that there were not the people that there are today. There was still the French who worked well." Karim also mentioned that the quartier Maarif, where his shop was located, used to be a center for foreigners and that his street used to be well-frequented. Now, he complained, Maarif has become a poor extension of Guathier, a quartier that caters to the "upper middle class versus the very middle class of Maarif."

In another conversation, Karim and I talked about how shops and restaurants have changed over the past decade in Casablanca. I mentioned the number of new cafés.

> Karim: In the past, someone could create anything and it worked. Now, with globalization, a lot of things have changed.
> Author: You mean because of competition?
> Karim: Yes, competition. We are very close to Europe. We feel what is going on there.

Looking around at the garish café in which we were having coffee, with its video screen, cushioned chairs, and an upstairs for couples seeking privacy, he commented, "In the past, they built cafés that were simple, but now if you don't build a café like this, it is not going to succeed."

In contrast to their romanticization of the past, young Moroccans in the global middle class express their admiration for the lifestyle, the political freedom, and, perhaps above all, the business environment offered in industrialized countries. As a young journalist, the son of a respected leftist intellectual, said, "There will be a change in Morocco when there is a party that supports the truth based in the law." Karim decided to open a dry cleaners after watching a program about laundromats in France. Likewise, he learned the business through contacts he made in France. However, he favored the Anglo-Saxon model of liberal market capitalism.

Karim: There are French who go to Great Britain for the day to work. They leave at five in the morning, they are in England at six, they do their work, and then they come back.

Author: What kind of work?

Karim: Anything, they are young. In France, they are very attached to the state. There is all of the unemployment, etc. . . .

Author: The U.S. also has a lot of problems.

Karim: Yes, but that is everywhere. The European Union marches at a speed, Europe can't catch up. Europe, with the exception of England, is behind.

The problem for Karim, as the owner of a small enterprise, was that he could derive ideas for his business from France or England, but in Morocco, he lacked state structural support, access to capital so that he could reinvest in the business, and a market trying to become more informed. He complained that the state assisted large foreign companies like Thompson and McDonald's but not small companies like his own. "I pay about 4,000 dhs a month on electricity alone. Imagine, if I had to pay rent on top of that [his family owns the property]. After the 20 percent tax on profits, local taxes, and the bills, I do not earn a lot. I regret occasionally that I did not sell the *pat-porte* [down payment on rent] for 2 million dhs and then rent the space for a couple of thousand dhs a month."

For those with fewer resources than Karim, namely, someone like Abdelkrim, or those with more resources, such as entrepreneurs seeking international customers, social relations are fundamental to access to the global market. For Abdelkrim, finding a job in a private company in import/export means much more than formal education. During the period I was living in Morocco, he spoke with several foreigners about launching an export business. "Chances are passing me by," he once said to me. "I am watching chances pass me by." The most consistent potential partner was an American named Stephen, who asked him to send him wood products in the United States. Abdelkrim would go to Essaouira (a seven-hour bus ride) to collect the products on his day off and then send them to Stephen. As I understood the details of the business from Abdelkrim, he would pay himself for his trips there as well as phone calls to the United States. He succeeded at extracting money (and not enough to pay his expenses) from Stephen only after harassing him. Eventually, Stephen shut Abdelkrim out, and Abdelkrim moved on to other American partners, who promised to set him up with an office and a fax in Morocco. They then decided they were too busy for the business. "Just give me a chance, I told them. The wood products would just be a small, small [gesticulating to emphasize how small] part of their business. Just give me office space in the U.S., I told them, and I would sell the products."

He also tried to work with a well-off Moroccan friend of his and a Taiwanese businessman trying to open an import company in Morocco. Abdelkrim wanted to export Taiwanese products to West Africa to compete with more expensive French goods: "French goods are so expensive, and Taiwanese products are cheap. I told him [the Taiwanese businessman] to open an office in Mauritania. I called my friends and they said, Abdelkrim we need photos, we need a catalogue. But he is too afraid. He is moving very slowly [in Morocco]. He only wants to do business with people he knows. I tell him that he can succeed because he is not Moroccan, that Moroccans trust a foreigner. But he does not want to take the risk. I do not like that. I told him just to give me a chance."

With his friend, he wanted to import motorbike helmets and sell them at a fixed price. "The problem is that they come into the country without organization. Some sell them at much cheaper prices than others." The friend refused.

Hannah Arendt (1976, 302) writes of how the refugee, denied the opportunity to participate in common human enterprises, becomes simply a human being, "without a profession, without a citizenship, without an opinion, without a deed by which to identify and specify himself — *and* different in general, representing nothing but his own absolutely unique individuality which, deprived of expression within and action upon a common world, loses all significance." Unemployment or economic insecurity in Morocco should not be equated with the dislocation and chaos of postwar Europe, but the issues that Arendt lists as fundamental to participation in our world when discussing apatrides are the same issues facing young Moroccan men and women. Leaving a trace on the world, fulfilling a destiny, and expressing an opinion that bears meaning are all indicative of the dilemma that faces both the Moroccan young, urban, educated and the Moroccan state. Karim, the owner of the dry cleaners, once described the public university as "a factory, with thousands of students in ampitheaters. Of the five thousand students, perhaps one hundred to two hundred are interested in their studies. The students are not able to reconcile the difference between the university and their own life. They are not able to study because they must strive to be at the university and then they must go back where they came from. They ask themselves, Why am I going to study if I am going to be unemployed?"

At one point, I started to push Abdelkrim to think beyond the job at the hotel. He had once told me, "Do you know the Guynemer and another new hotel just here on Anfa? They have offered me jobs, but I couldn't do it. I really love my hotel. I really do. I know every inch. If there is a nail, I know when it was put in." Yet, he continued to explore plans to go to the United States. He was waiting at one point for an American he had met at the hotel to arrange a visa for him, and we diverged into a conversation about his plans. Abdelkrim had helped the American move around when he was in Casablanca and had even arranged a room at a hotel on the beach, where the American preferred to stay. The visa had not come, but Abdelkrim had already planned for a departure and for life in the United States. He would move his grandmother to Tetuoan and put her apartment in his sister's name to avoid allowing his father, for whom he shows little respect, to take control of it. With just a visa and no job at a company, he wanted to return to literature, which he believes is his calling. The job at the hotel, a perversion in his life, had to end. "It is as if you moved from turning on the television to Channel 2, skipping Channel 1," referring to the second channel as his hotel job and Channel 1 as his missing vocation. "I do not want that for you," Abdelkrim said to me. "It is like you in your studies. You love your studies and you do not have time for anything else. I liked the university because I had confidence. I would answer every question. The answers were just there."

In 2001, Abdelkrim married a guest at the hotel, a woman from Canada who had come often to Morocco and offered Abdelkrim a chance to leave, perhaps to return to his studies. However, when he went for his immigration interview at the Canadian embassy, his application was turned down. His wife returned to live in Canada and he remained in Casablanca.

The desire for meaning and the sense of its absence find as much expression among successful midlevel managers and entrepreneurs as among the unemployed or insecurely employed. In his mid-thirties, Azzedine studied engineering in France and returned to find a managerial position in a then foreign-owned manufacturing firm (the firm has changed hands several times since Azzedine started working there). The eldest of nine children, he was born in Errachidia (in the south-central region of Morocco) to a Berber family and spoke Tamazight at home. His father worked as the director of a primary school. The father quit school before the lyceé, but secured a job in education forty years ago when the state, desperate for educated labor, hired teachers who had completed the *6me niveau* (basic education). Unlike Abdelkrim, who always wore inexpensive corduroy pants and button-down shirts, Azzedine sported a jacket and slacks and wire-rimmed glasses.

When Azzedine came back to Morocco after completing his studies, he claimed he wanted to do something for his country, similar to the discourse of Moroccan intellectuals who returned from France in the 1980s. Now, he feels that there is nothing he can do, and his current goal is to "see the world," figure out his possibilities, and then decide where he would like to live. He explained, "I do my work well. I am responsible in three areas and I want to learn. But I am not able to negotiate the salary. There are men who do not work as much but are able to negotiate wages. I am not able." I protested that he earns a good salary, much better than most of his peers. Life in the United States is expensive and hard, and he may not be able to find the same quality of job.

> Azzedine: But I want to be a waiter in a restaurant.
>
> Author: Are you able to do that?
>
> Azzedine: For several years, yes. Not for a long time. I am able to work in engineering. I am able to work with the wind. I want to see business in the U.S., in a developed country. I did not make it here and I am not sure that I am going to succeed. . . . It is not a question of salary, in fact, it is a question of liberty.
>
> Author: Liberty as the possibility of living apart from the family?
>
> Azzedine: *Non,* it gives me great pleasure to live with my family. There is no freedom of press here, or freedom of expression. When I see the discourse of foreign investment, I say it's the blah, blah. It is necessary to clean up the administration, decrease interest rates, and put to work the society.
>
> How many people in your sample want to leave for the U.S., 100 percent?
>
> Author: Not all, maybe 90 percent [smiling]. There is a difference between men and women. The women are more content to stay here and the men want to leave. The men who earn 1,500 dh/month [like Abdelkrim] want to leave for money. When I speak with people like you, who earn a half-decent salary, they are frustrated.
>
> Azzedine: *Voilà,* that is the word, it is frustrating.

As we walked out, he declared the café too "snob." I replied that the owner must be earning a profit, because the café was packed. He snapped,

"He should be asked if he pays taxes. He should be asked how he earns money."

The Search for a Counter-Morocco

I am scared to look into the future. — Abdelkrim

The search for a counter-Morocco through connection to the globe represents the darker side of cosmopolitanism (Appadurai 1996; Held and Archibugi 1995) and of the flow of consumer goods, cultural artifacts, images and symbols, and media technologies (Ossman 2002). Arjun Appadurai writes that the new role of imagination in social life is to allow individuals to fantasize about possibilities through contact with the media and migrants. He adds that "what is implied is that even the meanest and most hopeless of lives, the most brutal and dehumanizing of circumstances, the harshest of lived inequalities are now open to the play of the imagination" (1996, 54). However, he leaves off here, with a conception of imagination as a social practice similar to imagination for Benedict Anderson (1991), or part of the new politics of community.

I suggest that the consciousness of the global middle class represents a middle-class follow-up to Marxist alienation. Not able to translate their individuality through the nonlocated, ambiguous arena of the globe, these men and women become just individuals, representing nothing but themselves. In the inverse equation of citizen and enterprise put forth by Arendt regarding refugees, these men and women fulfill their unique individuality only by turning away in idealization and fantasy from established collective representation and common national enterprise.

A sales clerk in a Meditel store, a store that sells cell phones: You see what I do. This is not my level. I have a bac plus 4. Yet, I went to one of the best business schools here. I spent 200,000 dh for nothing. You have to have connections in Morocco. I was better than the others, but they had connections. There are people who work at the headquarters of Meditel who have the bac plus 2.

> Author: Why did you come to work here?
> Clerk: I was unemployed for a year. I suffered a depression. In the end, I took this. There are ten distributors of Meditel in Morocco. They announced they had jobs. I went after it and I had an interview after twenty days. But this is not . . . This is what I have to tolerate.

People come in here and smoke, and I have to say please, stop smoking. People treat the store like a trashcan. It is difficult in Morocco because I am different. I want to leave because there is a difference of cultivation. It is better to be like the others. I want to leave because I want to do an MBA. I want to do marketing. My husband wants to leave for a better standard of living. My sister-in-law and sister live in the U.S. My sister-in-law works and my sister is studying. And they are very, very happy there. Because of that, we want to leave.

One day, I showed up at a café to meet Abdelkrim, and he told me that he had written down some notes for me but had forgotten them at home. He had shared a bottle of vodka with a guest that weekend and was still suffering from a hangover. However, when Noureddine, his friend, showed up at the café, Abdelkrim started to discuss extemporaneously his theory of identity: "Watch this. I will say one word and he will say the other." "Crisis," he said to Noureddine, who looked clueless. "Hey, what am I talking about?" "Identity," Noureddine responded. "I am always talking about the crisis of identity and people are telling me, 'Shut up, Abdelkrim.'" He then pointed to an ashtray on the table and said:

Moroccan youth are 55 percent full and 45 percent a void. They want to reject everything that is their parents and their family, their heritage. But this is impossible. What do they do to fill this void? They watch television. Moroccans, I assure you, watch six hours a day of television. The youth take from television to fill their identity. Do you know the series *Guadalupe* [the central character in a Mexican telenovella]? This series has done something horrible in Morocco. When the actress came to Morocco — she was invited by the princess — millions went to Rabat to see her. Sometimes when I am talking to a girl or a man, I feel like I have seen this behavior before, and then I realize that this has come from *Guadalupe* or an Egyptian movie. A guy will tell me that he has a girlfriend and that she is really sweet but she is having problems with her family. It is not real. I tell you, there is a real crisis of identity. The youth are fleeing from the past and from Morocco. They hate what is Moroccan and want to be something else [i.e., an actor in an Egyptian or Mexican drama]. They are rebelling against authority, which they see as the family [imitates a teenage or twenty-something child insulting his parents]. But in reality, what they are angry at, it is beyond the family. It is [whispers] the government.

Our parents did not take us to a café, they did not take us to a restaurant, they did not teach us how to make love to a woman. Where do we learn about these things? From the television. . . . No, Moroccans do not have money. From the *parabole*, people start to have high aspirations. Yet, the material means are not moving along with them. The superstructure is moving much faster than material means. The two must move in parallel. Moroccans do not accept the reality, what is fact. Instead, they want to buy clothes. Egyptians admit that they are poor, they accept it. In Morocco, we cannot accept it.

On a return visit to Morocco, after the years of conducting dissertation research, I mentioned to Karim that I felt that the desire to leave had increased. He responded: "Yes, the reason is that people want too much, more than the country can give them. They take on the customs of Europe, they speak in French. Myself, I speak more than half the time in French. The problem is that people forget that Morocco is still a poor country in Africa. Me, I am trying to build a modern dry cleaners, but clients are not— they say the prices are too high. But twenty, thirty years from now, Morocco will, is going to change completely, this [pointing down to the floor] is going to be Europe."

I told him that I knew Moroccans and Algerians living in Washington, D.C., with diplomas working in coffee shops and unable to pay their bills (*musarif*). "Yes," Karim responded, "most, except for one or two who come back, are disappointed. But the people who go there to do their studies, they do their studies, they marry, and they are happy. But most of those who go to make money come back disappointed."

In conceptualizing globalization and perhaps even in formulating and lending support for policy, we must take into account disappointment as well as the restless aspiration for change, both of which persist regardless of location. The owner of an athletic club who lives part time in California compared his unease in both countries, as well as his appreciation. In his comments, he responded not as much to the expected benefits and drawbacks of a particular place as to his increasingly common experience of living between places:

> Life in the U.S. is too stressful, too expensive. Everything costs so much. Here, life is cheaper. You can have a good life here. You know, in the U.S., people don't help each other. Here, people help each other because they want to. In the U.S., if you miss a payment, two payments, they sell your house. Here, they talk to you. In the U.S., people volunteer because they need to do something. Here, people want to help.

In the U.S., people want more, better. And things are so expensive. A couple that makes $100,000 a year can't make it anymore. Here, people are content with a little. They just need a little. In the U.S., I have to wonder if things are fair. Look at O. J. Simpson. It is clear he killed his wife, but he hired expensive lawyers.

If there were a strong governor in Casablanca, then he could change things in a week. People don't clean the streets because it is menial work and it pays low. In the U.S., people clean the streets because it is the thing to do. They just do it. Here, if a strong man was to show that you clean the streets for the beauty, to be proud, the young people would do it. It is not cultural. Culture is, well, it will take fifty years to move from couscous to a hamburger. That is culture. I think in one week things could change. I see it already.

Summary

This chapter situates together the groups described in chapter 3 on the basis of a common condition of alienation. The principal argument is to not make causal assumptions about the origins of alienation, namely, that discontent, which in the Arab World sometimes takes form in Islamic political activity, is simply the effect of economic pressure and political corruption and will go away if the economy grows and corruption disappears. Market reform has replaced the identity between individual fulfillment and national potential with the nonidentity of individual and global economy. The consequence is a population dependent economically on further reform and private investment but unable to translate a particular space and historical moment in terms of themselves. They respond in their behavior by not participating in the political or social life of the nation and, alternatively, by fantasizing about the possibilities in an alternative realm, a counter-Morocco.

The consciousness of the global middle class implies that a reduction in unemployment rates for university graduates may palliate immediate discontent, but that the existential restlessness in all likelihood will persist. With this idea in mind, I have argued not to abandon alienation in social theory because we no longer can discuss consciousness as an essence to be revealed through truth. We can, through exploring class formation, reconsider the relation among expressed alienation, class formation, and class politics, and implicitly, the politics to which we would give intellectual credence as social theorists and sociologists.

For instance, we can question the accuracy of a prevalent liberal notion that the state can, through regulating global investment and trade and supporting local civil and educational institutions, rebuild the middle class.[8] This notion follows the logic that redistribution of resources should revive a middle class in OECD and middle- and low-income countries that has been battered by the declining value of wages and deterioration of working conditions (for example, doctors and teachers in the United States). Yet, if the modern middle class of these critiques cannot be revived, then we should consider the political and economic ramifications of a new middle class constituted by the very conditions being criticized.

In the conclusion, I outline the possible politics of the global middle class. In fact, the global middle class may represent the economic counterpart of the translational and transnational culture that Bhabha discusses regarding Third World migrants to the West. If these men and women now become identified socially by connection to global capitalism, and if they existentially live not by identity with a transcendent arena but in a non-located, unstable space outside the nation, then they too are migrants. The politics of the global middle class derives from this experience, rooted not as much in cultural identification as in the effort to achieve existential purpose through economic security and social recognition.

Conclusion:

Economic Insecurity and

Social Formation

The ideas I have presented reflect years of ethnographic research and qualitative interviews conducted primarily in Casablanca, Morocco. They also reflect the desire to develop a critical understanding of the social impact of global market capitalism. In concluding, I want to suggest potential political implications of an evolving global middle class. Although I offer ideas about how political consciousness might take shape, I do not claim to predict the future. Rather, I want to show how a theoretical framework derived from substantial empirical research can attenuate existing theories of future communities and political action (see Agamben 1993; Bailly and Nancy 1991; Hardt and Negri 2000).

This kind of framework can point to a historical movement not guided by an underlying telos or idealism but by social processes produced in a given economic and political context. In other words, a sociological approach can avoid falling into structurally determined or philosophically argued prediction while not dismissing speculation on the future altogether. I suggest that sociology has the potential to illuminate when we return to theoretical approaches like Critical Theory that integrate structural analysis with interpretation of subjective meaning in the world. Such an integration allows us to understand the dynamic between structure and consciousness and how, if questioning the possibility for change, the latter may come to influence the former.

The argument I have laid out here originates in a dichotomy between the modern middle class and the global middle class. The modern middle class emerged in an epoch when the state attempted to control the organization of the economy and society, imposing an ideology of nation building to legitimize policies that ranged from political oppression to the development of school curriculums. The class created from policies of development and modernization saw itself as the vanguard of progress, the appointed leadership of a largely illiterate, agricultural nation.

As external pressures due to mounting debt and (mostly) European interest in new labor and export markets forced the triangle of power among state, economy, and society to disintegrate, the role of vanguard for the middle class fell apart, if not in substance through education at least in political and social importance within larger Moroccan society. The adoption of a structural adjustment program in 1983 and a subsequent climb in unemployment and low-paying, unstable employment among university and high school graduates dispossessed this population of the preconceived historical mission of its predecessor.

The state, under the ultimate leadership of the king, certainly has remained the most important institutional authority in the country. Yet, more actors, particularly international ones, now participate in decision making. Policies in turn reflect the exogenous demands of the WTO, a free trade accord with the European Union, and the conditions of the IMF, World Bank, and other creditors. Without the interdependence that existed between the legitimation of state power and the creation of a modern middle class, the future of the new generation of educated men and women has become a secondary consideration, a political and social problem of joblessness and a failure of training that should be solved increasingly by private actors. This new position of educated men and women within the political economy of Morocco has yielded both a sociostructural and a subjective impact that conflict with conventional theoretical assumptions about the middle class.

Structurally, efforts to promote integration in the global market economy have pushed the diplômés to seek employment in the service sector in addition to the occupations of the older middle class, tying the fate of this generation to levels of foreign and domestic investment and the more general organization of the private sector rather than the political power of the regime. As a consequence, a system of social evaluation has evolved in connection with participation in the global economy. Aspects of personal comportment, from manner of articulation to dress, that are in turn interrelated with education, family, and income (Bourdieu 1987), are now not associated with a specific career in the administration. Rather, they indicate capacity to manage contact with foreign companies and grasp financial instruments and techniques of marketing and manufacturing.

Specifically, this generation has become fragmented into two more coherent social groups of entrepreneurs and midlevel managers and the unemployed and temporarily or insecurely employed. The third group is a more mixed population, encompassing the traditional occupations of the modern middle class as well as the salaried professionals and small-scale *commerçants* in the private sector.

Although similar to the new middle class of advanced industrialized nations or the petite bourgeoisie of Marx in their structural heterogeneity, the groups share a common subjective position founded in loss of attachment to the nation-state. An individual, in this case, an individual like other educated, ambitious men and women, experiences a loss of the ideal of progress through rational activity within the nation. The withdrawal of state intervention, state power, from the social structure and the ideal of self-realization (with social mobility as its material manifestation) then becomes the catalyst for reconstitution of this subjective position and the critical center, so to speak, of the existential challenge of this generation.

The loss of the ideal of human potential offered in national development and the foreclosure of material possibility is the same loss and foreclosure of possibility that underpins the psychic condition of melancholy (Freud 1981). The reflexivity of the subject is formed at the moment of loss (Butler 1997), when human potential becomes the ego-object and conscience the critical examination of the fulfillment of potential. The tension between conscience and ego results in ambivalence, a condition that plagues the entire global middle class. Melancholy is thus a social process in Morocco, a replacement for the trajectory of social mobility within the nation-state. It is the psychic imprint of the lost ideal of human potential (see Butler 1997), an "internal" mimicking of the social ideal held up by the state in the postcolonial era.

Ambiguity, loss of principle and purpose for the global middle class, is not, however, negation of class formation, but its very underpinning, one based on liminality in relation to the nation and awkward dislocation within the global economy. Historically, social instability and material insecurity mean that the global middle class cannot live through the role of actor in the global market economy with material or existential authority or claim, as did the modern middle class, progress within the "sameness" of self, history, and space. In fact, by encouraging decisions about everything

from professional training to retirement plans to funds for children's education (that have become popular in Morocco), liberal market capitalism sets
the conditions for another social loss. In the instability and insecurity of
global capitalism, the economic actor, like the citizen in the modern nation,
may become what is lost, and thus also the determining factor in new social
consciousness. Following the trajectory of loss and subsequent ambivalence, having "refused" the nation-state, the global middle class may turn
away from decision making and responsibility and from the global economic elites who through it attempt to claim their own legitimacy. They
thus may provide the moment, in their alienation and rootlessness, for a
new political path. This path would unfold in a conceptual direction and
with a politics very different from theoretical and actual class conflict of the
past. In the next section, I outline the basic arguments framing the conceptual direction and in the following section discuss the political implications.

Social Theory and Economic Insecurity

Everybody is looking for something to make them okay with their life. Happiness, no,
satisfaction, is always inside. We can find it. It is just a question of time. Sometimes, it can
come late. It has come late for me. Like me, I am like in prison or something. A lot of
people dream to have my job. But not a lot of people dream to have my salary. I could go
out of Morocco and have more resources, but that may not do it. This is why I am telling
you it is inside of you. The problem is time. After 30, everything goes so quickly.—
Abdelkrim

The notion of a global middle class is founded on larger theoretical arguments about social transformation in a period of global market integration.
But there is a caveat: these ideas in no way should suggest resolution,
answers to questions about subjectivity, class, society, and alienation. They
represent instead consideration of the internal contradictions within global
capitalism. They connect trade liberalization, market reform, diversifica-
tion of consumption possibilities, and development of technology and services to the unintentional cultivation of modes of behavior and thought
that conflict with the needs of an expanding market. More directly, these
ideas encourage addressing the sociopsychological effects of global capitalism by theorizing the relationship between economic insecurity and the
social meaning of human potential.

Integrating the structural element of economic insecurity with a subjective position constituted through political economic valuation of human

potential, the first broad conceptual argument is to continue to ask questions about class. I contend here that class represents an intellectually viable and politically fruitful methodological and theoretical approach to the social dimension of globalization, globalization implying the specific historical period in which we live. The global middle class reflects the contradictions of economic globalization in a peculiarly intensive way, opening up possibilities for theoretical speculation and debate. The subjective identification with an ideal of human fulfillment and material advancement binds the global middle class materially both to white-collar and technical jobs that promise security and status and to the consumer goods distributed in expanding trade and privatization. The alienation of this class is indicative of what might go wrong in the path of market integration to promote growth and cultivate a popular base marked by enthusiasm for neoliberal values and understanding of neoliberal economic practices.

The second broad argument concerns analyzing the social relations that evolve between different groups and different classes within the new organization of economic and political power and the rise of a dominant ideology. The abstract language of global market integration as well as the empirical details of its effects hide the transformation of relations between economic and political elites and the middle class.

In the past, the state invested dually in mobility and the ideal of emancipation because a modern middle class possessed of both social stability and self-identity within a political economic system legitimized authority by governing elites over society, economy, and polity. Influenced by dependence on state investment and the ideologies of modernization and nationalism, members of the modern middle class, even if in political opposition, did not question the existence of the state or the necessity of elite leadership (even in Marxist movements). Rather, they criticized the management of the state and the political goals of the king and specific individuals and parties. In other words, the position of elite leadership seemed interchangeable, open for contestation and replacement.

In contrast, contemporary state divestiture from responsibility for personal well-being and individual social status and economic security implies a profound rupture between political and economic elites and nonelite populations. Sustained economic growth in global market integration requires a consumer-oriented middle-income population, but the young, urban, educated do not function as a thematic image for the nation or for the political legitimacy of a ruler (of course, with the unemployed, it can be the opposite). In more profound social and political terms, the absence of an overarching political and social community, of a society composed of different individuals but united in nationhood, means that local nonelites and elites lack common representation. The exclusion of representation extends as well to transnational economic elites who offer material opportunities and signifiers of social status through consumer goods and media, but not responsibility for a located social environment. The social and political bond between elites and nonelites thus falls apart globally and locally, leaving only economic benefit and exploitation (see Hardt and Negri 2000).

Conceptually, we have to consider the importance of this rupture to social formation, regarding both what we call new formation and how we define it. The modern middle class represents a modern class because its members translate external change, development, in terms of themselves. Conversely, the young, urban, educated make up the global middle class because they share the same inability to equate collective representation and the external environment with steps of individual change. They are individuals who represent nothing but themselves.

The political path they might pursue would reflect the collapse of elite-driven representation and responsibility. The political goal of the global middle class would be to attain access to services formerly subsumed within the province of the state but that now, increasingly, come from the non-located, heterogeneous social relations that signify and support globalization. Ultimately, their politics would entail creating institutions structurally and philosophically supportive of these social relations and the issues of human potential and economic security that so obsess them.

The Politics of a Global Middle Class

Before discussing a possible political philosophy and policy position of a global middle class, we should first reconsider the basic fusion between the social structure of modern societies and political ideology and organization. The twentieth-century middle class, in the name of social justice and individual equality in the collectivity, propelled the rise of democracy and market capitalism in the nation-state and, conversely, buttressed the authoritarian state and a state-controlled economy. The decline of the economic security of the modern middle class and of the younger generations of urban educated has led to images of a society bifurcated into rich and poor. In Argentina and Morocco, for instance, media and popular discourse refer to the economically and socially declining middle classes as *nuevos pobres* or *nouveaux pauvres*.

Behind this discourse is the assumption that we must use conventional categories of rich, middle class, and poor in economic reform. Yet, waning objective and subjective attachments to the institutions of the nation-state have weakened the significance of "equality within the collectivity" in shaping public behavior and influencing political decisions, and thus the applicability of these categories. In Morocco, the state has not taken the issue of equality seriously enough to carry forth with any significant redistribution of income, yet the ideals of opportunity and emancipation still underpin nationalism and nation building. In contrast, we must ask if and how to continue to think about the dichotomy of equality and inequality and how to connect economic conditions to the language of individual emancipation in the global market economy.

Policy-wise, we should not draw on a cause-and-effect sequence regarding middle-class behavior, either in the conservative sense of regulating private life to make middle-class families more stable or the liberal sense of ensuring a middle-class economic position to offer stability to modern society. Representing the liberal-left position, James K. Galbraith (2000, 4) writes that without government regulation of private industry, the United States has transformed "from a middle-class democracy into something that more closely resembles an authoritarian quasi-democracy, with an overclass, an underclass, and a hidden politics driven by money." To Galbraith, members of the middle class, and he shares here the views of much of the labor movement and the left, are more likely to maintain stable families, vote, work efficiently and well, and express contentment with their lives. Rising inequality in wages and job security has "lifted the veil of ignorance" about equality among individuals and encouraged political forces, enticed by the resources of business lobbies, to punish rather than support individuals for falling behind (4). Inequality becomes a matter of political choice, capable of being challenged through policy direction but alive through the perceptions of politicians and citizens alike.

However, the middle class of these functions — social, political, and economic stabilization — may no longer exist. We perhaps can think instead of a global middle class that functions to support the global market economy, in a pure economically liberal form of individuals desiring the right to opportunity, to move where this opportunity is located, to consume, and to engage in entrepreneurism. The politics associated with participation in liberal market capitalism relate to the insecure foundation of individual and collective rights and, more directly, material and social reward within this economic system.

Looking further, through giving rise to a global middle class, global market integration may create its own form of "gravedigger." More than the "morphology" of globalization (see Castells 1996), it may be the relationship between the global middle class and global business elites, structured through economic obligations and options, that makes the greatest imprint on subjectivity and social consciousness and, ultimately, political behavior.[1] Loss of the historical moment of the middle class in the nation-state has temporally corresponded with the rise of the abstract, universal consumer, saver, and investor as a deliberately apolitical, asocial ideal. Yet, like the deliberately political and social ideal of national citizen, the ideal of an economic actor is stymied by the material and social conditions inherent in maintaining global market integration. The permanence of individual insecurity both encourages economic practices, like saving and investing, and undermines the stability of social reward related to these actions.

The evolving present and future loss would underpin the substance of the individual in globalization and, likewise, suggest directions for the organization and ideals of political movements. The politics of a global middle class in globalization would in fact address three interrelated questions concerning the future. The first returns to the image evoked in the first chapter of the Palestinian attempting to cross borders and establish residency. Mahmud Darwish's (1988) isolated, confused narrator asks, "I am not a citizen here and I am not a resident. Therefore, where am I and who am I?" The narrator then concludes, "You realize that you are present philosophically, but you are absent legally" (94). For young Moroccan men and women, the statement becomes You realize you are present legally, but you are absent philosophically. Any theory and strategy of politics for the global middle class must confront this absence, and not as a nostalgic return but as an embrace of the challenge the global market economy presents to the subject.

In other words, this effort would not entail returning to the "I" grounded in the physical, temporal, and bounded social world of the nation-state. The second question thus relates the fading I of the nation-state to the collapse of a located social system. This relation has, in fact, already determined the possibility for a new substance of individual meaning. Without the boundaries negotiated in the individual's relation to the state, without the modern fixation of self-fulfillment at a particular moment and in a particular place, individuals cannot equate social differentiation and the contingent denial of the other with an interpretation of self-fulfillment.

Individuals in this situation no longer strive to achieve the security of the autonomous individual and therefore no longer justify reward within a social order at the expense of someone else. Rather, they perceive a world through the existence of the other, who provides fulfillment in acts of acknowledgment, inclusion, and material support. The political theme of the global middle class, the low hymn that now stands as detachment from the nation-state, becomes the claim to social recognition and resource security (meaning health, education, income, and so on) in the world. This claim transforms into a right through the establishment of global institutional standards of economic and social security and global philosophical-political valuation of each individual.

The third question thus entails relating individual fulfillment and happiness to the relationship between economy and polity. The global middle class has emerged in the change in relative power between the market economy and the state. Distance between elites and nonelites and the potential rejection of decision making as individual meaning challenges the power of the economy over political life. However, the temporal and substantive organization of an individual life exists outside of a system of collective representation, of a nation, hindering the return of modern organization of political power.

If this is the moment for new organizations and possibilities for social power, long subsumed under the state and the economy, then political movements and eventually institutions should address the historical trends that have given rise to a global middle class. They should ask how to confront loss as a social process and how to champion existential meaning within the social relations and the dissemination of values, images, and artifacts that give rise to globalization. The answer to both questions may be to relate social power to subjective position in the globe. This relation would form by forgetting ideals in favor of what Agamben (1993, 43) calls "the only ethical experience . . . the experience of being (one's own) potentiality, of being (one's own) possibility." The individual experience of potentiality would reflect a global organization of possibility that rejects conceptualizing the role of the individual or collectivity within a larger structure, and thus explicit direction toward a nation, global market economy, or otherwise. In this case, the only clear direction that remains is the future.

Notes

1 Global Market Capitalism

1 Of course, the flip side of this remark is how remarkably few examples of positive social impact World Bank and IMF officials bring up in their official speeches and press conferences. They tend to discuss prescription and blocked or slow progress far more than actual proof of success.

2 Stiglitz writes, "From 358 million in 1990 to 208 million in 1997, using China's admittedly lower poverty standard of $1 a day" (2002, 181–81).

3 Abdessalam Yassine recently published a book in English called *Winning the Modern World for Islam* (2000). In the book, he calls the nation-state a "prison that limits you, ties you up, and blocks your impetus" (149) but also emphatically encourages patience and not violence in the transformation to Islamic government.

4 Although the absence of a strategy permeates conversations public and private, arguments in the press about developing a strategy for the future seem more forthright and urgent, particularly since September 11. For example, Abdelrahman al-Rashed, the former editor in chief of the Arabic daily *Sharq al-awsat*, criticized Saudi politicians for not promoting innovative thinking and following through with social and economic programs. He called on Saudi politicians to "produce a program that reflects creative thinking and not just quick responses that echo what is said here and there" (9 June 2003, 18).

5 King Mohammed VI has allowed, among others, Abraham Serfaty, who served the longest sentence among the participants in the Marxist movements of the 1970s, to return from exile in France.

6 Dynasties in Morocco have risen and fallen on adherence to different Islamic schools and, of course, ability both to consolidate the tribes under single rule and maintain Moroccan isolation from foreign influence. The Idrissides (788–1055), the first dynasty, founded Fez and brought together Berber tribes under single rule. The Almoravides (1055–1147)

established Marrakech and invaded Spain. They were followed by the Almohades (1130–1269), a Berber dynasty that propagated a strict practice of Islam, or the doctrine of the *muwahhadīn*. Under Yacoub Al Mansour, the Almohades ruled Morocco and conquered Spain during the Golden Age of both Jewish and Muslim thought, art, and commerce. They were replaced by the Merinides (1258–1465), a scholarly dynasty. After military defeats to Spain and Portugal, they themselves were replaced by the Saadians (1520–1660), a Cherifien dynasty from the Dra' Valley. The Alaouites, from the Tafilalet region and also descendants of the Prophet, turned their military efforts inward, and through several sultans, brought Arab and Berber tribes under the authority of the *makhzen*.

7   By nation-state, I mean the establishment of a modern political apparatus that assumes through force and policy control over the entire territory and attempts, in an effort to legitimize its authority, the creation of a national culture and society.

8   Saad Eddin Ibrahim (1994), reflecting common intellectual interest in the Arab World, refers to the "social contract" that has been broken between the state and university graduates in his discussion of Islamic political activity in Egypt.

9   This perception manifested itself through affiliation with different ideologies of development, whether Western, Islamic, nationalist, or a combination of principles of authenticity and reform.

10   As Judith Butler (1997, 198) explains, the withdrawal of social regulation and power is what produces the internal space of the psyche, and the loss of these forces is the initiating point of power and regulation for the subject: "The subject is produced, paradoxically, through this withdrawal of power, its dissimulation and fabulation of the psyche as a speaking topos. Social power vanishes, becoming the object lost, or social power makes vanish, effecting a mandatory set of losses."

11   Butler (1997, 198) writes: "By withdrawing its own presence, power becomes an object lost — 'a loss of a more ideal kind.' Eligible for melancholic incorporation, power no longer acts unilaterally on its subject. Rather, the subject is produced, paradoxically, through this withdrawal of power, its dissimulation and fabulations of the psyche as a speaking topos. Social power vanishes, becoming the object lost, or social power makes vanish, effecting a mandatory set of losses. Thus, it effects a melancholia that reproduces power as the psychic voice of judgement addressed to (turned upon) oneself, thus modeling reflexivity on subjection."

12   Emphasizing this point through literary device, in *La Malediction*, Rachid Mimouni (1994) shows his protagonist, who studied medicine in France, being pursued by his brother, who has become an extremist.

13   Bourdieu (1984, 106) equates social homogeneity with social class: "Constructing, as we have here, classes as homogeneous as possible with respect to the fundamental determinants of the material conditions of existence and the conditionings they impose therefore means that even in constructing the classes and in interpreting the variations of the distribution of properties and practices in relation to these classes, one consciously takes into account the network of secondary characteristics which are more or less unconsciously manipulated whenever the classes are defined in terms of a single criterion, even one as pertinent as occupation."

14   The population unemployed for 12 months or more (the *chômeurs de longue durée*) increased in Morocco from 69.6 percent of total unemployed to 74.8 percent in 2000. Likewise, the average period of unemployment rose from 34 months to 41.6 months during the same time period (from *Les Indicateurs Sociaux* 2000).

15   Fassi, that is, from Fez, one of the imperial cities and the center of culture, in the sense of personal cultivation as well as arts and letters, in Morocco. This is a category used in opposition to Berber and 'rubi, which signifies "from the countryside," and thus baser, less sophisticated in manners and knowledge. Fassi dominance in Moroccan elites has diminished as bureaucrats of 'rubi origin who have benefited from opportunities in the administration emerge as political and economic leaders. This rise in status may not appeal to either members of the old elite or their progeny. A young journalist from a prominent Meknes family told me to look at the names of current ministers, few of which signify Fassi origin. He also mentioned shifts in the student population at his private high school. When he was there, about eight years ago, the students were fair in their complexion and hair color, two other markers of Fassi descent. Now, he remarked, they are darker, obviously 'rubi. "Where," he asked, "could their parents find the money to send them there [to an expensive private school] if not from corruption?"

16   The urban population ages 30–34 that has never married increased in Morocco from 30.8 percent in 1994 to 40.6 percent in 1998. The average age at marriage in urban areas has increased for men from 31.2 years old in 1994 to 32.6 years old in 1998 and from 26.9 to 28.3 years old for women (*Les Indicateurs Sociaux* 2000).

17   Abdellah Laroui is one of the greatest living historians and social thinkers of the Arab World. He has written extensively on Moroccan nationalism and Arab intellectual thought.

18   Tocqueville (1945, 105) writes, "As social conditions become more equal, the number of persons increases who, although they are neither rich nor powerful enough to exercise any great influence over their fellows, have nevertheless acquired or retained sufficient education and fortune to satisfy their own wants . . . they are apt to imagine that their whole destiny is in their own hands."

19   Homi Bhabha (1994, 223) summarizes this position of cultural difference against the "specularity" of social class in *The Location of Culture,* writing that "the present moment [is] the insignia of other interstitial inscriptions of cultural difference . . . *to assume an effective political identity or image* — the limits and conditions of specularity have to be exceeded and erased by the inscription of otherness."

20   As an example in Morocco, writing in the early 1980s, Mark Tessler (1982, 81–82) argued that if the regime does not allow for more democratization, university and high school students unable to find jobs or rise to positions of power will join the opposition, creating the same political instability that existed in the early 1970s. This did not happen, despite growing and more evident disparities in income and extraordinarily high unemployment rates. Part of my project has been to explain why.

2 National Development

1   Daoud and Monjib themselves are prominent leftist intellectuals. Daoud used to write for a leftist magazine called *Lamalif* before it was shut down by the Ministry of the Interior in 1988–89.

2   *Fqih* means in English "legist, expert of *fiqh* (jurisprudence, religious law)" as well as teacher in Quranic schools. This title requires formal Islamic education, which in Morocco would be at al-Qurawayyiin, the oldest university in the world in fact, in Fez.

3   The *salafiyya* movement (from the term *al-salaf al-salih*, or "pious ancestors") originated in the ideas of the Iranian thinker Jamal ad-Din al-Afghani (1839–97), the Egyptian Muhammed 'Abduh (1849–1905), and his follower, the Syrian Rashid Rida (1865–

1935). Salafism is based on a differentiation between "the essential doctrines of Islam and its social teachings and laws" (Hourani 1991, 308). The essential principles of Islam — belief in God, in Muhammed as the last of a line of prophets to whom God's word was revealed, and moral responsibility and judgment — are inflexible, whereas the customs, laws, and mores of the day should be interpreted through the Quran, through the *shari'*, or Islamic law, and human reason and altered to suit the above principles. Hourani cites a quote from 'Abduh that summarizes the goals of Islamic reformism. 'Abduh's life was to "liberate thought from the shackles of imitation (*taqlīd*) and understand religion as it was understood by the community before dissension appeared; to return, in the acquisition of religious knowledge, to its first sources, and to weight them in the scale of human reason, which God has created in order to prevent excess or adulteration in religion, so that God's wisdom may be fulfilled and the order of the human world preserved; and to prove that, seen in this light, religions must be accounted a friend to science, pushing man to investigate the secrets of existence, summoning him to respect established truths and to depend on them in his moral life and conduct" (1991, 308; quoted from Rida 1931, 1: 11). The salafiyya movement's most prominent spokesmen in Morocco were 'Abdallah ben Driss Senoussi, Bouchâ'ib ad-Doukkali, and, later, 'Allal al-Fassi, the grand *za'im*, or charismatic leader, of the Istiqlal Party. See Munson (1993) for a history of Islamic reform movements in Morocco.

4   For a general history of Morocco, see Laroui (1977a).

5   For a general history of the period of French occupation in the region, see Hourani (1991). Specific details of this paragraph are drawn from chapter 16.

6   The treaty in 1856 established a standard 10 percent ad valorem duty on imports and a fixed tariff on exports, effectively ending the sale of monopolies by the sultan to elite royal merchants (Schroeter 1999, 90–91).

7   Germany, 1890–91; England, 1892; Spain, after another war in 1893; France, 1892, 1902; Spain, 1896; England, 1901. The last in this series of increasingly damaging treaties was the Algesiras Convention of 1906, which established equal trade rights for participating European countries for the next half-century (A. Laroui 1977b, 251–52).

8   A. Laroui writes, "Let us not forget the two decisive reasons: these men came too late in a country weakened economically and politically divided and above all they were too few. What could twenty, at maximum fifty, men accomplish, individuals who were half-educated and without distinctive talent, grappling with an administration that was relatively sizable, archaic, complex, almost ritual, and perhaps did not survive except for these very same characteristics?" (1977b, 289).

9   A. Laroui (1977a, 344), analyzing the progression of North African history, declares: "The Maghrib had produced neither a modern capitalism nor, it follows, a bourgeoisie. Colonial Europe lent it one, but on condition that this European bourgeoisie enjoy exclusive privileges, that bourgeois law, bourgeois freedoms, bourgeois economy and administration remain a closed sphere, forbidden to Maghribis. They have no need of them anyway, it was said. This policy, one might think, ought logically to have enabled two societies to coexist. But in the eyes of the colonial establishment the coexistence was essentially provisional, for after going through a phase of enlightened despotism, the one society, it was thought, would transform itself into an adult bourgeois democracy, while the other, after a period of slow disintegration under the benevolent control of the military, would degenerate into an anthropological reservation. An aid to growth, on the one

hand, a speeding up of regression on the other — this, the colonial ideologists tried to make themselves and others believe, was the judgment of history. The condemned society was expected to work to its last breath for the society that would survive it."

10   This backing waned after Independence, for as Waterbury (1970, 105) comments, "The Istiqlal [in the late 1960s] no longer holds the practical appeal for the commercial class that it once did, for it has accomplished its task, the protectorate regime has been sent packing, and the Europeans are gradually liquidating their enterprises voluntarily."

11   Jamil Salmi (1985, 30) cites statistics that between 1933 and 1955, the number of students enrolled in *niveau primaire général* rose from 21,900 to 314,800; in *niveau primaire professionnel* 1,300 to 7,500; and in *secondaire* 608 to 6,712.

12   Experiencing a 150 percent increase, population growth in Morocco over thirty years equaled growth in France during the period 1700–1850 (Gruner 1984, 167).

13   Figuring out exact numbers of classes or social groups can be a frustrating, in fact, futile exercise. However, I can cite guesses and loose figures from several scholars. John Waterbury (1971) estimated that during the 1960s, among the Moroccan elite there were about 1,000 men: 100 in the army, 450 in the Ministry of the Interior, 300 high-ranking fonctionnaires, 130 prominent politicians and union leaders, 100 important members of economic organizations, independents, and the 'ulema. Waterbury does qualify the 1,000, as he cannot account for overlap among these divisions (86). Mark Tessler (1982, 37–38) offers a slightly different picture, a common image in Morocco of concentric circles. The first, in the center, is the king, the second is composed of about 200 political party and union leaders and senior officials in ministries; these are "highly educated individuals" from urban bourgeois families. The next circle consists of 600–700 men, some of whom are rural notables, others regional and local leaders, and others in military and security, business leaders, and members of the 'ulema. The last circle is of the local and rural subelite, or *qaids*, influential sheikhs, leaders of approximately 800 local councils, grassroots party officials, and parliament members. Tessler gives a total, rough, figure of 5,000.

14   Rates of domestic investment jumped in the postcolonial period, averaging an annual growth rate of 11 percent between 1965 and 1973, and 10 percent between 1973 and 1980. In the 1980s, annual growth rates of domestic investment dropped to 2 percent (1980–85) and 3.6 percent (1985–90; Pfeifer 1999, 58). Domestic borrowing in Morocco rose from 192 million dirhams (net) in 1970 to 1.521 billion dhs in 1978, and external borrowing rose from 268 million dhs in 1970 to 5.194 billion dhs in 1977, dropping off to 3.365 billion dhs in 1978 with government efforts to control the budgetary crisis (from *Morocco: Economic and Social Development Report,* 1981, table 5.1). Phosphate mining and export was and still is controlled by the state (OCP). With the oil crisis, the price of phosphates tripled between 1973 and 1974. In addition to the boom in mining receipts, a jump from 674 million dh (1969 prices) to 1.684 billion dh in 1982, construction, industry, the administration, and transportation, all sectors heavily influenced by public enterprise, all expanded during the 1970s. Agriculture, as is still the case, fluctuated with weather conditions, and decreased slightly during the 1970s, from 4.087 million dh in 1971 to 3.991 million dh in 1982. During the 1970s, Morocco more than quadrupled its imports of cereals, from .36 million tons in 1970 to 1.65 million tons in 1980 (from Morrisson 1991, 133). The state granted a raise of 26 percent to civil servants' wages in 1975 and, in the same year, began to subsidize sugar and oil. Faced with unrest and rising prices due to the oil crisis of the late 1970s and drought, the state raised wages of civil servants again by 10

percent in 1979, and the minimum wage by 30–40 percent (from *Morocco: Economic and Social Development Report* 1981).

15   The period of repression in the 1960s and 1970s, a period of omnipresent internal security and surveillance and a dearth of public information, ripped away at human rights and shattered opposition groups. In the ultimate measure, Hassan declared emergency rule from 1965 through 1970, suspending the legislature to assume their powers himself. Even after he put a halt to emergency rule, he permitted the formation of governments from primarily monarchist and right-wing parties (for example, Union Constitutionel) and elevated Driss Basri, his loyal minister of the interior, to greater and greater authority. He did not retreat from his harsh suppression of opposition until during the worst of a period of severe economic difficulty, in the late 1980s. At that point, he allowed the release of political prisoners and began to loosen control over the press and the establishment of NGOS.

Opposition parties, led by fervent nationalists like ben Barka, battled with Hassan to circumscribe his power. Despite emergency rule and ben Barka's assassination in 1965, the leftist opposition, in the form of the USFP as well as smaller Marxist parties, still presented a challenge well into the early 1970s. In 1971 and 1972, the king faced two attempted coup d'etats by the military and responded by jailing or executing members of the armed forces, opposition Marxist parties, and dissident intellectuals. However, as in India under Indira Ghandi, Chile under Pinochet, and Indonesia under Suharto, periods of political darkness corresponded with the growth of the middle class. King Hassan utilized a substantial spurt of growth in the mid-1970s and increased spending dramatically to cement relations with his allies among elites and foster alliances with nonelites to cultivate his own security.

Marocanisation, the policy of mandatory majority (50 percent) Moroccan ownership and management (majority of board of trustees, and the president of the board), was initiated by the Dahir of March 2, 1973, which itself defined a Moroccan company, determined the activities, and established the procedures to implement and finance marocanisation (see El Oufi 1990, chap. 3). This Dahir followed on the Dahir of November 14, 1959 that subjected foreign companies to Moroccan law and established their offices as Moroccan subsidiaries. In the larger sense, it gave the Moroccan state the right to control foreign capital within the country's borders, making it illegal to transfer profits without the permission of l'Office des Changes. In 1973, among the sectors subject to marocanisation were almost all commercial industries: in the tertiary sector, banks, insurance, transportation, service agencies, material production and automobile companies, and in manufacturing, automobiles again, leather, chemical products, construction, electronics, and some agricultural industries such as forestry. Also included were hotels and restaurants, artisanal industries, import/export businesses that are either part of the producing company or industries exempt from marocanisation, and foreign companies that had concluded an arrangement with the state in state-controlled industries, such as mining and tourism.

16   El Oufi (1990), analyzing the marocanisation loans and the type of investor by occupational category, determined that 2 percent of the total active population that could be called middle class (*couches moyens*) participated in marocanisation. Only seven hundred investors with middle-income resources benefited from the loan program. On the other hand, the largest investment of capital, more than 40 percent, in marocanisation came from upper-echelon administrators, businessmen (about 14 percent), and those not de-

claring a profession, but whom El Oufi surmises to be wealthy (139n.). Whereas the smallest investment unsurprisingly came from workers in manufacturing and the service sector (under 2 percent each), investment from professionals was not much greater (about 5 percent; 139–40).

17   Mohamed Lahbabi (1970) claimed that 77 percent of youth ages 15–19 (2 out of 3) and 87.8 percent of youth 20–29 (9 out of 10) were illiterate; 5 percent of those ages 15–19 (1 out of 20) and 2 percent of those ages 20–29 (1 out of 50) possessed a certificat d'études.

18   *Les Indicateurs Sociaux* (1993, 166). In 1970, Egypt had a literacy rate of 32 percent, Jordan 54 percent, Tunisia 28 percent, and Algeria 25 percent. Morocco's rate, the lowest, was 21 percent (*Human Development Report 1998* 2002).

19   For example, in 1980, Morocco's infant mortality rate (per 1,000 live births), at 99, was comparable to others in the region — 120 for Egypt, 98 for Algeria, 109 for Turkey — but much higher than Tunisia at 71, Jordan at 41, and the average of middle-income countries at 68. As of the 1990s, Morocco's infant mortality and birth rates were slightly higher than those of countries with comparable per capita GDP (*World Development Report* 1997; Morrisson 1991, 22).

20   Morrisson (1991, 27) calculates a drop of 12.4 in the percentage of the population living in poverty between 1970 and 1982, from 42.4 to 30 percent. There are higher rates of poverty in rural areas, although this gap, because of migrant remittances, public works in rural areas specifically concerning irrigation and transportation, and migration itself to urban areas and overseas, has narrowed. Poverty rates remained higher than those of other middle-income countries in the region, such as Tunisia and Algeria (19.9 percent of the national population in 1985 and 12.2 percent of the population in 1988 versus 26 percent of the population in Morocco; from *World Development Report* 1998–1999).

21   In 1979, a World Bank study reported that 28 percent of the urban population and 45 percent of the rural population lived below the absolute poverty level, measured at 1,275 dhs per capita annual income. These percentages supposedly totaled 7 million people out of a population of a little under 20 million. The total population according to the 1982 Census was 20,354,000: 8,671,000 urban and 11,683,000 rural (*Population An 2062* 1991. A chart in the same volume estimates the 1980 population at 19,332,000).

22   The World Bank (1981, 223) followed Kuznets in qualifying growing inequality as part of economic development: "A deterioration in expenditure distribution is a commonly observed phenomenon during economic development. . . . This pattern is said to be due to migration from the rural areas to the towns, where income distribution is more uneven. In the case of Morocco, the phenomenon of rural migration seems to have played only a relatively small part."

23   His figures do not add up, but the suggestion is that the wealthiest segment of the population spends almost 50 percent of total expenditures, whereas the poorest 40 percent of the population spend 11.1 percent (Cherkaoui n.d.).

24   *The Economic and Social Development Report* (1981) divides household expenditure into three classes: households spending less than 600 dh a year, which rose from 0.5 to 2.9 percent in the 1960s; households spending 600–4,200 dh a year, which dropped from 78.3 to 49.2 percent; and households spending more than 4,200 dh, which rose from 21.2 to 47.9 percent. Presumably, in addition to factors of growth and household definition, households increased their income and thus their consumption.

25   In 1956, there were 318,995 students enrolled in primary, 10,490 in secondary, and 3,792

in postsecondary schools. By 1980, there were 2,170,237 students enrolled in primary, 797,110 in secondary, and 93,851 in postsecondary. The increases in numbers of students should not hide the fact that most Moroccan children during this period never attended secondary school, representing close to 80 percent of the population ages 12–18 in 1980 (Salmi 1985, 60). Participation in education also differed widely among provinces, with Casablanca and Rabat claiming the highest levels of student attendance and enrollment (61).

26   Waterbury (1970). Statistics vary in Morocco, as in many other countries. However, general trends are unmistakable. For example, a USAID report by Abdelghani Sbihi and Mohammed El Aouad (1994, 11–12) list higher numbers for primary education in 1953–54: 182,000 for public and 232,770 for both public and private, and for secondary education, 33,893 in the public system and 44,128 in both public and private. In 1959–60 total figures had risen to 722,215 and 67,207, respectively. Jamil Salmi (1985) cites statistics that are slightly higher than those in at least the 1970–71 and 1980 *Annuaire Statistiques*. The 1980 *Annuaire* lists enrollment in *primaire* in 1975–76 at 1,475,006 in the public system and 1,547,647 in both public and private, and in 1979–80, 1,984,672 students in the public system and 2,051,862 in both public and private. However, his chart demonstrates the dramatic change in participation in education in the twenty-five years after Independence.

27   Again, even if figures differ from one source to another, the general trend remains the same.

28   Tessler (1982, 77) reports that in 1968, 11,000 Moroccans were pursuing advanced education, 7 percent of them in religious education, and 3,000 overseas, mostly in France. Of this 11,000, 18 percent were women. Ten years later, in 1975, most students (74 percent) were still majoring in either letters, law, education, or social science. In 1979, there were 70,000 Moroccans in advanced education, 5 percent in religious schools.

29   The rate of activity among the urban male population age 15 years or more decreased steadily, from 83.1 percent in 1960 to 76.4 in 1971 to 75 in 1982 to 74.5 percent in 1990. Among the urban female population, rates of activity increased from 12.1 to 19.5 to 23.1 to 23.9 percent (*Population et Emploi* 1992, 55).

30   The number of salaried workers rose from 1,128,600 in 1960 to 2,429,919 in 1982, whereas the number of independent workers increased at a relatively slower pace, from 1,103,500 in 1960 to 1,504,121 in 1982. The percentage of *aides familiaux* and *travailleurs indépendants* represented 28 and 20 percent of total employment in 1982 versus 45 percent for *l'emploi salarié* in the same year. Overall, salaried workers rose from 38.24 percent in 1960 to 40.78 percent in 1971 to 45 percent in 1982 (*Population et Emploi* 1992, 55).

31   He naturally defended his leadership, declaring, "The people understand that progress and prosperity are conditioned by the State, a strong State, just and devoted to the general interest, and that the fight for power, in instigating instability, opens the way to regression, to decadence. There is no lack of examples of countries reduced to powerlessness" (*Discours Années* 1962–63). After criticizing the men who tried to depose him, he also declared, "I remain as always convinced of the necessity of uniting all hearts, of rehabilitating all good will. But from now on, I will be more vigilant. Those that have not participated in our past conflicts will be able to bring into our future battles a contribution that will never be considered negligible" ("Former une nation homogène demeure notre objectif," 4 January 1963, in *Discours Années* 1962–63). The head of a small, relatively

homogeneous country, Bourguiba succeeded more than any other Arab leader in creating a secular society with a sizable middle class. This social transformation since Independence may have facilitated economic reform but did not, in the form of mass political resistance or increasing public disgruntlement, inspire a challenge to Ben Ali's suppression of opposition leaders and parties, human rights, and a public sphere.

32 See Ralf Dahrendorf's discussion of the new middle class in *Class and Class Conflict in Industrialized Societies* (1959).

33 Laroui, following his belief in the evolution of Reason in history, sees the Muslim community of the Hegira and its descendants as incapable of meeting modern demands. Likewise, the monarchy, landlords, and bourgeois elites never sufficiently evolved in Morocco to propel the society forward in history. Faced with domination, the population would ignore the makhzen rather than resist through conflict, a technique that Laroui again wishes to leave in the past.

34 I focus here on the two most prominent political thinkers of post-Independence Morocco, Mehdi ben Barka and al-Fassi. Ben Barka belonged to Istiqlal until 1959, when he and a group of left-leaning intellectuals and professionals created UNFP. This choice is not to discount less prominent political activists or writers but to facilitate explaining the different ideological positions in Morocco at the time. In fact, students of Moroccan politics will not find the choice original at all. Years ago, Ernest Gellner wrote an article entitled "The Struggle for Morocco's Past" (1961) that he began with the sentences: "There are at present two dominant political parties and trends in Morocco. The key figure of one is Allal al-Fassi, and of the other, Mehdi ben Barka" (from *Middle East Journal* 15, no. 1: 79).

35 Involved in resistance activities from his teens, ben Barka differentiated himself from the more religious, more conservative faction of the nationalist movement led by Allal Al-Fassi in that he favored bilingual education and declared himself agnostic: "The young dirigeant [of le Parti National] makes himself known by his new approach [style] vis-à-vis tradition. His behaviour becomes more individualistic, more liberal. He who learned the voluminous Koran by heart before the age of ten becomes agnostic even in conserving a profound attachment to Arab-Islamic culture. . . . Mehdi is a modernist who intends to rid Islam of old wives' tales, superstitions, and fatalistic beliefs which he regards as responsible for the weakening of the Umma, the Muslim community. Mehdi sympathizes with salafisme, which he confounds in Morocco with nationalism. . . . 'Religion is one thing but the cultures and the civilizations which give birth to religions are a fundamental given of political life,' declares Mehdi to his friend Lentin. This secular and pragmatic approach to religion will characterize his political path" (quoted in Daoud and Monjib 1996, 76–77).

36 Ex-political prisoners have created a mini-industry of accounts of prison and human rights abuses, a phenomenon that a young entrepreneur once described to me as a "preoccupation with the past. All this thinking about the past does no good for the present and the future."

37 With distance from Independence and more access to education, the generations born around Independence were expected to resist the regime if their material desires were not satisfied. In an analysis of politics in Morocco, Mark Tessler (1987, 79) cites a survey in the 1960s that found students highly optimistic about their career possibilities. He speculates, as do other political scientists studying development, "Third generation elites [who have been educated after Independence] tend to be trained in the humanities and liberal professions, rather than in the technical fields where cadres are still sorely needed; and thus,

despite their high educational levels, they are likely to have difficulty finding jobs consistent with their aspirations. One consequence of this is a continuing shortage of trained personnel in many specialized fields. But the inevitable frustration and increased alienation of third-generation elites is of equal or even greater significance."

Tessler also comments on the fourth generation, the one on which I have focused my research. He offers several possibilities for their political behavior. They could become, as in other Arab countries, less nationalistic and more interested in cultural reform, even though the overwhelming majority of this generation would be educated in Morocco. They could become more attached to Arabism and Islam, being educated much more in Arabic than previous generations, and likewise be "less open to the external world than their predecessors and . . . not have the high cultural levels of their elders. They will, on the other hand, be more representative of the nation and less distant and alienated from nonelites" (78). I found the situation to be less clear and more complex, with most of the people I interviewed being much more open to the "external world" because of cultural globalization and economic necessity, despite, yes, not being in some instances as well-educated as previous generations.

38   *Homo faber* is "strictly speaking, unpolitical, and will incline to denounce action and speech as idleness, idle busybodyness and idle talk, and generally will judge public activities in terms of their usefulness to supposedly higher ends — to make the world more useful and more beautiful" (Arendt 1958, 208).

39   Lahbabi was arrested in 1980 along with Abderrahim Bouabid.

40   "Notre politique vise à émanciper l'individu, c'est une politique qui le protège de l'ignorance. . . . Il est évident que tout développement et tout progrès sont fonction de l'extension de la culture et de la généralisation de l'enseignement" (King Hassan II, 3 March 1962, quoted in Salmi 1985, 45).

41   Stefania Pandolfo (1997, 7) writes of *Le passé simple,* "A text written along the edges of the chasm itself, in the interstitial zone of a 'thin line' inscribing the border between Orient and Occident, Tradition and Modernity, Arab and French, and in the vision of the fracture which hurled a portion of the subject's history into a grammatical *passé simple* — tense of separation, and of uncanny returns." This tense in French is past historic, an action completed and separated from the actor.

42   Quoted from the English translation (Chraïbi 1990, 6).

43   Most teachers, whether accurate or not, argue that in the past, teachers had better training as well as the material means and the intellectual freedom to teach students how to synthesize material and develop an argument (whereas today students ostensibly cannot). The director of a private lycée in a lower-middle-income area told me, "They [teachers] have become les fonctionnaires. For them, it is income that poses the problem. There is no compensation or bakshish [under-the-table income]. If you ask why teachers do not teach well, they would answer, If you give us the means to improve our situations, to buy materials. Salaries bother teachers, and now they gather their things at the end of class and that's it. They do something else outside [work at a second job]. Before, the teacher would work relentlessly. Today, they do manual labor."

44   The SMIG in fact by 1994 was three times its value in 1981, reflecting the politics of promising economic security and the reality of weak or negative economic growth. The increases in the minimum wage also exceeded growth in GNP per capita, which was the equivalent of 70 percent of the SMIG in 1980 and 55 percent in 1995. Although not well

documented, a drop in the wages relative to the minimum wage has resulted as well from companies hiring more and more nonqualified, noncontractual labor to reduce costs. In the mid-1980s, half of the companies in manufacturing were paying an average salary less than the SMIG to nonqualified workers (Jaïdi 1995, 20–21). A 1979 World Bank report listed the percentage of industrial enterprises paying salaries under the SMIG in 1978. Not unexpectedly, smaller enterprises, those under forty-nine employees, paid the least in wages. Companies in plastics, leather, textiles, clothing, and machinery were among those that paid all or most of their employees under the minimum hourly wage. The companies that tended to pay better were in wood, office supplies, and other industrial products.

45   Zartman (1987, 29–30) perceives the Moroccan middle class entirely in terms of state political interests and related policies: "There are some signposts for the restructuring of the social basis of the new political system with emphasis on the middle class (while keeping fences mended with traditional notables of city and countryside). Most important were the Five Year Plan for 1973–77 and the Moroccanization *dahir* (decree) of March 2, 1973, which specifically referred to the creation of a middle class of managers and directors to fill in the gap between rich and poor. Even after the plan was scrapped because of general economic conditions, the urban land and housing policy continued to favor middle-class growth, and the continued availability of credits for Moroccanization and for small and middle-sized enterprises (PME) worked in the same direction. Indeed, even the economic policy toward army officers, which includes the attribution of land and housing and the opening up of business opportunities, is calculated to bring them into a broader middle-class base for the polity. Similarly, the ten-fold increase in the civil service during the reign of Hassan II is another measure of the growth of the middle class directly under the control and in the service of the monarchy."

3   *New Social Groups*

1   *La Vie Economique,* 14 June 1996, 20–22. *La Vie Economique* is one of the country's most prominent weekly economic newspapers.

2   After a sit-in outside the palace, the king pushed Driss Basri, the interior minister, to find the striking unemployed doctorates jobs.

3   For example, see Stiglitz (2002) or the literature from organizations like Public Citizen and the AFL-CIO for a more popular critique of global market integration.

4   According to Stephen Rose (2000), between 1979 and 1997, income for the bottom tenth rose 2.7 percent, for the bottom half 10.8 percent, and for the top tenth 29.9 percent. In 1999, the lowest quintile possessed an average wealth of $42,200, or 4.1 percent of total wealth, and the top 1 percent possessed $5,104,800, or 24.9 percent of the total wealth. The middle class shrank between 1979 and 1997, from 44.4 to 38.4 percent of the population, but the portion of the population that is well-off also rose, from 34.2 to 40.7 percent of the total population. The percentage of the population that is poor (a total of about 21 percent) remained the same, causing the greatest controversy.

5   As of 1990, service sector employment in the United States was about 75 percent of total employment, with manufacturing dropping close to 20 percent (Standing 1999).

6   For a similarly nostalgic view of an older middle class and critique of current trends, see Paul Krugman, "For Richer: The Disappearing Middle Class," *New York Times,* 20 October 2002.

7   Employment share of textiles and clothing industry in total manufacturing increased in Morocco from around 25 to 38 percent between 1985 and 1995. Textile and clothing manufacturing are important in the region in general, employing by far the largest number of workers among manufacturing subsectors. Employment share for textiles is 18.9 percent and for wearing apparel 10 percent. By comparison, the employment share in food is 18.1 percent and in iron and steel 7.1 percent. Value-added and output have decreased over time in both sectors, however, without any other manufacturing sector rising to take their place (*Economic Trends in the* MENA *Region* 1998).

8   Perhaps one indicator of Morocco's stable progress during the 1990s appeared during the financial crises of 1997 and 1998. As Asian stock markets and currencies plunged in value, the small but developing stock market in Morocco posted gains. The stock market rose by 48 percent in 1997 (IMF press release, 31 March 1998). A *New York Times* article suggesting potential bargains in bottomed-out emerging markets cites a top portfolio manager (Joyce Cornell, the lead portfolio manager for Scudder Emerging Market Growth Fund) as encouraging investment in the Middle East, particularly in less well-known stock markets like that of Morocco (Jonathan Fuerbringer, "The Markets in Turmoil: The Emerging Markets," *New York Times,* 6 September 1998, 4).

9   The average annual growth rate of GNP in Morocco was .6 percent between 1998 and 1999, whereas in Egypt, the growth rate was 5.7 percent and in Tunisia 6.2 percent (*World Development Report* 2000–2001).

10   Morocco's dependence on rain is so acute that an end to the drought in 1996 led to a stunning growth rate of 12 percent in the GDP. This is opposed to a 1.2 percent average annual growth rate between 1990 and 1995. In addition, a 65 percent increase in agricultural output in 1994 corresponded with an 11 percent increase in real GDP (1996: 37), whereas in 1992 and 1993 the growth rates of GDP were −4.4 and −1.1 percent, and for agriculture −36 and −6.2 percent (World Bank 1996, 30).

11   Statement by Mohammed Daïri, alternate executive director for Morocco (28 April 2003, www.imf.org).

12   In a move that shocked World Bank officials as well as politicians and intellectuals in Morocco, the king published a letter written to him in 1996 from James Wolfensohn, the head of the World Bank. The letter expressed disappointment in Morocco's progress on the social front.

13   Al-aslah Wattajdid joined the Mouvement populaire démocratique et constitutionnel in 1996 to enter into the political system and then ran separately in the 2002 elections, coming in third in terms of seats won nationally. After winning 42 out of 325 seats, a jump from 14 in the previous parliament, the PJD decided not to join a coalition with the leftist USFP. See Munson (1993) for Sheikh Yacine's history of resistance against King Hassan. After Yacine wrote a letter asking the king to respect the duties of Islam and thus correct his behavior, the king sent him to a psychiatric hospital. Yacine did not stop making public statements or attempting, through his followers, to take over student unions at universities and organizing campus demonstrations and information fairs (where tables were set up with political literature as well of the writings of Islamist radicals such as Sayyid al-Qutb). His party was linked to the 1997 demonstrations for more buses at the university in Casablanca, and the state accused his followers of organizing the students to move out onto the street.

14   This coalition is called the Koutla and is composed of Istiqlal, the nationalist party that led

the political struggle for Independence, Union Socialiste des Forces Populaires (USFP), Parti de Progrés et Socialisme (PPS), and Organisation Demoqratique d'Action Populaire (OADP).

15   For reflections of this viewpoint, see editorials and articles published in the *New York Times* such as Elaine Sciolino, "At a Traumatic Moment, Morocco's King Is Mute" (27 May 2003), or Aboubakr Jamaï (editor of *Le Journal*), "Morocco's Choice: Openness or Terror" (31 May 2003). From an institutional standpoint, the IMF 2003 Article IV evaluation focuses part of its report on the "Successful democratic transition [that] has been the overriding priority of Moroccan authorities during 1998–2002." The IMF commended the Moroccan government for improved transparency and accountability, gestures that "augur well for policy implementation" (IMF 2003, Article IV Consultation).

16   Morocco's labor force grew at a rate of 3.39 percent between 1965 and 1995 and is projected to grow at a rate of 2.52 percent between 1995 and 2025, compared to projections of 2.35 percent in Egypt, 3.90 percent in Jordan, and 1.9 percent in Tunisia (*World Development Report* 1995). The average annual growth rate in the population (now at about 30 million) between 1980 and 1990 was 2.2 percent, and between 1990 and 1995 2.0 percent, a minor decline. In other countries of the region, the drop was somewhat higher; for instance, Egypt with 2.5 to 2.0 percent, Algeria 2.9 to 2.2 percent (during a virtual civil war), and Tunisia 2.5 to 1.9 percent (*World Development Report* 1997). In Tunisia, the overall unemployment rate in 1999 was 15.6 percent; in Saudi Arabia, the unemployment rate in 2000 was 15 percent; and in Jordan, the unemployment rate in 1999 was 14.4 percent (*Arab Human Development Report 2002* 2002).

17   ONA is invested primarily in mining, insurance, distribution sectors, and agribusiness. The company earned 1.2 billion dh in profit and 16 billion dh in revenues in 1998.

18   For example, a strike at the Jordache factory in Casablanca in 2000 was stopped in part by government intervention.

19   See an International Confederation of Free Trade Unions (ICFTU) report dated September 1999, on a strike at the AVITEMA egg production plant in the province of Temara, 30 km outside of Rabat. The police supposedly beat the striking workers and did arrest twenty-one union members, including the general secretary of the plant union and a member of the administrative committee of the UMT-Rabat regional association.

     The SMIG was about 8 dh an hour in urban areas (less than a dollar) in 2000–01 and the SMAG about 45 dh a day in agriculture.

20   See "Kingdom of Morocco: Private Sector Assessment Update," World Bank Report (15 December 1999), for a survey of enterprises and reported constraints on the growth of small businesses. The greatest constraint business owners felt they faced was in the behavior of the administration, followed by market share.

21   Basic goods include food, clothing, and housing; secondary goods include transportation and communication, health and medical supplies, household appliances, and nonessential food items.

22   In the use of temporary labor, companies risk low motivation and underproductivity and create disincentives for management to invest in training and organization. See *Growing Faster, Finding Jobs* (World Bank 1996).

23   This drop compares with 16 to 13 percent in Egypt but differs from countries like Jordan, where government consumption was 22 percent of GDP in 1995 (*World Development Report* 1997).

24   Driss put his name on a list presented to the government by unemployed doctorates. He finally received word that he had a job after I finished my dissertation research, in 1998.

25   The exceptions are the French mission and the American School.

26   Wright (1997) uses characteristics of skill and authority to locate different types of employees within the class structure. He argues that managers, because of their income and responsibility of control over employees for the benefit of the company (owner), occupy a position distinct from the working class. Skill and expertise also differentiate an employee within the dynamic of exploitation/class relations. Skilled workers receive a "rent" for their talent and expertise, and in his illustration of class relations, it is the expert manager who is in the location closest to capital and nonskilled workers are in the location closest to the working class.

27   Reich outlines three categories of workers in *The Work of Nations* (1991). These categories of symbolic-analytic services, routine production services, and in-person services reflect the trends of contemporary economic internationalism, in which most workers remain dependent on investment in the local economy but some, the first category of symbolic analysts, can sell their labor, both virtual and real, all over the world.

28   There were about five hundred students at Ecole Superiure de Gestion in 2002–2003 and almost sixteen hundred alumnae. The school boasted eighty-five professors (a ratio of about 6:1) as well as a connection with ESG Paris, and 20 percent of its graduates continued their education (3ème cycle) in the United States, Canada, or France (from *L'Etudiant Marocain* 2002–2003). In contrast, there were 8,744 students enrolled in les grandes écoles and institutes in 2000–2001 and 246,905 students enrolled full time at levels 1er and 2ème cycles in the ensemble of state universities in 2000–2001. There were 14,724 students enrolled in the 3ème cycle during the same academic year (*Annuaire Statistique du Maroc* 2001).

29   Women make up half the student bodies of faculties of medicine and law and therefore do and will hold a place in these traditional middle-class professions. Women graduating from humanities or social science departments, however, work mostly in secretarial and clerical positions, which in Morocco still bear a stigma for men. I did not interview female doctors or lawyers. The women bureaucrats and teachers I knew worked in temporary positions, or as substitutes or stagaires, and I thus included them in the unemployed.

   An article in the March 21, 1997 edition of *La Vie Economique*, drawing from a 1994 report of the Ministry of Justice, stated that there are almost three hundred (252 as of 1994) women magistrates out of a total of 3,000 and almost one thousand women (820 in the report) lawyers out of a total of more than 6,000. In another article from this edition, the paper stated that women make up almost 10 percent of the posts in the Ministry of Foreign Affairs, concentrating particularly in the department for multilateral cooperation and the department for the UN and international organizations. Excluding a member of the royal family, Lalla Aïcha, no woman has served as ambassador, although of the 173 women diplomats in 1994, six occupied posts of the highest grade in the foreign service, or *ministre plenipotentiare* (34). Women also hold 35 of the 325 seats in the lower house of Parliament after the elections of 2002, which mandated that 10 percent of new deputies be women.

30   See Ibaaquil (1996) regarding parents' aspirations for their children.

31   See Singerman (1995) for an analysis of social contacts in Egypt.

32   See Bennani-Chraibi (1994) for an account of family obligations and parental support for chômeurs.

33 I have changed the names of the men and women I interviewed.

34 The strikers had sent King Hassan II a letter for his birthday and the king's response was that there should be no expectation of a job in *la function publique*. Suggesting his disappointment in the king's position, Driss mentioned that Hassan II had talked about the success of Moroccan athletes in his latest Discours. Driss then cracked, "I did karate for five years. I should have continued with that. We had the idea at the sit-in to put on shorts and T-shirts."

35 At the beginning of the conversation, Driss offered me some details about the current sit-in at UMT headquarters (summer 1997). He told me that the first round of 184 doctorates had been offered positions in ministries but refused posts that were not in *enseignement supérieure*. The government responded with a threat to dissolve the offer if they did not take the jobs before a certain deadline. The second round of 130 that conducted a hunger strike still had not received employment despite the promise of the king. The UMT group, which numbered between 150 and 250, of which about 60 are women, were still waiting. There were reports that the minister de l'education superièure would give a concours in September as a way of eliminating demand. Driss responded, "We have passed so many exams. It is us who should give the exams, not take them. You know it is illegal to give an exam to someone with a doctorate. And they do not even know how they will do it. I spoke with someone in the Ministry and he said that there is a commission in progress to study the issue. When jobs become available, they will be in education, health, social work, and justice. The positions in foreign affairs are reserved for *les grandes familles*. People don't have money to buy cigarettes and they see these beautiful cars. They ask how they got there. But no one opens their mouth."

36 Of the men and women I interviewed who had worked or were working as stagaires, only one had secured a full-time position after an internship (he worked in a government ministry). One woman had worked as an intern in another ministry for five years without becoming *titularisé*, the equivalent of receiving a permanent contract. She earned 1,600–1,700 dh/month after taxes (about 2,000 dh/month gross). The ministry renewed her contract each year, but if she left to study or for any other purpose, she was not guaranteed the job when she returned. She also told me that as of 1997, there were 1,700 *civilistes*, or interns, waiting to be promoted. Like others in her situation, she felt trapped in a professional quagmire. She could not advance within the ministry except for a fortuitous change in circumstances; she could not leave unless she had another job, particularly because of high unemployment rates; and she could not pursue an advanced degree to make herself more marketable because, first, she would lose the job she had, and second, the degree program she wanted to enter, in computer systems, required that she come from a post that is titularisé.

37 Statistics on marriage in 1982 are from *Annuaire Statistique* (1996); statistics on marriage and fertility rates from 1994 and 1998 are from *Les Indicateurs Sociaux* (2000).

38 The boats crossing Gibralter symbolize and measure, for Europeans and Moroccans alike, the level of economic and social pressure in Morocco. For example, a front-page article in *Le Monde diplomatique* that analyzed the first two years of Mohammed VI's reign offered as preliminary evidence of the young king's success statistics on Moroccan illegal immigrants stopped at European coasts. Out of 2,039 illegal immigrants stopped in 2000, 70 percent were Moroccan (Ignace Dalle, "Le Maroc attend le grand changement," *Le Monde diplomatique*, June 2001, p. 1).

4   A Generation of Fuyards

1   Freud (1957, 244) describes the mental features of melancholia as "profoundly painful dejection, cessation of interest in the outside world, loss of the capacity to love, inhibition of all activity, and a lowering of the self-regarding feelings to a degree that finds utterance in self-reproaches and self-reviling, and culminates in a delusional expectation of punishment." He differentiates melancholia from mourning in that the object lost in the latter is conscious (namely, the death of a loved one) and thus the ego can recover as the libido detaches from the object. Melancholia is the reaction to loss of a loved one or an ideal (in the case of my research), but occurs in much less clear and certain conditions than mourning. Freud writes in "Mourning and Melancholia" that "one [the analyst] cannot see clearly what it is that has been lost, and it is all the more reasonable to suppose that the patient cannot consciously perceive what he has lost either. This, indeed, might be so even if the patient is aware of the loss which has given rise to his melancholia, but only in the sense that he knows *whom* he has lost but not *what* he has lost in him" (245).

2   The electoral process changed for the 2002 elections in that ballots listed individuals and not parties. The intention of this change was to discourage local corruption. However, despite more transparent elections, voting participation declined from the 1997 elections, from 58 to 52 percent.

3   Hannah Arendt (1976), on whose work Agamben relies heavily, discusses throughout her work the idea that the nation-state depends on participation in a homogeneous order of production and political organization. The fate of Jews, Gypsies, and refugees after World Wars I and II showed how much our understanding of "being" had become dependent on inclusion in a particular web of legal, political, and social rights. Stripped of these attributes through exile and exclusion, a man or woman loses the rights constitutive of being human: "Not the loss of specific rights, then, but the loss of a community willing and able to guarantee any rights whatsoever, has been the calamity which has befallen ever-increasing numbers of people. Man, it turns out, can lose all so-called Rights of Man without losing his essential quality as man, his human dignity. Only the loss of polity itself expels him from humanity" (297). As Agamben points out in his critique of Arendt, she focuses on the political order, whereas Foucault concentrates on the self. Agamben brings them together in an analysis of the interrelationship of power over the body and political power. Here, I want to bring together the organization of political authority with power over the symbolism of occupation and social mobility to psychological life. In the current period of market integration and neoliberalism, this life specifically refers to the Western liberal, semimystical unfolding of self-potential that marks the stages of life negatively or positively and creates "internal" conflicts of despair, depression, and repression or periods of bliss and a surfeit of happiness.

4   Omnium Nord Afrique (ONA) is the largest company in Morocco, with multiple holdings in sectors ranging from fishing to automobiles.

5   See Baudrillard, "The Mirror of Production" (1988) for a critique of Marx as proponent (and, for Baudrillard, dupe) of production as determinant of history and consciousness.

6   Fowzia's circumstances changed over the years after my dissertation research, as she eventually had three children and started to work as the director of a small private school in Rabat. Her new concern then became money, as she told me she received not more than the SMIG of 1,600 dh for her work.

7   Hussein, the owner of the market research firm, once complained that those with income to invest put their money into cafés, which have become increasingly elaborate and popular in Casablanca, particularly with freer relations between men and women. Cafés to Hussein were an unproductive investment.

8   An idea championed by the AFL-CIO, whose Web site on Labor Day, 2003 defined unions as "The best anti-poverty, equal opportunity, family security, middle-class-building program for working families."

Conclusion

1   In *The Rise of the Network Society* (1996), Manuel Castells describes global disunification, or social distantiation based on different organizations of time and space. The first is built through flows of information and capital and fostered by ever-accumulating power, and the second, of populations and territories excluded and included in the metanetwork according to need, derived from biological time and the traditions, customs, and culture, as well as the labor of the locality. Networks are the "new social morphology of our societies, and the diffusion of networking logic substantially modifies the operation and outcomes in process of production, experience, power, and culture" (469). To be part of the network — and this occurs all over the world among managers, technicians, some professionals, and business elites (the enterprisers) — is to be in a position of domination. The structure of this network, its spatial form and technological connection, influence more than specific social interests and the organization of societies and relations among different groups and individuals. "Presence or absence in the network and the dynamics of each network *vis-à-vis* others are critical sources of domination and change in our society: a society that, therefore, we may properly call the network society, characterized by the preeminence of social morphology over social action" (469).

I have adopted perhaps a more traditional theoretical approach than that of Castells, in that I start with the relation between inequality in material conditions and the constitution of subjectivity, and subsume networks, use of technology, the Internet, and so on, within the formation of larger social groups. In another sense, I do give preeminence to social action over social morphology. Political conflict and interest thus extend to more than global market integration and the domination of a global wired elite, motivated by the profits of global investment and trade and the anxiety of global competition, over the disorganized and dominated masses, who turn to identity movements in order to express resistance.

References

Abercrombie, Nicholas, and John Urry. 1983. *Capital, Labour, and the Middle Classes*. London: G. Allen and Unwin.

Abbott, Andrew. 1988. *The System of Possessions*. Chicago: University of Chicago Press.

Abouzeid, Leila. 1987. *'M ilfil*. Beirut: Dar Afaq Jadida.

———. 1989. *Year of the Elephant: A Moroccan Woman's Journey toward Independence and Other Stories*. Austin, Texas: Center for Middle East Studies.

Activité, Emploi et Chomage. 2000. Rabat: Direction de la Statistique.

Adam, André. 1968. *Casablanca: Essai sur la transformation de la société marocaine au contact de l'occident*. Paris: Editions du CNRS.

Adorno, Theodor W. 2000. *Negative Dialectics*. New York: Continuum.

Agamben, Giorgio. 1993. *The Coming Community*. Trans. Michael Hardt. Minneapolis: University of Minnesota Press.

———. 1995. *Homo Sacer: Sovereign Power and Bare Life*. Trans. Daniel Heller-Roazen. Stanford: Stanford University Press.

Ajami, Fouad. 1998. *Dream Palace of the Arabs: A Generation's Odyssey*. New York: Pantheon.

al-Fassi, 'Allal. 1966. *Al-Naqd al Dhati*. Beirut: Dar al-kashshat.

al-Mutanabbī. 1967. *Poems of al-Mutanabbī*. Trans. A. J. Arberry. London: Cambridge University Press.

Anderson, Benedict. 1991. *Imagined Communities: Reflections on the Origins and Spread of Nationalism*. 2nd ed. London: Verso.

Annuaire Statistique. 1980. Rabat: Direction de la Statistique.

Annuaire Statistique. 1996. Rabat: Direction de la Statistique.

Annuaire. Statistique. 2001. Rabat: Direction de la Statistique.

Appadurai, Arjun. 1996. *Modernity at Large*. Minneapolis: University of Minnesota Press.

Arab Human Development Report 2002. 2002. New York: UNDP.

Arendt, Hannah. 1958. *The Human Condition*. Chicago: University of Chicago Press.

——. 1976. *The Origins of Totalitarianism*. New York: Harvest.

Ashford, Douglas. 1973. "Second and Third Generation Elites in the Maghrib." In *Men, State, and Society in the Contemporary Maghrib*, ed. I William Zartman. London: Praeger.

Ayache, Albert. 1997. *Etudes d'histoire sociale marocaine*. Rabat: Okad / Al Asas.

Bailly, Jean Christophe, and Jean-Luc Nancy. 1991. *La comparution: Politiqué à venir*. Paris: C. Bourgois.

Banque Centrale Populaire. Division du Marche des Particuliers et des Professionels. 2000. "Intervention de la Banque Populaire dans le financement des jeunes." 10 February.

Bataille, Georges. 1986. "The Notion of Expenditure." In *Deconstruction in Context*, ed. Mark Taylor. Chicago: University of Chicago Press.

Baudrillard, Jean. 1988. *Jean Baudrillard: Selected Writings*. Stanford: Stanford University Press.

Ben Barka, Mehdi. 1959. "Problèmes d'édification du Maroc et du Maghreb: Quatre entretiens avec El Mehdi Ben Barka, recueillis par Raymond Jean." *Tribune Libre* 52. Paris: Plon.

Ben-David, Dan. 1993. "Equalizing Exchange: Trade Liberalization and Income Convergence." *Quarterly Journal of Economics* 108, no. 3: 653–679.

Bennani-Chraibi, Mounia. 1994. *Soumis et Rebelles: Les jeunes au Maroc*. Casablanca: Editions le Fennec.

Bhabha, Homi. 1994. *The Location of Culture*. London: Routledge.

Bourdieu, Pierre. 1984. *Distinction*. Trans. Richard Nice. Cambridge, Mass.: Harvard University Press.

Bourguiba, Habib. 1977. *Discours Années 1962–63*. Tunis: Secrétariat d'Etat à l'Information.

Bourquia, Rahma, Mokhtar El Harras, and Driss Bensaïd. 1995. *Jeunesse estudiantine marocaine, valuers et stratégies*. Rabat: Publications de la Faculté des Lettres et Sciences Humaines.

Bowles, Samuel. 2002. "Globalization and Redistribution: Feasible Egalitarianism in a Competitive World." In *Inequality around the World*, ed. Richard Freeman. London: Palgrave.

Brenner, Robert. 1976. "Agrarian Class Structure and Economic Development in Pre-Industrial Europe." *Past and Present* 70: 30–75.

Butler, Judith. 1997. *The Psychic Life of Power*. Stanford: Stanford University Press.

Castells, Manuel. 1996. *The Rise of the Network Society*. Oxford: Blackwell.

"Les Cent Jours de Mohammed VI." 1999. *Jeune Afrique L'Intelligent*, 14 November.

Centre Marocain de Conjoncture. 1993. *Le Marche du Travail: Pression croissante de la demande et deceleration des oeuvres d'emploi*. Bulletin 9, May.

——. 1996. *Consommation des Ménages: Dynamique des comportments*. Bulletin 14, March.

——. 1998. "Consommation." Letter 79. September.

Chatterjee, Partha. 1993. *The Nation and Its Fragments: Colonial and Postcolonial Histories*. Princeton: Princeton University Press.

Cherkaoui, Abdelmalek. N.d. *Indicateurs Socio-economiques du Maroc*. Casablanca: Shoof Publications.

Chraïbi, Driss. 1954. *Le passé simple*. Paris: Denoel.

——. 1990. *The Simple Past*. Trans. Hugh Carter. Washington, D.C.: Three Continents Press.

Citations de S. M. Hassan II. 1981. *Discours du Trône*, ed. Mustapha Sehimi. Rabat: Société Marocaine des Editeurs Réunis.

Clement, Jean-François. 1986. "Morocco's Bourgeoisie: Monarchy, State and Owning Class." *Middle East Report* 142 (September–October): 13–17.

Consommation et Depenses des Menages, 1984–1985. 1987–1991. Rabat: Secretariat d'Etat au Plan, Direction de la Statistique.

Cox, W. Michael, and Richard Alm. 1999. *Myths of Rich and Poor: Why We're Better Off Than We Think.* New York: Basic Books.

Dahrendorf, Ralf. 1959. *Class and Class Conflict in Industrial Society.* Stanford: Stanford University Press.

Daoud, Zakya, and Maâti Monjib. 1996. *Ben Barka.* Paris: Michalon.

Darwish, Mahmud. 1988. *Yowmiyyat il-huzn il-'di.* Beirut: Dar 'uda.

Deneoux, Guillain P., and Abdelslam Maghroui. 1997. "The Political Economy of Structural Adjustment in Morocco." In *Economic Crisis and Political Change in North Africa,* ed. Azzedine Layachi. Westport, Conn.: Praeger.

Discours et interviews de S. M. Hassan II. 1962–1963. Rabat: Ministère d'Etat Chargé de l'Information.

di Tella, Rafael, and Robert MacCulloch. Forthcoming (2004). "The Consequences of Labor Market Flexibility: Panel Evidence Based on Survey Data." *European Economic Review. The Economic Development of Morocco.* 1966. Washington, D.C.: World Bank.

Economic Policy Institute. 2000. "Economic Snapshots." January. Web site presentation. www.epinet.org/content.cfm/webfeatures_snapshots_archive_snapshotsarchive.

——. 2001. "Economic Snapshots." 21 December. http://www.epinet.org/content.cfm/web features_snapshots_archive_snapshotsarchive.

Economic and Social Development Report. 1981. Vol. 1. Washington, D.C.: World Bank.

Economic Trends in the MENA Region. 1998. Washington, D.C.: World Bank.

Eddin Ibrahim, Saad. 1994. "Islamist Political Movements." Lecture. Center for Middle East Studies, University of California, Berkeley, fall.

El Oufi, Noureddine. 1990. *La Marocanisation.* Casablanca: Editions Toubkal.

——. 2000. "L'impératif social au Maroc: De l'adjustement à la regulation." *Critique économique,* no. 3 (autumn).

Esping-Andersen, Gosta. 1990. *The Three Worlds of Welfare Capitalism.* Princeton: Princeton University Press.

——. 1992. "Post Industrial Class Structures: An Analytical Framework." Working Paper 1992/38.

L'Etudiant Marocain. 2002–2003. Casablanca: L'Etudiant Marocain.

L'Evolution Economique du Maroc dans le Cadre du Deuxième Plan Quadriennal (1954–57). 1958. Casablanca: L'Etudiant Marocain.

Fanon, Frantz. 1967. *Black Skin, White Mask.* New York: Grove.

Firebaugh, Glenn. 1999. "Empirics of World Income Inequality." *American Journal of Sociology* 104, no. 6: 1597–1630.

Freud, Sigmund. 1957. "Mourning and Melancholia." In *The Standard Edition of the Complete Psychological Works of Sigmund Freud,* vol. 14. Trans. and ed. James Strachey. London: Hogarth.

Galbraith, James K. 2000. *Created Unequal.* Chicago: University of Chicago Press.

Gaudio, Attilio. 1972. *Allal al-Fassi, ou l'histoire de l'istiqlal.* Paris: Editions Alain Moreau.

Gellner, Ernest. 1961. "The Struggle for Morocco's Past." *Middle East Journal* 15, no. 1: 79–90.

Giddens, Anthony. 1973. *Class Structure of the Advanced Societies.* London: Hutchinson.

——. 1995. "The Growth of the New Middle Class." In *The New Middle Classes,* ed. Arthur J. Vidich. New York: New York University Press.

Gramsci, Antonio. 1971. *Selections from Prison Notebooks.* Trans. Geoffrey N. Smith and Quintin Hoare. New York: International.

Gruner, Roger. 1984. *Du Maroc traditional au Maroc moderne: Le contrôle civil au Maroc, 1912–1956.* Paris: Nouvelles Editions Latines.

Grusky, David B., and Jesper B. Sorenson. 1998. "Can Class Analysis Be Salvaged?" *American Journal of Sociology* 103, no. 5: 1187–1234.

Hardt, Michael, and Antonio Negri. 2000. *Empire*. Cambridge, Mass.: Harvard University Press.

Harvey, David. 1989. *The Condition of Postmodernity*. Oxford: Blackwell.

Held, David, and Daniele Archibugi, eds. 1995. *Cosmopolitan Democracy: An Agenda for a New World Order*. Oxford: Polity.

Hourani, Albert. 1991. *A History of the Arab Peoples*. Cambridge, Mass.: Belknap.

Human Development Report. 1998. New York: UNDP.

Hussein, Taha. 2001. *Mustaqbal i-thuqafa fi-misr* (The future of culture in Egypt). Tunis: Dar Maaraf.

Ibaaquil, Larbi. 1996. *L'école marocaine et la compétition sociale*. Rabat: Editions Babil.

Les Indicateurs Sociaux. 1993. Rabat: Direction de la Statistique.

Les Indicateurs Sociaux. 2000. Rabat: Direction de la Statistique.

International Confederation of Free Trade Unions (ICFTU). 1999. "In the Forefront of the Battle." Trade Union World (briefing), 10 January.

International Monetary Fund (IMF). 1998. Press release, 31 March.

———. 1999. Article IV Consultation. Washington, D.C.: International Monetary Fund.

———. 2001. Article IV Consultation. Washington, D.C.: International Monetary Fund.

———. 2003. Article IV Consultation. Washington, D.C.: International Monetary Fund.

———. 2003. Article IV Consultation. Washington, D.C.: International Monetary Fund.

Jaïdi, Larbi. 1995. "Le Marché de l'Emploi: Ses tendances et ses mécanismes." Unpublished paper.

Jameson, Fredric. 1991. *Postmodernism, or The Cultural Logic of Late Capitalism*. Durham, N.C.: Duke University Press.

Jones, Charles R. 1997. "On the Evolution of the World Income Distribution." *Journal of Economic Perspectives* 11, no. 3: 19–36.

Lahbabi, Mohamed. 1970. *Les années 80 de notre jeunesse*. Casablanca: Editions Maghrebines.

Laroui, Abdallah. 1974. *La crise des intellectuels arabes: Traditionalisme ou historicisme?* Paris: Maspero.

———. 1977a. *The History of the Maghrib: An Interpretive Essay*. Princeton: Princeton University Press.

———. 1977b. *Les origines sociales et culturelles de nationalisme marocaine*. Paris: Maspero.

———. 1982. *L'Ideologie arabe contemporaine*. Paris: Maspero.

Levinas, Emmanuel. 1989. *The Levinas Reader*, ed. Seàn Hand. Oxford: Blackwell.

———. 1998. *Of God Who Comes to Mind*. Trans. Bettina Bergo. Stanford: Stanford University Press.

LMS Conseil. 1997. "Etudes sur les salaires des cadres." Unpublished report. Casablanca.

Marx, Karl. 1988. *Economic and Philosophic Manuscripts of 1844*. Buffalo, N.Y.: Prometheus.

Milanovic, Branko, and Yitzhak Shlomo. 2000. "Does the World Have a Middle Class?" World Bank working paper.

Mills, C. Wright. 2002. *White Collar: The American Middle Classes*. Oxford: Oxford University Press.

Mimouni, Rachid. 1994. *La Malediction*. Paris: Stock.

Montagne, Robert. 1948–1950. "Naissance du Proletariat Marocain." *Cahiers de l'Afrique et l'Asie* 3.

Morrisson, Christian. 1991. *Adjustment and Equity in Morocco*. Paris: OECD.

Munson, Henry. 1993. *Religion and Power*. New Haven: Yale University Press.

Nancy, Jean-Luc, and Tracy B. Strong. "La Comparution." *Political Theory* 20, no. 3 (1992): 371–398.

"1999–2000 Stagnation." 2000. *Bulletin Centre Marocain de Conjoncture*. June.

Ossman, Susan. 2002. *Three Faces of Beauty: Casablanca, Paris, and Cairo*. Durham, N.C.: Duke University Press.

Pandolfo, Stefania. 1997. *Impasse of the Angels*. Chicago: University of Chicago Press.

Pfeifer, Karen, et al. 1999. "Reform or Reaction? Dilemmas of Economic Development in the Middle East." Issue of *Middle East Report* 210 (spring).

Population An 2062: Stratégies, tendances. 1991. Rabat: CERED.

Population et Emploi. 1992. Rabat: CERED.

Qabbani, Nezar. 2000. *'Safir la ttalib t'shira dkhul* (Birds do not require a visa for entry). Beirut: Nezar Qabbani Publications.

Reich, Robert B. 1992. *The Work of Nations: Preparing Ourselves for Twenty-First Century Capitalism*. New York: Vintage.

Resilience and Growth through Sustained Adjustment: The Moroccan Experience. 1995. IMF Occasional Paper.

Rodrik, Dani. 2000. "How Far Will Economic Integration Go?" *Journal of Economic Perspectives* 14, no. 1 (winter): 177–186.

——. 2002. "Feasible Globalizations." Unpublished paper.

Rose, Stephen J. 2000. *Social Stratification in the United States: The New American Profile Posters, a Book-and-Poster Set*. New York: New Press.

Rousseau, Jean-Jacques. *Social Contract*. Trans. Maurice Cranston. Baltimore: Penguin.

Salāwī, Ahmad b. Khalīd. 1954–1956. *Kitāb al-istiqsāʿ fī īakhbār al-Maghrib al-Aqsā*. Vol. 9. Casablanca: Mansurat Wizarat al-Taqafiyya wa-l-Turat. Trans. in *Archives Marocaines*. Vol. 30–33. Paris: Ernest Leroux.

Salmi, Jamil. 1985. *Crise de l'Enseignement et Reproduction Sociale du Maroc*. Casablanca: Editions Maghrebines.

Sbihi, Abdelghani, and Mohammed El Aouad. 1994. *Besoins en Formation au Maroc*. Washington, D.C.: USAID report. April.

Schroeter, Daniel J. 1999. "Royal Power and the Economy in Precolonial Morocco: Jews and the Legitimation of Foreign Trade." In *The Shadow of the Sultan: Culture, Power, and Politics in Morocco*, ed. Rahma Bourqia and Susan Gilson Miller. Cambridge, Mass.: Harvard University Press.

Serhane, Abdelhak. 1995. *Les Proletaires de la Haine*. Paris: Publisud.

Singerman, Diane. 1995. *Avenues of Participation*. Princeton: Princeton University Press.

Skocpol, Theda. 2000. *The Missing Middle: Working Families and the Future of American Social Policy*. New York: Norton.

Standing, Guy. 1999. *Global Labour Flexibility: Seeking Distributive Justice*. New York: St. Martin's.

Stewart, Frances. 2000. "Income Distribution and Development." UNCTAD X Roundtable on Trade and Development: Directions for the Twenty-first Century, 12 February.

Stiglitz, Joseph E. 2002. *Globalization and Its Discontents*. New York: Norton.

Tessler, Mark. 1986. "Image and Reality in Moroccan Politics." In *The Political Economy of Morocco*, ed. I. William Zartman. New York: Praeger.

Tocqueville, Alexis de. 1945. *Democracy in America*. New York: Knopf.

Tucker, Richard. 1978. *The Marx-Engels Reader*. New York: Norton.

Waterbury, John. 1970. *The Commander of the Faithful*. New York: Columbia University Press.

Weber, Max. 1958. *The Protestant Ethic and the Spirit of Capitalism*. Trans. Talcott Parsons. New York: Scribner.

White, Gregory. 1988. "The Advent of Electoral Democracy in Morocco's Constitutional Monarchy? The Constitutional Referendum of 1996."

World Bank. 1981. *Morocco: Economic and Social Development Report*. Washington, D.C.: World Bank.

——. 1996. *Growing Faster, Finding Jobs*. Washington, D.C.: World Bank.

——. 1999. "Kingdom of Morocco: Private Sector Assessment Update." Working Paper. 15 December.

World Development Indicators. 1995. Washington, D.C.: World Bank Publications.

World Development Report. 1995. Washington, D.C.: World Bank Publications.

——. 1997. Washington, D.C.: World Bank Publications.

——. 1998–1999. Washington, D.C.: World Bank Publications.

——. 2000–2001. Washington, D.C.: World Bank.

——. 2003. Washington, D.C.: World Bank.

Wright, Erik Olin. 1997. *Class Counts*. Cambridge, England: Cambridge University Press.

Yassine, Abdessalam. 2000. *Winning the Modern World for Islam*. Trans. Martin Jenni. Iowa City: Justice and Spirituality Publishing.

Zartman, I. William, ed. 1987. *The Political Economy of Morocco*. New York: Praeger.

Zartman, I. William, Mark A. Tessler, et al., eds. 1982. *Political Elites in Arab North Africa*. New York: Longman.

Zghal, Abdelkader, et al., eds. 1980. *Les Classes Moyennes au Maghreb*. Paris: Editions du Centre National de la Recherche Scientifique.

Index

'Abduh, Muhammed, 147 n.3
Abouzeid, Leila, 60–61
Abroad: desire to go, increase of, 133; job opportunities, 97; studying, appeal of, 93
Actors, political, global middle class as, 125–26
Adam, André, 13
Ad-Doukkali, Bouchâ'ib, 147 n.3
Administrators, children of, 92
Adorno, Theodor W., 17
Agamben, Giorgio, 30, 112, 144, 160 n.3
Agriculture, Morocco's dependence on, 75–76
Aïcha, Lalla, 158 n.29
Al-Afghani, Jamal ad-Din, 147 n.3
Alaouite dynasty, 9, 145 n.6
Al-Fassi, Allal, 51, 53–56, 147 n.3, 153 nn.34–35
Alienation: condition of, 134; of educated youth, 5–6, 8–10, 33, 123; of entrepreneurs, 20; in global market integration, 19; and global middle class, 108, 131, 134, 140; and identification with the state, 124–25; interdisciplinary conception of, 31;

and local elite power, 113; in market reform, 118–24; and self-confidence, 120–21; and social structure, 104–5; of unemployed, 20
Al Mansour, Yacoub, 145 n.6
Almohades, dynasty of, 145 n.6
Almoravides, dynasty of, 145 n.6
Al-Rashed, Abdelrahman, 145 n.4
Ambivalence: about market reform, 113; of global middle class, 138
Americans, nineteenth-century, and educated Moroccans, 29–30. See also United States
Anderson, Benedict, 131
Anxiety: about present, 1–2; and sense of statelessness, 7–8
Appadurai, Arjun, 131
Arabic, speaking, versus French, 36
Arab World: learning through Western culture, 55; market reform in, 4–5; petite bourgeoisie in, 28
Arendt, Hannah, 52, 59, 128, 131, 160 n.3
Argentina, income distribution in, 70
Arkoun, Mohammed, 5
Ashford, Douglas, 56–57

Social loss, and liberal market capitalism, 139. *See also* Loss

Social mobility, and privately educating children, 23–24

Social organization, during market reform, 5

Social origin, and competition for jobs, 21–22, 38

Social relations: analyzing, 140; for entrepreneurs, 127–28; and global market integration, 19

Social structure: and alienation, 104–5; impact of market integration on, 11–12

Social theory, and economic insecurity, 139–41

Social transformation: and market reform, 74–77; middle class as deterrent to, 27

Soussi origin, Moroccans of, 22

Stability, political, in Morocco, through market reform, 6

State: authority of, 54–55; and economic actors, 137; and economic security, 50; and entrepreneurial spirit, 100–101; and global middle class, 112–18; identification with, 124–25; legitimacy of, 113; and market and social intervention, 69; power of, ambivalence about, 113; reform of management of, 3; and subjectivity and consciousness, 108–12

State actors, 77, 79

Stateless, university graduates as, 7–8. *See also* Identity/identification; Loss

Stiglitz, Joseph, 4, 155 n.3

Structural adjustment program, 137

Symbolic-analysts, as category of workers, 87–91

Taxes, and trade with Europe, 39–40

Teachers: quality of life of, 84; on social judgment of past, 64

Temporarily employed, as social group, 138. *See also* Unemployed

Tessler, Mark, 147 n.20, 149 n.13, 152 n.28, 153 n.37

Thinkers, Islamic, and market reform, 5

Trade, European, with Morocco, 39

Traditional occupations, 91–95. *See also* Jobs

Transformation, of middle class in Morocco, 10–13

UGTM (Union Génèrale du Travail Marocain), 79

Ulema ("Islamic scholarly elite"), on contact with non-Islamic world, 38

UMT (Union Marocaine du Travail), 79

Unemployed: alienation of, 20; characteristics of, 95–98; on entrepreneurs, 102; media coverage of, 97; as result of market reform, 12; as social group, 25, 99, 138; social origins of, 22; university graduates, attitudes of, 82–83. *See also* Unemployed

Unemployment: and King Hassan, 79; and noncitizenship, 4; and private sector, 79–80; as way of life, 95–96

Unemployment rates, urban, 76–77

Union des Syndicats Confederés (CGT), 41

Union Générale du Travail Marocain (UGTM), 79

Union Marocaine du Travail (UMT), 79

Union Marocaine de Travailleurs (UMT), 24

Unions, workers affiliation with, 41–42, 78–79

United States: attending schools in, 83; disappointment of Moroccans in, 133–34; income distribution in, 70; and Moroccan middle class, 29–30

University, public, interest level of students at, 128–29

University graduates: alienation among, 33, 123; and initiative, 103; job expectations of, 121–22; job opportunities for, 81, 104; political dissension of, 6–7; and public sector jobs, 82; as social group, 99; and state actors, 79; as stateless, 7–8; unemployment among, 77. *See also* Lycée graduates

Urban unemployment rates, 76–77

Waterbury, John, 44, 48, 149 n.10, 152 n.26

Weber, Max, 8

White-collar work: labor market for, 80; and loss of social identity, 118; surge in, 49–50; value assigned to, 21

Wolfensohn, James, 156 n.12

Women, employed: and capital, 87; charac-

Shana Cohen is a Senior Research Fellow in Social Policy and Social Care at Sheffield Hallam University.

Library of Congress Cataloging-in-Publication Data
Cohen, Shana.
Searching for a different future : the rise of a global middle class in Morocco / Shana Cohen.
Includes bibliographical references and index.
ISBN 0-8223-3351-1 (cloth : alk. paper)
ISBN 0-8223-3387-2 (pbk. : alk. paper)
1. Middle class — Morocco. 2. Globalization — Social aspects — Morocco. 3. Globalization — Economic aspects — Morocco. I. Title: Rise of a global middle class in Morocco. II. Title.
HT690.M67C64 2004   305.5′5′0964 — dc22   2004005067